MOBILITY WORK IN COMPOSITION

MOBILITY WORK IN COMPOSITION

EDITED BY
**BRUCE HORNER,
MEGAN FAVER HARTLINE,
ASHANKA KUMARI,
AND LAURA SCENIAK MATRAVERS**

UTAH STATE UNIVERSITY PRESS
Logan

© 2021 by University Press of Colorado

Published by Utah State University Press
An imprint of University Press of Colorado
245 Century Circle, Suite 202
Louisville, Colorado 80027

All rights reserved
Manufactured in the United States of America

 The University Press of Colorado is a proud member of the Association of University Presses.

The University Press of Colorado is a cooperative publishing enterprise supported, in part, by Adams State University, Colorado State University, Fort Lewis College, Metropolitan State University of Denver, Regis University, University of Colorado, University of Northern Colorado, University of Wyoming, Utah State University, and Western Colorado University.

∞ This paper meets the requirements of the ANSI/NISO Z39.48-1992 (Permanence of Paper).

ISBN: 978-1-64642-019-3 (paperback)
ISBN: 978-1-64642-020-9 (ebook)
https://doi.org/10.7330/9781646420209

Library of Congress Cataloging-in-Publication Data

Names: Horner, Bruce, 1957– editor. | Hartline, Megan Faver, editor. | Kumari, Ashanka, editor. | Matravers, Laura Sceniak, editor.
Title: Mobility work in composition / edited by Bruce Horner, Megan Faver Hartline, Ashanka Kumari, and Laura Sceniak Matravers.
Description: Louisville, Colorado : University Press of Colorado, [2020] | Includes bibliographical references and index. | Summary: "Takes mobility to be the norm, rather than the exception to a norm of stasis and stability. Both in-depth investigations of specific forms of mobility work in composition, as well as and responses to and reflections on those explorations"— Provided by publisher.
Identifiers: LCCN 2020051274 (print) | LCCN 2020051275 (ebook) | ISBN 9781646420193 (paperback) | ISBN 9781646420209 (ebook)
Subjects: LCSH: English language—Rhetoric—Study and teaching (Higher)—Social aspects. | Academic writing—Study and teaching (Higher)—Social aspects.
Classification: LCC LB1575.8 .M63 2020 (print) | LCC LB1575.8 (ebook) | DDC 808/.0420711—dc23
LC record available at https://lccn.loc.gov/2020051274
LC ebook record available at https://lccn.loc.gov/2020051275

Cover illustration by Excellent backgrounds/Shutterstock.

CONTENTS

Acknowledgments   ix

Introduction: Mobility Work in Composition
Bruce Horner, Megan Faver Hartline, Ashanka Kumari, and Laura Sceniak Matravers   3

PART ONE: CASE STUDIES IN MOBILITY

1. Mobile Knowledge for a Mobile Era: Studying Linguistic and Rhetorical Flexibility in Composition
   Christiane Donahue   17

2. Marking Mobility: Accounting for Bodies and Rhetoric in the Making
   Ann Shivers-McNair   36

3. Small m– to Big M–Mobilities: A Model
   John Scenters-Zapico   51

4. Managing Writing on the Move
   Rebecca Lorimer Leonard   67

5. "Pretty for a Black Girl": AfroDigital Black Feminisms and the Critical Context of "Mobile Black Security"
   Carmen Kynard   82

6. Composing to Mobilize Knowledge: Lessons from a Design-Thinking-Based Writing Course
   Scott Wible   95

7. Rethinking Past, Present, Presence: On the Process of Mobilizing Other People's Lives
   Jody Shipka   112

vi CONTENTS

8. Imagine a Schoolyard: Mobilizing Urban Literacy Sponsorship Networks
   Eli Goldblatt   127

PART TWO: RESPONDING AND MOBILIZING

9. The Work of Mobility
   Anis Bawarshi   147

10. Mobility at and beyond the Utterance
    Andrea R. Olinger   154

11. (Im)Mobilities and Networks of Literacy Sponsorship
    Laura Sceniak Matravers   160

12. Resisting the University as an Institutional Non-Place
    Timothy Johnson   167

13. (T)racing Race: Mapping Power in Racial Property Across Institutionalized Writing Standards and Urban Literacy Sponsorship Networks
    Jamila M. Kareem and Khirsten L. Scott   174

14. Mobilizing Connections across Disciplinary Frames
    Megan Faver Hartline   182

15. Social Movement Friction and Meaningful Spaces
    Patrick Danner   189

16. Mobility through Everyday Things
    Ashanka Kumari   195

17. Staging Ingenuity: A Pedagogical Framework of Mobilizing Creative Genre Uptake
    Elizabeth Chamberlain   201

18. Genre Uptake and Mobility: Making Meaning in Mobilized Contexts
    Keri Epps   208

19. Regarding Our Disciplinary Future(s): Toward a Mobilities
Framework for Agency
    Rick Wysocki   216

20. Making Mobility Work for Writing Studies
    Rachel Gramer and Mary P. Sheridan   223

    About the Authors   231
    Index   237

ACKNOWLEDGMENTS

The project for which this book represents the most recent iteration began in early 2016, when contributors for this collection came together for the first time to share their ideas on how mobility studies might connect to our work in rhetoric and composition. Since that time, our contributors have presented their ideas at the 2016 Thomas R. Watson Conference on Rhetoric and Composition as well as discussing, workshopping, emailing about, and revising their writing to hone their conceptions of mobility in composition, the (for now) final versions of which appear in this collection of essays. We thank them not only for their writing about mobility, but also for their willingness to take a long-term, iterative mobilities approach to our work together. Thanks also to Rachael Levay at Utah State University Press for her generous support for this project and to Laura Furney, Beth Svinarich and Daniel Pratt, also of Utah State University Press, for helping us see the book through to completion. Thanks as well to our reviewers, who provided valuable suggestions on earlier versions of this collection.

We are grateful to the University of Louisville's Committee on Academic Publication, which provided funding in support of this project, and to Glynis Ridley, the University of Louisville English Department Chair, and colleagues at the University of Louisville, for their support and encouragement. We thank Sara P. Alvarez and Jaclyn Hilberg for their attention to detail and editorial assistance. We also gratefully acknowledge the Thomas R. Watson Endowment for support in research in rhetoric and composition.

MOBILITY WORK IN COMPOSITION

INTRODUCTION
Mobility Work in Composition

Bruce Horner, Megan Faver Hartline,
Ashanka Kumari, and Laura Sceniak Matravers

Composition teachers, scholars, and writing program administrators have long been concerned with matters of mobility, whether in terms of transnational writing program administration; translingual and transcultural writing; (dis)abilities; the role of written language in knowledge mobility; interrelationships between literacy, careers, and identity; mobile composing practices; writing and immigration; or the interrelations of literacy practices, technologies, locations, and mobilities.[1] Such scholarship has advanced understandings of the role writing and its teaching play in maintaining and transforming social identity and shaping knowledge production and its mobilization. But while mobility is regularly invoked as a phenomenon characterizing students, literacy practices, knowledge transfer, texts, and even writing programs, what constitutes mobility as a phenomenon that might link these itself remains unexamined.

Responding to this state of affairs, this collection advances a mobilities perspective on work in composition. We see a mobilities perspective offering a framework by which to articulate relations between seemingly disparate concerns in composition by providing an alternative inflection of these concerns—a mobilities paradigm. The term *mobilities* itself offers a name for what seem to be related concerns: the "globalization" of higher education and, with it, writing programs; the transnational movement of students and faculty; the mobilization of knowledge about composition as it travels (or doesn't) from research articles to policy proposals to pedagogical and compositional practices; the circulation of texts and ideas, and the role of language and literacy in the movement of not just texts and ideas but also of people, geographically and socially; and of course the mobility of capital shaping the conditions within which composition work takes place and with which that work contends.

However, in suggesting a common feature to these concerns, mobility studies also provides a different inflection to them. Ordinarily, in

DOI: 10.7330/9781646420209.c000

composition studies, these concerns are understood as matters requiring adjustment or accommodation: how we might best (ethically and pedagogically) accommodate a more transnational student body; how we can avert the mistranslation of knowledge in efforts at its implementation in teaching; how we can smooth the career paths of students and faculty; and how and why we (and others) should accommodate differences in literacy and language practices. Mobility, in other words, is approached as a problem to be solved in order to return to what we imagine should normally happen.

But a meaningful application of a mobilities perspective involves adopting a mobilities paradigm (Sheller and Urry 2006), whereby the phenomena of the movement and transformation of knowledge, people, identities, ideas, languages, texts, bodies, and institutions no longer represent deviations from a norm to which they are to be accommodated (cf. Faist 2013, 1638). Instead, our confrontations with these phenomena can lead us to recognize their mobility as itself the norm—not something to be accommodated to a norm of stability, or "sedentarism," but instead, the expected, to which any apparent stability must itself be reconciled (Sheller and Urry 2006). While adopting such a paradigm maintains attention to these phenomena, it casts their mobility in a different light. Rather than their mobility *per se* constituting a feature distinguishing them from the norm, the specific dynamics of their mobility come to the fore: the conditions and relations shaping mobility as well as producing different kinds (paces, means, meanings, experiences, effects) of mobility (e.g., sanctioned vs. unsanctioned), understood as "ontological absolutes" (Adey 2006, 76).

In other words, in rendering mobility itself the norm rather than deviation from the norm, a mobilities paradigm opens up mobility itself to investigation—again, not as a deviation or exception to be accounted for, but rather, in terms of the various forms mobility takes. Just as the New Literacy Studies (NLS) is characterized by its insistent pluralization of *literacy* to *literacies* (Lillis and Scott 2007) to mark differentiation among what had hitherto been understood as a noncount monolith ("literacy") into various social practices, mobility studies—or at least those informing this collection—in rendering mobility the norm makes possible the differentiation among what is now a "countable": mobilities (see Glick Schiller and Salazar 2013). That, then, is one conceptual purchase to a mobilities paradigm.[2]

As also suggested by the comparison to NLS, in positing and then differentiating among various mobilities, a mobilities paradigm foregrounds material social practice—understood here as the location and source rather than simply the means of manipulating, or manifesting, what are understood to be stable languages, classrooms, bodies, identities, texts, and knowledge. Thus, for example, a mobilities paradigm identifies language as located in and the (always emerging) outcome of practices, rather than as a preexisting entity that writers use or write in. Even the apparent stability of a language is rendered as the outcome of ongoing efforts (sedimentation) that themselves change, by reinforcing but relocating specific usages as part of what we thereby can justifiably term "common practice."

One further consequence of adopting this mobilities paradigm is that mobility is no longer understood as synonymous with movement, at least not as movement is ordinarily conceived. Instead, stasis and movement are understood as relations within mobility (see Adey 2006, 86–87). Whereas a sedentarist paradigm imagines a world of solids that may or may not on occasion move or be moved, and whose movement merits attention as a break from the norm, a mobilities paradigm sees a world of fluidity—a sea, as it were, of currents in and on and with which various entities contend. In such a world, even those entities that appear stable are necessarily mobile—like boats at sea—in order to maintain their seemingly stable position. Stasis, rather than the assumed norm, becomes a point of inquiry, something to be accounted for. A further consequence of adopting a mobilities paradigm is that more attention is drawn to the forces shaping—setting the pace, direction, quality, and effects of—mobility, thereby producing diverse kinds of mobilities, ascribed different kinds of value, enacted by different means, and carrying quite different meanings (e.g., the mobility of the itinerant laborer vs. the mobility of the idle global rich). In place of a mobile/immobile binary, a range of mobilities appears for our consideration, each of them also fluctuating in character (Sheller and Urry 2006, 212–14).

Understanding composition work as mobility work thus means understanding the work not only in terms of movement or its absence—contributing (or not) to the upward social mobility of students, say, or facilitating the transfer of writing skills across diverse sites—but in terms of the transformations effected by processes of any such movement on what moves (or is moved or seems/is kept still); shifts in the pace and direction of such movements; and differences in such directions and pace (see Leander et al. 2010). Instead of imagining some students, for example, as "stuck" versus those whom we see as "going far," we can investigate what produces the appearance of being stuck (given mobility as the norm), and ways that going far may constitute a kind of stasis in itself, or rely on kinds of friction that keep those going far nonetheless "in place," like sailors struggling to remain "on course."

Further, in assuming and seeking out the mobile in the seemingly stable, a mobilities paradigm enforces a historical view of our work and the academic and social institutions and locations in and with which we work as mobile, however seemingly s(t)olid. And that identification itself assumes a range of often conflicting pressures contributing to the specific course and character of the mobility of these institutions and locations and relations of relative degrees and kinds of mobility. If place is an event, as Tim Cresswell (2002, 26) suggests, then, from a mobilities perspective, it is a continually unfolding event of shifting character in response to tides of movement and pressure.

In insisting on the historicity of even such seemingly timeless entities as institutions and locations, recognition of their mobility would, on its surface, appear to offer hope of change. That hope would, however, need to be tempered by the clear historical evidence of apparent continuity, that is, a lack of change. At the same time, a mobilities paradigm makes possible the identification of any appearances of continuity as the ongoing results of ongoing efforts; and hence, results that are inevitably partial, temporary, and vulnerable to contrary efforts, as illustrated in this collection by Eli Goldblatt's chapter on the shifting status and hopes of Moore School and plans for a vacant lot, John Scenters-Zapico's description of the strategies deployed by university administrators to keep him and his writing programs in a permanent state of limbo, and Carmen Kynard's account of the effect of a student's website on the otherwise seemingly inevitable and willful blindness among students to the color caste system.

As suggested by this insistence on the mobile character of all phenomena, however seemingly recalcitrant, a mobilities paradigm offers provocative inflections to questions of research methodologies in composition (and other fields—see Spinney 2015), as well as to matters of curricular design and pedagogy and our theories of language, language difference, writing development, and knowledge mobilization. Rather than assuming a stable language/skill/identity/body/institution/site/ environment/pedagogy/curriculum, we start from the premise of all these as always and inevitably fluid and relational to one another and transformed in and through practice. Such a starting premise changes the sense of all these and our work: who the "we" are who do that work, what that work looks like, and how we might recognize it, as illustrated by the example of the work accomplished by a student's reiteration of a "common" usage (see Donahue's discussion of *reprise-modification* and

Ann Shivers-McNair's discussion of the role of her own mobility in discussing her research). A mobilities paradigm provides not just a way of identifying a particular feature of contemporary social experience, and the involvement of the study and teaching of composition in that experience; a mobilities paradigm calls on us to rethink the terms in which we see ourselves, our work, and the location of our work by removing our sense of the stability of the foundation of all these, and by posing an alternative foundation that runs counter to dominant understandings of what "foundation" means and might consist of. As heady and vertiginous as such a shift may feel like and be, it also promises a more adequate rendering of the unsteady state in which we find ourselves.

MOBILE PROCESSES FOR MOBILITY WORK: CHARTING THE COURSE OF THE COLLECTION

In keeping with the premise of a mobilities paradigm of the fluid and relational character of ideas as well as other phenomena, this collection is designed to both allow for and illustrate the dynamics of knowledge mobilization as ideas move and are in the process transformed through relocation. For what a mobility studies paradigm claims about ideas and phenomena applies equally to itself: Rather than constituting a stable foundation on or from which to build or draw, a mobility studies paradigm is itself subject to and, indeed, dependent on ongoing and diverse reworkings even in efforts to maintain a sense of "a mobilities paradigm."

This has two consequences: first, the term "mobility" is inflected quite differently across the chapters. However disconcerting, those inflectional differences illustrate the mercurial character of mobilities itself, though we would add that it is possible and, in fact, common if unacknowledged, for individual contributions to those collections claiming a stable foundation to inflect differently, and thereby remake, that foundation through those inflections. This does not, of course, mean any or everything can, should, or does represent scholarship in mobility studies. Rather, it means that mobility—in the sense articulated above as the norm—serves as the point of departure for research projects taking diverse directions. Hence, the collection provides not so much a set of how-to's but, instead, diverse engagements with the dynamics of mobilities and responses from various perspectives on those engagements. What binds the work of the chapters in this collection as a collection is that the mobilities addressed are those worked in composition (broadly construed). Mobilities offers a particular inflection to composition, and composition inflects (works) mobilities.

As editors of this collection, we nonetheless faced the peculiar challenge of attempting somehow to capture, as it were, what we and our contributors otherwise insist is mercurial in character. We addressed this challenge during the collection's development and in the organization of the contributions in the collection you are now reading. First, what are presented here as finished chapters represent the culmination of an extended process of not only the expected drafting and revision of individual chapters, but also of extended, and repeated, conversations by the authors about one another's drafts and revisions. These conversations first began at a symposium held at the University of Louisville, and continued at the 2016 Thomas Watson Conference on Rhetoric and Composition, where revised versions of symposium drafts, and essays responding to them, were subjected to extensive and broad discussion by the several hundred teacherscholars attending the conference, in addition to pre- and post-conference and symposium exchanges between the editors and the authors. While a collection cannot capture the various turns the drafts, and conversations about them, have taken, we see traces of these in the chapters and responses presented here, knowing as well that readers will subject these to further twists as they take up what these present.

The organization of the collection into two parts is meant to encourage readers to adopt a mobilities perspective toward the work presented, and to forestall any temptation to see the matter as settled. In the eight chapters comprising part 1, the questions raised by a mobilities perspective are explored across key issues in rhetoric and composition, including translingual and multilingual literacies, digital and professional writing pedagogies, and community literacy. These chapters map threads of mobility that stretch across subfields, showing what a mobilities perspective brings to our work. The responses making up part 2 take up again, to revise, practices of thinking from a mobilities perspective presented in the chapters comprising part 1. In each of these response chapters, authors draw on two or more of the chapters in part 1 to continue exploring mobility work in composition. By this two-part organization, we hope to encourage, if not capture, a mobilities dynamic of ideas and knowledge at odds with the conventional and expected debate dynamic of argument and counterargument, claim and rebuttal; a dynamic that, instead, asks us to look again, and (inevitably) differently, at what we thought we knew and to rework it.

The authors of chapters in part 1 offer ways of thinking about *how* to use mobility to find connections and mark differences. Christiane Donahue offers a model for using a mobilities perspective to find and employ points of connection across subfields to better illuminate studies of writing and language, depicting the possibilities of such research through her analysis of how mobile connections between transfer and translingualism can deepen understanding of both practices. Ann Shivers-McNair, however, cautions scholars to not assume mobility is a given, but instead mark it in their research, attending to who and what counts as mobile and is allowed to move to the potential exclusion of others. Other chapter authors show how a mobilities perspective affords them new possibilities for considering the temporal and spatial mobility of people, writing, and ideas. John Scenters-Zapico uses his professional transition from Texas to California as a case study to explore how a mobilities paradigm might illuminate the complexities of workplace mobilities for individual faculty and larger trends related to how and why faculty move institutions (and don't). Rebecca Lorimer Leonard uses literacy "management" as a frame for examining the physical and linguistic mobility of both Nimet, a multilingual migrant writer from Azerbaijan living in the United States, and her writing, depicting Nimet's struggles with institutional management of literacy learning seen in the pronunciation classes she was required to attend for her nursing degree, and the successes of her personal literacy management, which illuminates the depth and complexity of her multilingual capacity. Carmen Kynard uses Pretty for a Black Girl, a website created by a first-year writing student, Andrene, to highlight how the mobilization of black women's vernacular technological creativity respatializes dominant white, neoliberal imperatives of higher education that maintain racist boundaries/binaries. Beyond temporal and spatial mobility, scholars depict instances of *knowledge mobilization* (the processes of knowledge distribution and uptake and the transformations wrought on knowledge by those processes): mobilizing ideas and people to create new understandings of how we teach, practice, and use writing alongside other communities. Scott Wible depicts how his use of design thinking in the writing classroom encourages students to learn to mobilize knowledge production for collaborative solution building with and for community partners, emphasizing how rhetoric and composition scholars might use this methodology for conducting socially transformative research. Jody Shipka analyzes the composition processes of the Inhabiting Dorothy project in which participants remediate strangers' memory objects, mobilizing them for a new audience and purpose, ultimately arguing for a more dynamic focus for composition research, theory, and practice that treats agency, action, and collaboration as distributed amongst both human and nonhuman entities. Eli Goldblatt maps the network of actors who are mobilizing to sponsor literacy development through the redesign of the schoolyard of an underserved Philadelphia school, calling for and showing the importance of a deeply relational, networked approach toward creating community change, strengthening social mobility through literacy, and reinventing a neighborhood and those working and traversing its space. In each of these chapters, scholars reveal the complex ways mobility is already working across rhetoric and composition, making the processes of spatial, temporal, and knowledge mobilization more visible.

The responses making up part 2 take up again, to revise, practices of thinking from a mobilities perspective presented in the chapters comprising part 1. In each chapter, scholars draw on two or more of the chapters in part 1 to develop when and how mobility might be used within rhetoric and composition. Anis Bawarshi draws on all the case studies from part 1 to explore the *work* of mobility in composition studies, showing how mobility shifts the emphasis of composition studies from the inhabiting/performing of a standard to the trans-acting/work of communication across difference. Following his chapter, several authors pursue questions of how the work of communicating across difference might be taken up, exploring the mobility of people, places, and activities within the study of literacy practices. Andrea Olinger juxtaposes Lorimer Leonard's case study with Donahue's theorizations about mobility to conceive of linguistic and literate repertoires as co-constructed by individuals and institutions, and thus as inherently mobile. Laura Sceniak Matravers focuses on the complicated (and sometimes paradoxical) relationships between acts of literacy, agency, and (im)mobilities using Goldblatt's conception of networked literacy sponsors to consider how Lorimer Leonard's and Kynard's case studies exemplify context as agentive. Timothy Johnson further explores institutional contexts in his discussion of "non-places," as portrayed in Scenters-Zapico's and Lorimer Leonard's chapters, showing how non-places use solitude and similitude to render important elements of intellectual and literate activity invisible. Jamila Kareem and Khirsten L. Scott use critical race theory and Jan Blommaert's theory of sociolinguistic scales to explore the respective presence and absence of race in Kynard's and Goldblatt's chapters; they claim that attention to race is necessary to disrupt the boundaries of who can use what literacies under what circumstances and create greater literacy mobility.

Other chapters address how mobility might be used to cross research boundaries within and beyond the discipline. Megan Faver Hartline extends Donahue's use of mobility as a way to connect disparate disciplinary research frames by analyzing how community writing (Goldblatt) and design thinking (Wible) are already connected, arguing that such connections might be mobilized to continue developing stronger research practices that involve and work for community members. Patrick Danner reexamines the use of space in Kynard's and Scenters-Zapico's case studies, putting their chapters in conversation with social movement rhetorics and proposing a mobility model of such rhetorics as a way of understanding the recursive relationship between objects, space, and meaning-making. Ashanka Kumari rereads Shivers-McNair's case study through the lens of Scenters-Zapico's small m– to Big M–Mobility stages model to offer an alternative, multidimensional consideration of Shivers-McNair's methodology for conducting and interpreting research. Drawing on the genres described by Wible, Kynard, and Shipka, Elizabeth Chamberlain develops a pedagogical framework of creative genre mobilization for writing assignment design; she argues that the best writing assignment prompts are those that invite students to reimagine genres as a mobile framework. Keri Epps examines how the mobility models presented in chapters by Lorimer Leonard, Scenters-Zapico, and Donahue allow for a clearer understanding of the complex reciprocal relationship between mobility and genre uptake, and she argues that, by making the agents of genre uptake more visible, mobility models reveal the embedded power hierarchies that must be negotiated. Rick Wysocki, analyzing agencies and actors in Wible's, Shipka's, and Donahue's mobility case studies, demonstrates that a fluid and distributed understanding of agency is necessary for scholars in rhetoric and composition to mobilize their research to address contemporary challenges. Rachel Gramer and Mary P. Sheridan examine how Wible, Goldblatt, and Kynard take up mobility studies as a methodological framework alongside other disciplinary research frames, interrogating how mobility might be used by writing studies scholars to address the field's long-standing questions of power. All of the chapters in part 2 extend the study of mobility in composition studies by taking up and responding to the case studies of part 1, furthering the process of mobilizing disciplinary knowledge and demonstrating how these works are transformed when placed in conversation with one another.

As the contributions making up this collection make clear, composition's uptake of a mobilities paradigm is in its beginning stages. Accordingly, we offer this collection as provocation to the transformations we know will result from readers' mobilization of what we've presented as they take it into their own teaching and scholarly pursuits. All work in composition works with mobility. We invite readers to take up such mobility work in their engagements with this collection.

NOTES

1. See Martins 2015; Canagarajah 2013; Horner and Kopelson 2014; Young, Vieira, and Lorimer Leonard 2015; You 2016; Lu and Horner 2009; Kapp 2012; Pigg 2014; Lorimer Leonard 2017; Nordquist 2017; Wan 2014; Vieira 2016; Pandey 2015; Berry, Hawisher, and Selfe 2012.

2. Adey, in fact, warns that "if we explore mobility in everything and fail to examine the differences and relations between them, it becomes not meaningless, but, there is a danger in mobilising the world into a transient, yet featureless, homogeneity" (2006, 91).

REFERENCES

Adey, Peter. 2006. "If Mobility Is Everything, Then It is Nothing: Towards a Relational Politics of (Im)mobilities." *Mobilities* 1 (1): 75–94.

Berry, Patrick, Gail Hawisher, and Cynthia Selfe. 2012. *Transnational Literate Lives in Digital Times.* Logan, UT: Computers and Composition Digital Press / Utah State University Press.

Canagarajah, Suresh. 2013. *Translingual Practice: Global Englishes and Cosmopolitan Relations.* New York: Routledge.

Cresswell, Tim. 2002. "Introduction: Theorizing Place." In *Mobilizing Place, Placing Mobility: The Politics of Representation in a Globalized World,* edited by Tim Cresswell and Ginette Verstraete, 11–32. Amsterdam: Rodopi.

Faist, Thomas. 2013. "Debates and Developments. The Mobility Turn: A New Paradigm for the Social Sciences?" *Ethnic and Racial Studies* 36 (11): 1637–1646.

Glick Schiller, Nina, and Noel B. Salazar. 2013. "Regimes of Mobility Across the Globe." *Journal of Ethnic and Migration Studies* 39 (2): 183–200.

Horner, Bruce, and Karen Kopelson, ed. 2014. *Reworking English in Rhetoric and Composition: Global Interrogations, Local Interventions.* Carbondale: Southern Illinois University Press.

Kapp, Rochelle. 2012. "Students' Negotiation of English and Literacy in a Time of Social Change." *JAC* 32 (3/4): 591–614.

Leander, Kevin M., Nathan C. Phillips, Katherine Headrick Taylor, Jan Nespor, and Cynthia Lewis. 2010. "The Changing Social Spaces of Learning: Mapping New Mobilities." *Review of Research in Education* 34: 329–394.

Lillis, Theresa, and Mary Scott. 2007. "Defining Academic Literacies Research: Issues of Epistemology, Ideology and Strategy." *Journal of Applied Linguistics* 4 (1): 5–32.

Lorimer Leonard, Rebecca. 2017. *Writing on the Move: Migrant Women and the Value of Literacy.* Pittsburgh: University of Pittsburgh Press.

Lu, Min-Zhan, and Bruce Horner. 2009. "Composing in a Global-Local Context: Careers, Mobility, Skill." *College English* 72 (2): 113–133.

Martins, David S., ed. 2015. *Transnational Writing Program Administration.* Logan: Utah State University Press.

Nordquist, Brice. 2017. *Literacy and Mobility: Complexity, Uncertainty, and Agency at the Nexus of High School and College.* New York: Routledge.

Pandey, Iswari. 2015. *South Asian in the Mid-South: Migrations of Literacies.* Pittsburgh: University of Pittsburgh Press.

Pigg, Stacey. 2014. "Emplacing Mobile Composing Habits." *College Composition and Communication* 66 (2): 250–275.

Sheller, Mimi, and John Urry. 2006. "The New Mobilities Paradigm." *Environment and Planning A* 38 (2): 207–226.

Spinney, Justin. 2015. "Close Encounters? Mobile Methods, (post)Phenomenology, and Affect." *Cultural Geographies* 22 (2): 231–246.

Vieira, Kate. 2016. *American by Paper: How Documents Matter in Immigrant Literacy*. Minneapolis: University of Minnesota Press.

Wan, Amy. 2014. *Producing Good Citizens: Literacy Training in Anxious Times*. Pittsburgh: University of Pittsburgh Press.

You, Xiaoye. 2016. *Cosmopolitan English and Transliteracy*. Carbondale: Southern Illinois University Press.

Young, Morris, Kate Vieira, and Rebecca Lorimer Leonard, eds. 2015. "The Transnational Movement of People and Information." Special issue, *Literacy in Composition Studies* 3 (3).

PART ONE

Case Studies in Mobility

1

MOBILE KNOWLEDGE FOR A MOBILE ERA
Studying Linguistic and Rhetorical Flexibility in Composition

Christiane Donahue

INTRODUCTION

In this chapter, I use the mobilities paradigm as a research lens for exploring linguistic, rhetorical, and discursive flexibility—motors of writing knowledge "transfer" and translingual "competence." Mobility as a paradigm offers a way to return to the intellectual work of analyzing knowledge transformation; opens up "transfer" as a much deeper, more fluid phenomenon than we may have been able to trace so far; and affords ways to study translingual activity more systematically. Mobility of people demands translingual mobility of language resources; deep learning demands mobility and the adaptability of knowledge across contexts, frequently called "transfer." I explore the triangle of mobility—translingualism—transfer, offering "code" and "competence" as two detailed examples of how mobility can help us to carry out our research differently.

Mobility situates individuals in a changing world, moves us past "sedentarist" biases, connects knowledge mobility to degrees of speed, and helps to underscore the negotiated nature of dialogic activities called forth by these phenomena (see Adey 2006; Elliott and Urry 2010; Urry 2011; Verstraete and Cresswell 2002).[1] The related concept of mobilization, linked at its root to mobility but with a far more "activist" coloring, also drives our understanding of both translingual realities and writing knowledge "transfer." Mobility and mobilization together thus open us up to a real shift in how we think about language and knowledge in writing and the interactive, dialogic co-construction of meaning. In that mobility, it's the fluidity of linguistic models and the study of language-in-use (Bazerman 2004; Donahue 2008; François 1994, 1998; Horner 2016a) that is also giving us new ways to model writing knowledge adaptation.

DOI: 10.7330/9781646420209.c001

18   DONAHUE

I am not, of course, the first to connect "translingualism" and "transfer."[2] However, I offer some additional ways to think about how these two frames interact, and perhaps most important, how a linguistic perspective on (trans)lingual uses can illuminate aspects of knowledge adaptation and transformation. I explore the connections at a conceptual level—something the "mobility" paradigm allows me to do—to locate shared motives, shared terms and consequences, and shared resistances to, for example, oversimplified accommodationist or acculturative models. This exploration will lead us inevitably to *design* competence as the key to successful communication in a mobile and superdiverse (Vertovec 2007) world, in the tradition of the New London Group and as developed by James P. Purdy (2014), Wible (chapter 6), and others.

LINGUISTIC PERSPECTIVES AND MOBILITY

Understanding language-in-use—"linguality," if you will—is the foundation to understanding translingualism: flexibility of the language user in relation to the local or global context. French functional linguistics has, since the 1960s, focused on "language-in-use as the source of language models rather than looking first to structures and then to their manifestations" (Donahue 2004, 139). This linguistics model was originally developed by André Martinet in the 1960s as a move away from Saussurean linguistics. It focuses on utterances and uttering (*énonciation*) in ways not dissimilar to pragmatics and semiology, often via discourse analysis that attends to the systematic study of situated language use, language-in-activity (1960).[3] French functional linguists further this by focusing on the dynamic and dialogic ways language, spoken and written, does what it does.

Two key linguists, M. M. Bakhtin and Frédéric François, offer specific ways to operationalize the idea of mobility in terms of language, writing, discourse, and knowledge. Bakhtin's work, translated into French before English and first cited in France in 1966 by Julia Kristeva, was foundationally important to some in the field. Frédéric François, a student of Martinet's in the 1960s, was later deeply influenced by Bakhtinian thinking.

A—BAKHTIN

Bakhtin is generally well-known in writing studies, but his model of language-in-use is more obscure.[4] It highlights the speaker-writer's mobility in relation to the context of production and allows us to account for the relationships that make meaning construction in speech and writing possible. "Language," Bakhtin suggests, "enters life through concrete utterances (which manifest language) and life enters language through concrete utterances as well" (1986, 63). For Bakhtin, the central focus is on this dynamic interplay, always. It is about "speech *life*" (emphasis mine), resisting the Humboldtian version of communication as a transparent medium of thought, independent of its communication (1986, 67) and emphasizing instead the dialogic co-construction of meaning that occurs with every utterance. In other words, the life is in the utterance, not in preexisting units waiting to be deployed, dictionary-style.

Words and sentences, for Bakhtin, are the language units available for meaning construction, the units traditional linguistics has focused on (1986, 69); they are *not* the primary unit of interest for understanding language-in-use (see also Bawarshi 2016). These units "belong to nobody and are addressed to nobody" (1986, 99) and are not "realized" until they are utterances (1986, 83). *Utterances* are the units of speech communication we must analyze to understand co-construction of meaning (1986, 67, 71). Those utterances exist only in the "forms of concrete utterances of individual *speaking people*," never outside of this (1986, 71), and are always transformative, always mobilized; we study the traces of that mobilization.

When Bakhtin explores the expressive nature of communication, he emphasizes the absence of expression in words not "in-use," not "mobile-mobilized," if you will: They are neutral until the actual moment of use. This point is part, in French linguistics, of a deep understanding of language-in-use as not something to study as a "code" with all that carries of the static and stable sense of the extracted language principles of a system (see also Berthoff 1999). For Bakhtin, that contact is a permanent part of the co-construction of meaning: "our speech . . . all our utterances . . . is filled with others' words, varying degrees of otherness or varying degrees of our-own-ness" (1986, 89) which inhabit the utterance, moving among different "in-uses" over time or at a given point in time. Writing, in this language model, is always rewriting, always negotiation, always translation; language functions in this constant original-new relationship in which, as Lu and Horner have also suggested, anyone who uses language and language conventions simultaneously transforms them, and language use decisions "are shaped by and shape" contexts and social positions (2016, 208). These Bakhtinian ways of understanding language-in-use are particularly strong for studying and analyzing mobility within language users' actual practices, a lens for looking at utterances in their social contexts.

B—FRÉDÉRIC FRANÇOIS AND REPRISE-MODIFICATION

Bakhtinian thinking undergirds questions of linguistic, rhetorical, and discursive mobility (see for example Bawarshi 2016; Delcambre 2016; Donahue 2008; Donahue 2018; Schuster 1985).[5] But Bakhtin himself noted that utterances are very unwieldy units of analysis (1986, 82). French linguist Frédéric François, less well known to US readers, operationalizes utterances as *"reprises-modifications,"* a term that means simultaneous retaking-up-modifying: reprise, much like in music (François, personal communication, 2007; see also Horner 2016a), as the reuse of material, and modification as the transformation that occurs in the reprising moment, fluid ongoing discursive activity, but that can be identified, categorized, and studied. The term has the advantage of working in English as well as in French, though "reprise" in English is more usually associated with music only (Donahue 2008; François 1994, 1998).

If we consider the nature of composing in a dialogic frame via linguists such as Bakhtin and François, we can argue that activities such as composing, translating, or paraphrasing are activities that are in fact forms of translanguaging. *All* language use is always reuse, making the new from the existing: All composing is recomposing. Paraphrase, for example, is "para" (to modify) and "phrase" (to tell)—to tell in modifying, to modify in telling. So, paraphrase is in fact a mode of *reprise-modification*. Something like a "commonplace" is a distillation of cultural knowledges or truths into a simple phrase that is another mode of *reprise-modification*. Reprise, even "exactly as is (as in a quote or a duplicated passage)," is still modification (François 1998). Horner suggests that language-in-use works precisely this way, co-constructing meaning in part by partnering with or resisting the meanings in the language, all it carries with it, its dialogic "shot through" past (2016a, 6). Composing to understand, to construct meaning, is built on this relationship.

Reprises can be highly conventionalized—Donahue in a study of French and US student writing offers the example of linguistic reprises like "the" in front of "apple" in English or the conventions that guide where adjectives are placed in French—but the complex re-elaborations of a shared pool in a new utterance are more interesting (2008). An utterance *is* its history, its appropriated and developed meanings, its intertexuality at that moment in time. The 2008 study offered an example of a student sentence that could be analyzed for reprises-modifications at micro-, meso-, and macro-levels. The sentence *Combien de conflits résultent de l'incompréhension de l'autre? Tous!* [*How many conflicts result from incomprehension of the other? All!*]

taps the discourses of generations in literature and politics, the current references to openness to others and a pluralistic society, and the local texts of the assignment and the Emile Zola source text [the student] read, and his own situated sense of any individual word in the phrase, this particular combination of words, and the oratorical style of calls to action, just to mention a few of the many factors at play in this one sentence. (Donahue 2008, 319)

The "reprise"-simultaneous "modification" echoes Bakhtin's description of utterances as always simultaneously a reuse of parts from a language system (and thus never "original") and a transformation (always *new*). For François, utterances are always both shared (not original) and new (individual), or, as Pennycook suggests, always have sameness *and* difference (2010, 35). A speaker is not, Bakhtin notes, "after all, the first speaker, the one who disturbs the eternal silence of the universe" (1986, 69).[6] Language-in-use analyses that focus on linguistic flexibility, negotiating moves, or textual movements have used the tool of "reprise-modification" to successfully unpack what is a slippery phenomenon, one that exemplifies writers'—and texts'—"internal" mobility (that is, mobility as writer's agency and mobility as textual effectiveness) or the constraints and limits on that mobility.

C—FROM LINGUAL TO TRANSLINGUAL

If all discourse is reprise-modification, reuse in transformation, transformation in reuse, and language is only meaningful in use, then the "lingual" in translingual—its language-in-use—is *already* mobile. Translingualism becomes a heightened state of mobile language activity, built from the way language functions in *all* cases, from "lingualism," if you will, connecting the translingual to the functional-lingual and suggesting that all lingual is translingual. A translingual orientation, then, might be defined as a linguistic model that allows us to frame, study, and explain spoken and written language use with "language" not as a nation-state bounded discrete communicative tool but as meaning-making activity working across, within, and through what have traditionally been seen as individual languages but are now understood as always in translation and heterogeneously constructed.

The norm in this model, as in some applied linguistics models, is language difference and internal heterogeneity: "the variety, fluidity, intermingling, and changeability of languages [is] the statistically demonstrable *norm* [emphasis mine] around the globe" (Horner et al. 2011; see also Hall et al. 2006, Kramsch 2009). Translingualism builds from the mobile lingual root to a "trans" attention to language-in-use and connects us to translingualism as mobilization—the marshaling of linguistic knowledge and resources. This norm shares roots with the mobility paradigm in that mobility is seen not as a problem to be solved but as a new norm to be understood, both for its nature and for what it affords and constrains.

WRITING KNOWLEDGE REUSE, ADAPTATION, AND TRANSFORMATION: "TRANSFER" AND MOBILITY

Our study of "transfer," as a learning model intended to help explore and explain how knowledge acquired in one context is reused, adapted, transformed, or called forward in another, can also be inflected, changed, and transformed via the "mobility" and "mobilization" paradigms, operationalized by the particular linguistic approaches to research just explained. "Transfer" of writing knowledge can also be understood as mobilization (Le Boterf 1994; Perrenoud 1999). The kind of *writing* knowledge needed today is mobile knowledge, movement from mooring to mobility, a movement across not just time but space, and above all, a movement that only matters if the writer has imbued it with meaning. The "writing knowledge" in question can range from how to hold a pen to sophisticated intertextual know-how, or from structural or genre knowledge to knowledge of processes, values, or self as writer.

"TRANSFER?"

Developmental views of "transfer" construct an expansive learning model that demands learners' critical participation in a multidirectional interactive co-construction of knowledge that creates new practices and changes communities, rather than imagining individuals simply moving from one knowledge context to a (different) other and using what they know (Tuomi-Gröhn and Engeström 2003, 34–35). This interactive view complements any sense of knowledge as mobile in both the "movement" and the "flexibility" senses mentioned earlier—supple learning that generates meaningful movement. Initial models of knowledge transfer worked within a simplified metaphor of transport that designated an object, "knowledge," that moves from one point to another, apparently staying identical. Mobility research suggests that even in simple physical "transport" this is not true, nor is it true in relation to knowledge. No knowledge ever simply "moves" from one identifiable bordered place

Mobile Knowledge for a Mobile Era   23

to another but is always transformed in the process, and the places are themselves fluid and transformable, not neatly bordered. Remember that mobility without meaning is simply movement as represented by a transport metaphor; we might reverse this to suggest that the knowledge movement of "transfer" is not the same as knowledge *mobility* (see also Fenwick and Farrell 2012; Horner 2016b).

These initial models evolved over time into cognitive, dispositional, and situated models (for a full review of this evolution and each model, see Tuomi-Gröhn and Engeström 2003). Some of these evolutions are particularly useful to understanding mobility of knowledge and know-how. Beach (1999) reconceptualized "transfer" as "consequential transition" (Tuomi-Gröhn and Engeström 2003, 27) in an effort to shift emphasis from the individual learner to ecological contexts and multiple interrelated processes (2003, 27). For Beach, generalization "is not located within the developing individual, nor can it be reduced to changing social activities; rather, it is located in the changing relationships between persons and activities" (Tuomi-Gröhn and Engeström 2003, 27).[7]

French scholar Le Boterf offers an additional possibility for knowledge transformation as "savoir-mobiliser," which is both "knowing *to* mobilize" and "knowing *how to* mobilize," both in action and intentionally motivated (1994). Perrenoud (1999) similarly argues that *mobilisation* captures the work of transformative reuse of knowledge more effectively. He suggests that *mobilisation* does not postulate the existence of analogies, "*meme partielles*," between current and previous situations; it covers both the creation of original responses and the simple reproduction of *réponses routinisées*; describes mental work that is costly and often long; evokes *une dynamique* rather than *un déplacement* (a "moving to" or displacing); targets diverse obstacles (*cognitifs, affectifs, relationnels*); draws on situation-specific concepts and knowledge; and suggests orchestration of *ressources multiples et hétérogènes* (Perrenoud 1999, 11). All of these developments draw attention to the importance of focusing on, in essence, mobility—though that has not yet come up as a term in US work on knowledge transfer, interestingly.

MOBILITY, "TRANSFER," AND TRANSLINGUALISM

Up to this point I have outlined some thoughts on linguistic models, translinguistic models, and transfer models. In this section I consider some generative interrelationships among mobility, transfer and translingual perspectives: language use as part of composing, language as always re-use, and negotiation, translation, and writing knowledge transfer as undergirding these practices. I do so not to glorify these perspectives but to explore how they might enable additional ways to think about teaching and learning writing.

TRANSLINGUALISM AND "TRANSFER"

The "trans" in both transfer and translingualism already connects them to mobility via the movement embedded in the prefix. Consider these conceptual parallels:

- The kind of writing knowledge needed today is mobile knowledge; the kind of linguistic knowledge in a superdiverse context (Vertovec 2007) is also mobile knowledge.
- If "language can now be understood to be always temporal, contingent, emergent" (Horner 2016b, 67), it is by deep nature transformatively transferrable and mobile.
- The norm in language use is difference, modification, and heterogeneity (Horner 2016a, 17); the norm in knowledge co-construction is successful transfer; that is, in both cases the norm is the statistical norm, what *is*, which is a descriptive-linguistic way of understanding "norm" in contrast to the "normative" (cultural) norm imposed by an always-questionable sociocultural or ideological authority. In this understanding of norm, both translingual practice and writing knowledge transfer, in a long view, are *unmarked*: within a community's expectations for normal practice, going without notice.
- Cushman (2016) notes that translingualism does not automatically change things in terms of meta-work; similarly, "teaching for transfer" does not automatically engender aware meta-cognitive activity in student writers. "Orientation" is key to writing knowledge transfer via writers' dispositions, and key to understanding (trans)lingual practices.
- "Transfer" is hard to study, as is translingual activity. Each shifts and transforms; each is complex and mercurial.

Translingual work thus connects directly to the transformative, adaptive work of reusing acquired or constructed writing knowledge.[8] Translingual activity and knowledge transfer also share a tension between mercuriality and some degree of stability; the illusion of something stable is not always illusion. Difference as norm still implies sameness in some part. The mobility research offers a lens on this question, exploring the relationship between "mobility" and "moorings." Mobility scholars conclude that everything *is* mobile—mobility as norm—but at varying speeds. If we were to trace in minute detail the question of language evolution over time, we might see that indeed difference is the foundation of language-in-use over time, remembering that "foundations" are themselves not permanent. We would also, I suspect, note that "transfer" of writing knowledge is always occurring, over time, at differentiated speeds and in response to different moments of communicative need, sometimes so fast that we don't perceive it as transfer. But in both cases some part would be stable, or, say, more shared than different.

In agreement with Dunn (2001), Purdy (2014), and Wible (chapter 6), and renewing the New London Group's emphasis on design as grounded in the reuse of available designs in new ways, we might argue that design is the principle underlying composing today. Writers in a mobile world must *design* their communications, their meaning-making compositions (Cope and Kalantzis 2009). This design demands choice, and translingual choices are part of the design competence necessary for adapting knowledge to new contexts. Just as we learn to choose genres and modes, we learn to choose linguistic features, including words and syntaxes. Choices fall on a continuum of more common, generic, highly conventionalized or normed choices, what some scholars have called sedimentation (Lu and Horner 2013; Pennycook 2010), to more individual or specific ones. There are, of course, consequences to choices that in linguistic contexts seem at times more readily harshly judged than in other contexts, such as mode or genre, and constraints at many levels; in that sense, "choice" implies more agency than I intend.

That choice—that mobility—is also "transfer." The model Bakhtin offers for language use thus connects to what has been called "transfer" via those same actions at its heart: reinvention, renewal, and transformation of knowledge. More recent work on re-mediation builds equally from this sense of dynamic reuse. We might also include the different strategies for creating voice and constructing texts in a mobile world that Canagarajah (2003) has outlined—accommodation, transposition, and appropriation—which overlap with considerations of how writing knowledge "transfer" functions.

Translation is an activity that moves among "translingual," "transfer," and "composing" discussions freely, highlighting linguistic, rhetorical, and discursive mobility in various facets. We can study it as "reprise-modification." In the "writing knowledge transfer" domain, European scholars have proposed "translation" as a more robust and dynamic frame for accounting for knowledge reuse and adaptation across time and contexts (Hilaricus 2011); in translingual discussions, scholars have analyzed translation *as* writing.[9]

EXAMPLES THAT "WORK" THE MOBILITY IN TRANSLINGUAL AND TRANSFER RESEARCH QUESTIONS

I now offer two examples of terms that can serve as research frames for studying mobility: "code" (and code-switching or meshing) and competence. The mobility paradigm helps us to both *rethink* them as tools of research, as we identify the moves of "reprise-modification" that do the linguistic and discursive work of making meaning, and to *reclaim* them.

1—Code

If we consider the utterance as the unit of analysis, and reprise-modification as a tool for pulling apart the ways utterances are doing what they do, then in fact "code," "codeswitching," and "codemeshing" could be *research tools* for understanding the nuts and bolts of translingual practice and of some kinds of transfer rather than models of language practice themselves. That level of systematic close analysis is part of what has been largely missing from both the translingual and the transfer landscapes,[10] the former having focused primarily to date on ethnographic work and "key example" illustrations, the latter having shied away from utterance-level analyses, perhaps out of concern for the perceived acontextuality of textual studies. Codeswitching and codemeshing can be linguistic tools to study language dynamics that can work well with reprise-modification and with "transformed" knowledge, rather than metaphors, models of translingual practice, or tools for teaching.

"Code" as stand-in for "language" is well entrenched. Within the French functional linguistics community, however, it has been rejected as an accurate term for language. Calling a language a "code," meaning an "entity," is far from neutral; the very term "code" already indexes a particular view of language structure and function (see also Canagarajah 2013; Lu 2009). European linguists in the functional framework would argue that languages are not "codes" at all, the term "code" being linked to structuralist assumptions about coherent discrete sets of features that make up an identifiable language.

Code "switching" analyses in linguistics are generally rooted in contact linguistics, a research domain that studies, both descriptively and from interpretive-ideological stances, the question of what happens to language when populations—large or small—come into contact with one another. We know from the mobility and superdiversity studies of today that this "contact" has multiplied in time and laterally in space. Contact can be "light" or "heavy," with degrees of effect: minor code-shifting between languages that might begin with lexical borrowing can trigger "deep borrowing" at the morphosyntactic level, all the way to loss of a language, a "language shift" that can lead in fact to language death (Myers-Scotton 1993, 208).

The writing studies community has taken up the terms "codeswitching" and "codemeshing," with deep debate about them and the value or harm they bring to translingual work (for example, Guerra 2012; Lu 2009; Matsuda 2013; Young 2009). But as Lu points out, "codeswitching" (at least as it has been used in composition and some linguistics work) implies that languages, seen as codes, "are self-evident, discrete, and stable entities which are independent of actual language practices, something language users merely switch on and off without affecting their constitution" (2009, 285). Blackledge, Creese, and Takhi argue that we must move beyond "code" in analyzing contacts in order to shift from a focus on "languages as distinct codes to a focus on the agency of individuals engaging in using, creating, and interpreting signs for communication" (2013, 193). "'A language,'" they argue, "is a construct that is not useful to analysis of language practices, language-in-use" (191).[11]

Here we can return usefully to Bakhtin and François. In a nonstructuralist frame, the "code" in question can be no longer an overall descriptor of a stable language entity but a way of studying the bits (Bakhtin's "language system") that combine and recombine in an unending transformative mobile activity of production of *utterances*, and that are themselves not stable bits, as they construct their meaning partly in use. Bakhtin might argue for the pieces of a language *system* as code, as bits that can be combined and recombined, but languages themselves as constructed out of language-in-use, the site of mobility in terms of knowledge co-construction, reuse, and adaptation and rich translingual practice, both clearly established as the norm, not the "alternative" ways of doing discursive work in the world.

We must distinguish the difference between *"un code = une langue"* (which then allows "codeswitching" or "codemeshing" to describe language-mixing activities) *et "code" du point de vue d'une linguistique pragmatique-fonctionnelle* which would on the other hand be the description of how a system of "bits" (morphemes, phonemes, into lexicon, syntax) reprise-modify in meaning construction. As Bakhtin suggests, those bits, uninhabited until they are realized in utterances, distinguish this analysis from a systems analysis in, say, the sciences, as here even the bits that seem stable are in fact *modifiés* in their *reprises*: historically, socially, use-saturated bits (see also Blackledge, Creese, and Takhi 2013). The "re" and the "mix" in "remix" are both socially saturated,

28 DONAHUE

even as bits, not neutral by history (think of all the ways "re-" has been employed) and yet new in *this* use in ways that modify both bits as well as the whole—all modified with every appearance. Understanding code in this way directly influences our understanding of (trans)linguistic competence and offers more subtle insight into how discourse knowledge adaptation and transformation are at work, whether successfully or not.

2—Competence

Competence as a term has a difficult history. It has been associated with structural linguistics and the traditional distinction between "competence" (innate or acquired ability in the individual) and "performance" (what an individual does, shows, or performs at a moment in time). More recently it has become tied to normative assessment efforts to identify the stable, individual ways "knowledge" as entity can be possessed, including efforts to assess transfer. But a *mobile* understanding of competence can draw on translingual and adaptive transfer orientations. In a mobile paradigm, "communicative competence" (Molina 2011), for example, might designate a writer/speaker's dia- (or multi-?) logic ability to successfully communicate, the transformative ability to merge language resources. This is not the measurable, testable "ability" of the individual autonomous subject but the dialogic co-constructed activity that creates meaning in social contexts.

Recent work on competence has focused on its resistance to traditional models, as "communicative competence" (Leung 2005), "situated competence" (Jonnaert et al. 2006), "culturally situated cognitive competence" (Wang et al. 2004), or "multicompetence" (Hall et al. 2006). While earlier versions of competence were tied to transmission models of education and learning, with students as "cognitive wholes" (Jonnaert et al. 2006, 7), these new models focus on the "sociality" of competence, its fully engaged and socially situated dynamic (Leung 2005). In the culturally situated model of adaptive competence, four factors are at work: "cultural artifacts, cognitive domains, interpersonal contexts, and individual schemata" (Wang et al. 2004, 2). Situated competence is, for Jonnaert et al., "the action of the person in the situation," his or her adaptation; competence is neither internal nor external but inter-influential (2006, 16). These different lenses on competence support the need to see knowledge transfer as equally interactive, dialogic, and engaged, and translingualism as linguistic competence that is socially situated action.

The "multicompetence" model thus connects competence tightly to our understanding of *language* knowledge as "dynamic constellations of linguistic resources, the shapes and meanings of which emerge from continual interaction between internal, domain-general cognitive constraints on the one hand and one's pragmatic pursuits in his or her everyday worlds on the other, that is through language use" (Hall et al. 2006, 226), a model in which "elements of language knowledge are not a priori components belonging to stable, a-contexual systems" (226). In linking the sociocontextual conditions of language use with the way language develops and takes form, Hall et al. cite functional linguistics, psycholinguistics, and sociolinguistics as all providing strong evidence of language systems as fluid, malleable, and in dialogue with social context.

The center of writers' language competence has been presented by Canagarajah (2013) as a "merged proficiency," a mixed, meshed, negotiating reuse accompanied by a mindset of flexibility and de-centering—an orientation (Horner 2016a, 6) with mobility at its center. François (1998) describes "orientation" itself as a competence that is key to productive linguistic-discursive activity—again, a competence that can only be a *relationship* among language user, language in use, environment, and context. We orient in interaction; with, for, and through. We know that "dispositions" can foster writing knowledge reuse (see for example Bereiter 1995; Driscoll and Wells 2012; Horner 2016b; Perkins, Jay, and Tishman 1993), and that dispositions are also what translingual research can link to translingual orientations. Mobility as a writer-speaker's flexibility is thus grounded in competence as the writer-speaker's ecological interactions, intersubjectivity, and situated orientation to learning; that "flexibility" is both freed and constrained.

Mobility also engenders another kind of competence: flexibility, in the sense of openness to uncertainty (Horner 2016a, 10). All language users "let ambiguities pass" as needed; translingual or English as a Lingua Franca (ELF) speakers and writers might do so more markedly, Horner notes, but it is a difference of degree, not of kind (2016a, 18). In the introduction to their collection *Latest Trends in ELF Research* (2011), Archibald, Cogo, and Jenkins highlight Ehrenreich's use of what she calls "accommodation analyses" that show how, in diverse "lingua cultural" contexts, communication is in fact almost always successful only because of the negotiating strategies in use.

This leads Archibald, Cogo, and Jenkins to argue, as does Horner, that ELF is not a set of features, "a distinct set of forms" (Horner 2016a, 9), or a "type" of English, but a particular *use* of English—a set of processes of accommodation involving identity and negotiation (see also Friedrich and Matsuda 2010). We see that resistance to features-driven models echoed in Bakhtin's work on genres (1986, 61). Molina reminds us that principles of textuality (cohesion, coherence, intentionality, acceptability, informativity, situationality, and intertextuality) can be only partially in place and "significant pieces of information lost" (2011, 1249) in multilingual contexts, and yet successful communication can occur (1249). Communicative competence works with partiality, embraces possible contradictions, and so on (this is not new to communication analysts). Here we see another insight for transfer research: understanding what "adaptive reuse" does with partiality, for example, or gaps, and how the knowledge transfers all the same, giving new possibilities for studying transfer-enabling competence.

CONCLUSIONS

"Mobility" is uniquely useful in analyzing translingualism *and* "transfer." The mobility paradigm suggests that the study of linguistic adaptability might serve as a model for the study of knowledge adaptability, and knowledge transfer models might illuminate some (trans)lingual practices. Linguistics has not been central to US writing studies in the past few decades.[12] But French functional and Bakhtinian linguistics is foundational, as we have just seen, to the translingual discussion, and it should be conceptually foundational to the "transfer" one.

While "transfer" (and most alternative terms we've seen developed) is not a term in linguistics research, the concept underlies everything; language acquisition, construction, uttering, and function are always activities of adaptive transformation, whether routine or transformative (and even when routine is transformative). Generalization *is* a linguistics concept, and explains how children acquire language rules, in fact to the point of over-generalizing for periods of time (for example, using an "-ed" ending in "gived"). Language learning and discourse development are unavoidably built on knowledge reuse and adaptation, as the New London Group argued already in 1994. Those mechanisms are worth exploring in order to better understand how writers are in fact constantly developing, interacting, and transforming various parts of their writing competences.

One avenue for further work is in the ways "mobility" *can* be studied in the movements of reprise-modification mentioned earlier. For example, mobility can be a lens for textual analysis. The "mobility" inside a text, seen via manifestations of linguistic, rhetorical, and discursive flexibility, can be studied if we understand text in the linguistic frames presented. Studying "language-in-use" does not need to stop at the level of static textual features. We can study the ways in which an utterance does what it does for a given receiver. The dynamism of the text "is not 'in' the utterance . . . but in the interaction with the subject-using-language" (Donahue 2008) and the many eventual readers who will co-construct meaning with the text.

We have considered here only some aspects of translingualism and some of "transfer." Future research might include, for example, trying out the lens of intertextuality-as-mobility as a way to analyze transfer and translingual practices. Each idea we pursue should help us in trying to consider the intellectual components of both translingual practices and writing knowledge practices in a global/local mobility paradigm that might allow us to study systematically and illuminate that intellectual nature.

NOTES

1. It is also a phenomenon, in terms of linguistic knowledge and competence, that underscores the point that distinctions such as "first" or "second" language appear to be insufficient categories of analysis in this complex context of *contact* (Blommaert and Rampton 2011, 15); they don't meet the realities on the ground. See also Hall et al. re: "native" or "second" language users (2006, 231–232). The issues of mobility are complicated by class and socioeconomic status, as noted in this volume's introduction. See also Blommaert (2010) regarding circuits and scales of mobility.
2. See, for example, Baer 2013: Cao et al. 2010; Horner (2016a) building from DePalma and Ringer's (2011) notion of "adaptive transfer"; Ivancic and Hesketh 2000; Lorimer Leonard and Nowacek 2016.
3. See, for example, Hyland 2003.
4. The significant history and complicated, often conflicting controversy about "Bakhtinian" thought bears reference. Bazerman (2004) mentions needing to "recover" linguist Volosinov from Bakhtin and cites key works originally attributed to Bakhtin as clearly Volosinov's. François (1994) similarly attributes key works to Volosinov and to Medvedev but highlights the difficult historical trails to follow in identifying various authorships. I am drawing primarily from *Speech Genres and Other Late Essays*, not mentioned in the Bakhtin authorship debates though the ideas developed there are certainly indebted to earlier work.
5. A term I first heard used by Jonathan Monroe in *Writing and the Disciplines* (2003).
6. See also Calvet 2006, 7.
7. For other reconceptualizations see DePalma and Ringer 2011, Lave 1988, Greeno 1997, Hatano and Greeno 1999, Davydov 1990, Engeström 2001, Descheeper 2008, Meirieu and Develay 1996, and Astolfi 2002.
8. See, for example, Lu 2009, 287 about transformation and decision-making in language use or Kramsch et al. 2008.
9. For more in-depth explorations of the nature of translation, see Serres 1974; Malakoff and Hakuta 1991; Neubert and Shreve 1992.
10. With notable exceptions, of course. For "transfer," for example, see Beard 2017 or Fishman and Reiff 2008 (though the reliance continues to be largely on forms of student self-report), or Donahue and Johnson 2018, and for translingual activity, we might consider Canagarajah's ethnographic-perspective work or Pavlenko 2006. Empirical methods long used to study bilingualism might be usefully adapted here.

11. See, for earlier treatments of this topic, Young's 1990 *Language as Behaviour, Language as Code*.
12. One certain reason is historical, but another is the lack of frequent translation of writing studies work across nation-states and disciplines (cf. Horner, Necamp, and Donahue 2011).

REFERENCES

Adey, Peter. 2006. "If Mobility Is Everything Then It Is Nothing: Towards a Relational Politics of (Im)Mobilities." *Mobilities* 1 (1): 75–94.

Archibald, Alasdair, Alessia Cogo, and Jennifer Jenkins, ed. 2011. *Latest Trends in ELF Research.* New Castle on Tyne: Cambridge Scholars Publishing.

Astolfi, Jean-Pierre. 2002. "Savoir, C'est Pouvoir Transférer." *Cahiers Pédagogiques* 408 (9).

Baer, Linda. 2013. "Improving the Student Experience: How Big Data Can Influence Student Affairs to Spur Student Engagement." Critical Issues in Higher Education Conference, New York, October 29–30, 2013.

Bakhtin, Mikhail Mikhailovitch. 1986. *Speech Genres and Other Late Essays.* Austin: University of Texas Press.

Bawarshi, Anis. 2016. "Beyond the Genre Fixation: A Translingual Perspective on Genre." *College English* 78 (3): 243–249.

Bazerman, Charles. 2004. "Intertextualities: Volosinov, Bakhtin, Literary Theory, and Literacy Studies." In *Bakhtinian Perspectives on Language, Literacy, and Learning*, edited by Arnetha F. Ball and Sarah Warshauer Freedman, 53–65. Cambridge: Cambridge University Press.

Beach, King. 1999. "Consequential Transitions: A Sociocultural Expedition Beyond Transfer in Education." *Review of Research in Education* 28: 45–69.

Beard, Jill A. 2017. "An Examination of Student Perceptions of Knowledge Transfer in First-Year Composition." Dissertation, University of Tennessee at Chattanooga.

Bereiter, Carl. 1995. "A Dispositional View of Transfer." In *Teaching for Transfer: Fostering Generalization in Learning*, edited by Anne McKeough, Judy Lupart, and Anthony Marini, 21–34. Hillsdale, NJ: Lawrence Erlbaum.

Berthoff, Ann. 1999. *The Mysterious Barricades: Language and Its Limits.* Toronto: University of Toronto Press.

Blackledge, Adrian, Angela Creese, and Jaspreet Takhi. 2013. "Beyond Multilingualism: Heteroglossia in Practice." In *The Multilingual Turn: Implications for SLA, TESOL and Bilingual Education*, edited by Stephen May, 191–215. New York: Routledge.

Blommaert, Jan. 2010. *The Sociolinguistics of Globalization.* Cambridge: Cambridge University Press.

Blommaert, Jan, and Ben Rampton. 2011. "Language and Superdiversity." *Diversities* 13 (2): 1–22.

Calvet, Louis-Jean. 2006. *Toward an Ecology of World Languages.* Translated by Andrew Brown. Cambridge: Polity.

Canagarajah, A. Suresh. 2003. "Practicing Multiliteracies." *Journal of Second Language Writing* 12 (2): 156–162.

Canagarajah, A. Suresh. 2013. *Translingual Practice: Global Englishes and Cosmopolitan Relations.* New York: Routledge.

Cao, Bin, Sinno Jialin Pan, Yu Zhang, Dit-Yan Yeung, and Qiang Yang. 2010. "Adaptive Transfer Learning." *Proceedings of the Twenty-Fourth AAAI Conference on Artificial Intelligence.* 407–412.

Cope, Bill, and Mary Kalantzis. 2009. "Multiliteracies: New Literacies, New Learning." *Pedagogies* 4 (3): 164–195.

Cushman, Ellen. 2016. "Translingual and Decolonial Approaches to Meaning Making." *College English* 78 (3): 234–242.

Davydov, Vasily Vasilovich. 1990. "Problems of Developmental Teaching, Parts I-III." *Soviet Education* 30: 8–10.

Delcambre, Isabelle. 2016. "France." In *Exploring European Writing Cultures*, edited by Otto Kruse, Madalina Chitez, Brittany Rodriguez, and Montserrat Castelló. Working Papers in Applied Linguistics 10, Zurich University of Applied Science, Switzerland.

DePalma, Michael-John, and Jeffrey M. Ringer. 2011. "Adaptive Transfer, Writing Across the Curriculum, and Second-Language Writing." *Journal of Second Language Writing* 20 (2): 134–147.

Descheeper, Catherine. 2008. "Rapport à l'écrit, dimension pragmatique, ancrage disciplinaire, par ou passé l'acculturation aux discours universitaires?" [Relationships to writing, pragmatic dimensions, disciplinary anchoring: What path does acculturation to university discourses take?]. Presentation at a meeting of Journée Internationale du FLE (JIFLE), Université de la Réunion, Saint-Denis, Réunion.

Donahue, Christiane. 2004. "Student Writing as Negotiation: Fundamental Movements between the Common and the Specific in French Essays." *Writing in Context(s): Textual Practices and Learning Processes in Sociocultural Settings*, edited by Fillia Kostouli, 137–164. Amsterdam: Kluwer Academic Publishers.

Donahue, Christiane. 2008. *Écrire a L'Université: Analyse Compare, France-États Unis*. Villeneuve-d'Ascq, France: Presses Universitaires du Septentrion.

Donahue, Christiane. 2018. "'Responsive Understanding' and Receptivity to Global Writing Research." In *Writing for Engagement: Responsive Practice for Social Action*, edited by Mary P. Sheridan, Megan J. Bardolph, Megan Faver Hartline, and Drew Holladay, 261–266. Lanham, MD: Lexington Books.

Donahue, Christiane, and Lynn Foster Johnson. 2018. "Liminality and Transition: Text Features in Post-Secondary Student Writing." *Research in the Teaching of English* 52 (4): 359–381.

Driscoll, Dana Lynn, and Jennifer Wells. 2012. "Beyond Knowledge and Skills: Writing Transfer and the Role of Student Dispositions." *Composition Forum* 26 (Fall).

Dunn, Patricia. 2001. *Talking, Sketching, Moving: Multiple Literacies in the Teaching of Writing*. Boston: Heinemann.

Elliott, Anthony, and John Urry. 2010. *Mobile Lives*. Abingdon, VA: Routledge.

Engeström, Yrjö. 2001. "Expansive Learning at Work: Toward an Activity Theoretical Reconceptualization." *Journal of Education and Work* 14 (1): 133–156.

Fenwick, Tara, and Lesley Farrell, ed. 2012. *Knowledge Mobilization and Educational Research: Politics, Languages and Responsibilities*. London: Routledge.

Fishman, Jenn, and Mary Jo Reiff. 2008. "Taking the High Road: Teaching for Transfer in a FYC Program." *Composition Forum* 18 (Summer).

François, Frédéric. 1994. *Morale et Mise en Mots*. Paris: L'Harmattan.

François, Frédéric. 1998. *Le Discours et Ses Entours* [Discourse and Its Surroundings]. Paris: L'Harmattan.

Friedrich, Patricia, and Aya Matsuda. 2010. "When Five Words Are Not Enough: A Conceptual and Terminological Discussion of English as a Lingua Franca." *International Multilingual Research Journal* 4 (1): 20–30.

Greeno, James G. 1997. "Response: On Claims That Answer Wrong Questions." *Educational Researcher* 26 (1): 5–17.

Guerra, Juan C. 2012. "From Code-Segregation to Code-Switching to Code-Meshing: Finding Deliverance from Deficit Thinking through Language Awareness and Performance." In *61st Yearbook of the Literacy Research Association*, edited by Pamela J. Dunston, Linda B. Gambrell, Kathy Headley, Susan King Fullerton, and Pamela M. Stecker, 29–39. Oak Creek, WI: Literacy Research Association.

34   DONAHUE

Hall, Joan Kelly, Ann Cheng, and Matthew T. Carlson. 2006. "Reconceptualizing Multi-competence as a Theory of Language Knowledge." *Applied Linguistics* 27 (2): 220–240.

Hatano, Giyoo, and James G. Greeno. 1999. "Commentary: Alternative Perspectives on Transfer and Transfer Studies." *International Journal of Educational Research* 31 (7): 645–654.

Hilaricus, Janis R. 2011. "Toward a Sociomaterial Approach to Knowledge Transfer." Presentation at the International Conference for Organizational Learning, Knowledge and Capabilities (OLKC), Kingston upon Hull, UK.

Horner, Bruce. 2016a. "Reflecting the Translingual Norm: Action-Reflection, ELF, Translation, and Transfer." In *A Rhetoric of Reflection*, edited by Kathleen Blake Yancey, 105–124. Logan: Utah State University Press.

Horner, Bruce. 2016b. *Rewriting Composition: Terms of Exchange*. Carbondale: Southern Illinois University Press.

Horner, Bruce, Min-Zhan Lu, Jacqueline Jones Royster, and John Trimbur. 2011 "Language Difference in Writing: Toward a Translingual Approach." *College English* 73 (3): 303–321.

Horner, Bruce, Samantha Necamp, and Christiane Donahue. 2011. "Toward a Multilingual Composition Scholarship: From English Only to a Translingual Norm." *College Composition and Communication* 63 (2): 269–300.

Hyland, Ken. 2003. "Discourse Analysis in L2 Writing Research." *Journal of Second Language Writing* 12 (2): 165–170.

Ivancic, Karolina, and Beryl Hesketh. 2000. "Learning from Errors in a Driving Simulation: Effects on Driving Skill and Self-Confidence." *Ergonomics* 43 (12): 1966–1984.

Jonnaert, Philippe, Johanne Barrette, Domenico Masciotra, and Mane Yaya. 2006. *Revisiting the Concept of Competence as an Organizing Principle for Programs of Study: From Competence to Competent Action*. Montreal, QC: Oré/UQUAM.

Kramsch, Claire. 2009. *The Multilingual Subject*. Oxford: Oxford University Press.

Kramsch, Claire, Danielle Levy, and Genevieve Zarate. 2008. "Introduction." In *Précis du Plurilinguisme et du Pluriculturalisme*, edited by Claire Kramsch, Danielle Levy, and Genevieve Zarate, 15–26. Paris: Contemporary Publishing International.

Lave, Jean. 1988. *Cognition in Practice: Mind, Mathematics, and Culture in Everyday Life*. Cambridge: Cambridge University Press.

Le Boterf, Guy. 1994. *De la Competence: Essai sur un Attracteur Étrange* [About Competency: Essay on a Strange Attractor]. Paris: Editions D'Organisation.

Leung, Constant. 2005. "Convivial Communication: Recontextualizing Communicative Competence." *International Journal of Applied Linguistics* 15 (2): 119–144.

Lorimer Leonard, Rebecca, and Rebecca Nowacek. 2016. "Transfer and Translingualism." *College English* 78 (3): 258–264.

Lu, Min-Zhan. 2009. "Metaphors Matter: Transcultural Literacy." *JAC* 29 (1/2): 285–293.

Lu, Min-Zhan, and Bruce Horner. 2013. "Translingual Literacy, Language Difference, and Matters of Agency." *College English* 75 (6): 582–607.

Lu, Min-Zhan, and Bruce Horner. 2016. "Introduction: Translingual Work." *College English* 78 (3): 207–218.

Malakoff, Marguerite, and Kenji Hakuta. 1991. "Translation Skill and Metalinguistic Awareness in Bilinguals." In *Language Processing in Bilingual Children*, edited by Ellen Bialystok, 141–166. Cambridge: Cambridge University Press.

Martinet, André. 1960. *Éléments de Linguistique Générale*. Paris: Armand Colin.

Matsuda, Paul Kei. 2013. "It's the Wild West Out There: A New Linguistic Frontier in U.S. College Composition." In *Literacy as Translingual Practice*, edited by A. Suresh Canagarajah, 128–138. New York: Routledge.

Meirieu, Philippe, and Michel Develay. 1996. "Le Transfert de Compétences Analysé a Travers la Formation de Professionnels." In *Le Concept de Transfert de Connaissances en*

Formation Initiale et en Formation Continue, edited by Philippe Meirieu, Michel Develay, Christiane Durand, and Yves Mariani, 31–46. Lyon, France: CRDP.

Molina, Clara. 2011. "Curricular Insights into Translingualism as a Communicative Competence." *Journal of Language Teaching and Research* 2 (6): 1244–1251.

Monroe, Jonathan. 2003. "Writing and the Disciplines." *Peer Review* 6 (1): 4–7.

Myers-Scotton, Carol. 1993. *Duelling Languages: Grammatical Structure in Codeswitching.* Oxford: Clarendon Press.

Neubert, Albrecht, and Gregory M. Shreve. 1992. *Translation as Text.* Kent: Kent State University Press.

New London Group. 1996. "A Pedagogy of Multiliteracies: Designing Social Futures." *Harvard Educational Review* 66 (1): 60–92.

Pavlenko, Aneta, ed. 2006. *Bilingual Minds: Emotional Experience, Expression and Representation.* Toronto, ON: Multilingual Matters Ltd.

Pennycook, Alastair. 2010. *Language as a Local Practice.* London: Routledge.

Perkins, D. N., Eileen Jay, and Shari Tishman. 1993. "Beyond Abilities: A Dispositional Theory of Thinking." *Merrill-Palmer Quarterly* 39 (1): 1–21.

Perrenoud, Philippe. 1999. "Transférer ou Mobiliser Ses Connaissances? D'une Metaphore L'autre: Implications Sociologiques et Pedagogiques [Transferring or Mobilizing Knowledge? From One Metaphor to Another: Sociological and Pedagogical Implications]." http://www.unige.ch/fapse/SSE/teachers/perrenoud/php_main/php_1999/1999_28.html.

Purdy, James P. 2014. "What Can Design Thinking Offer Writing Studies?" *College Composition and Communication* 65 (4): 612–641.

Schuster, Charles I. 1985. "Mikhail Bakhtin as Rhetorical Theorist." *College English* 47 (6): 594–607.

Serres, Michel. 1974. *La Traduction* [Translation]. Paris: Les Editions de Minuit.

Tuomi-Gröhn, Terttu, and Yrjö Engeström. 2003. "Conceptualizing Transfer: From Standard Notions to Developmental Perspectives." In *Between School and Work: New Perspectives on Transfer and Boundary-Crossing*, edited by Terttu Tuomi-Gröhn and Yrjö Engeström, 19–38. Bingley, UK: Emerald Group Publishing.

Urry, John. 2011. "Social Networks, Mobile Lives and Social Inequalities." *Journal of Transport Geography* 21: 24–30.

Verstraete, Ginette, and Tim Cresswell, eds. 2002. *Mobilizing Place, Placing Mobility: The Politics of Representation in a Globalized World.* Vol. 9. Amsterdam: Rodopi Press.

Vertovec, Steven. 2007. "Super-Diversity and Its Implications." *Ethnic and Racial Studies* 30 (6): 1024–1054.

Wang, Qi, Stephen J. Ceci, Wendy M. Williams, and Kimberly A. Kopko. 2004. "Culturally Situated Cognitive Competence: A Functional Framework." In *Culture and Competence*, edited by Robert J. Sternberg and Elena L. Grigorenko. Washington, DC: APA Books.

Young, Lynne. 1990. *Language as Behaviour, Language as Code.* Amsterdam: John Benjamins Publishing.

Young, Vershawn Ashanti. 2009. "'Nah, We Straight': An Argument Against Code Switching." *JAC* 29 (1/2): 49–76.

2

MARKING MOBILITY
Accounting for Bodies and Rhetoric in the Making

Ann Shivers-McNair

Distinctions and boundaries are never disinterested: when someone is named as a witch, a factory worker, a rustic, or an illiterate, someone else profits from that distinction. When images are distinguished from texts, someone profits. . . . No body is disinterested. And that is why this work is central to rhetorical studies, which has always taken the study of partisanship as its province.

—Sharon Crowley (1999)

INTRODUCTION

This chapter focuses on the ways in which theories, methodologies, and practices intersect and inform each other in an approach to studying mobility. One of the central arguments I make here is that it is important not to treat "mobility" as a given. As potentially generative and capacious as "mobility" may be as a way of researching and teaching writing and rhetoric, "mobility"—like writing or rhetoric—is not a starting point we can assume. Like writing or rhetoric, "mobility" is *marked*, in the sense of the act of drawing boundary marks.[1] What counts as mobility? Who and what are mobile? What and who do *not* count? The marking of mobility is a boundary-marking practice that makes some bodies, traditions, spaces, and meanings matter at the exclusion of others. And because (as Sharon Crowley reminds us) boundaries are partisan, contested, and dynamic, the marking of mobility itself is both an ethical and a rhetorical concern.

But the marking of mobility is also a research concern: how do we study mobility in a way that accounts for mobility as *marked* rather than *given*? The marking of mobility in our research and teaching entangles the theoretical concepts and traditions we draw on, the methodologies and methods we draw on, and the people, spaces, places, things, and

DOI: 10.7330/9781646420209.c002

rhetorics we engage. In other words, how we mark mobility in the ways we study and teach writing and rhetoric shapes and is shaped by the definitions, knowledges, practices, bodies, spaces, and rhetorics we study and teach. I argue that in order to understand something like mobility, we need to account for this entanglement, for the many markings of boundaries, and for who and what are made to matter and who and what are excluded from mattering. Indeed, the concepts and assumptions we begin with are inflected, crossed, and entangled with the bodies and spaces and things we engage, even as the concepts and assumptions we begin also shape who, what, and how we engage. Thus, in this chapter, I assemble an onto-epistemological framework for attending to the marking of mobility and the making of bodies and rhetorics, and I apply the framework to an example from my research, concluding with implications for further study.

ONTO-EPISTEMOLOGIES OF MOBILITY WORK

In other contributions to this collection, mobility is discussed as or alongside creativity in making and design (Shipka, chapter 7; Wible, chapter 6) and linguistic transformation (Donahue, chapter 1). These inflections resonate with my own understandings of mobility and making as dynamic boundary-marking processes by which meanings, actions, and things are negotiated and renegotiated. And as Wible argues, we also need to attend to the mobility work happening in the choices of designers/makers when they identify "communities to engage and problems to pursue" (109). In other words, the way designers/makers/ writers conceive of the "community" or "audience" they are engaging is itself a boundary-marking practice that both includes and excludes, and that can and should be examined. Furthermore, as Carmen Kynard (chapter 5) and Anis Bawarshi (chapter 9) point out, not everyone experiences mobility in the same way: Mobility can be greatly constrained for bodies marked as other.

The politics of mobility is also operating in our research—specifically, in where we look for mobility (or making, or writing, or rhetoric), and in who and what count as mobile. Jan Blommaert and Bruce Horner argue for a reframing of mobility—of students, of institutions, and of knowledges—"not as a new phenomenon distinguishing some learners, knowledge, and IHEs [institutions of higher learning] from others but as an inevitable feature of all these" (2017, 5). Blommaert and Horner thus draw attention to the boundary-marking practices by which researchers located mobility in the "new" or emergent, and to what was missed and excluded—both in research and in pedagogical applications. In other words, where mobility is located and how mobility is marked is not solely a function of the communities we study, but also of where researchers look for mobility and how researchers mark the boundaries of mobility.

Accountability for boundary-marking processes has long been the concern of feminist, decolonial, and disability studies scholars in writing studies, and the framework for understanding the marking of mobility I am assembling here acknowledges and builds upon these traditions. Jay Dolmage reminds us that because structures, spaces, environments, and pedagogies are often created with a privileged, able-bodied, white male in mind, "disability is *created*, partially, as a result of the biases and proclivities of 'standard' or 'normal' structures," which is why disability studies calls out and intervenes in such boundary marks and the resulting exclusions (2009, 169). Stephanie Kerschbaum similarly calls for a dynamic view of difference "as rhetorically negotiated through 'marking difference'" (2014, 6). Indeed, as Crowley argues, "Distinctions and boundaries are never disinterested" (1999, 363). Or as Kristin Arola argues in articulating criteria for good, careful assemblages, it is important to "consider the relations that came before" (2016, n.p.) and who benefits from the assemblage, just as Ellen Cushman reminds us, in her articulation of decolonial rhetorics, that Western epistemologies are not neutral (2016), and Jennifer Sano-Franchini reminds us the traditions we cite and do not cite can erase non-Western rhetorical practices (2015). In other words, the boundary marks we draw shape who and what come to matter, and who and what are excluded from mattering—not only in physical spaces but also in onto-epistemological spaces.

Karen Barad, an interdisciplinary queer feminist scholar whose work has been taken up in rhetoric and writing studies, also emphasizes accountability to boundary marks as an intersectional concern, and she offers diffraction (drawing on the work of Donna Haraway [1992]) as both a vocabulary and a practice for accountability. In addition to providing a useful approach to accountability in knowledge-making, diffraction is a useful approach to engaging and theorizing mobility work, specifically, in acts of knowledge-making. Diffraction, Barad explains, is "the way waves combine when they overlap and the apparent bending and spreading out of waves when they encounter an obstruction" (2007, 28). Diffraction, like reflection, is an optic metaphor, but whereas reflection relies on a "black-boxing" (to borrow Latour's phrase [1999]) of light as a ray approximation, diffraction attends to the dynamic nature of light itself—and the fact that whether or not light behaves as a wave or particle is entangled with the measuring apparatus itself. Where reflection, as an optic metaphor, proceeds from assumptions of distance, prior-ness, and sameness (however mirrored, triangulated, or mediated), diffraction proceeds from the assumption that differences are marked *within* phenomena, that "subject" and "object" emerge *in* intra-action.[2]

For Barad (and for Haraway), diffraction is not only a way of describing how difference is marked, but also a methodology for theorizing difference that attends to "interference" patterns of waves from multiple sources, rather than privileging one perspective. Key to this approach is the understanding that "diffraction does not fix what is the object and what is the subject in advance, and so, unlike methods of reading one text or set of ideas against another where one set serves as a fixed frame of reference, diffraction involves reading insights through one another in ways that help illuminate differences as they emerge: how different differences get made, what gets excluded, and how those exclusions matter" (30). In this way, diffraction resonates with Peter Adey's articulation of the politics of mobility, in which mobility is differentiated and differential, "power is enacted in very different ways," and in which mobility is relational and experiential, and "it means different things, to different people, in differing social circumstances" (2006, 83). Adey suggests that the difference and relatedness in mobilities and the politics of mobility are the mechanisms by which "illusions of mobility and immobility are created" (83). In both Adey's and Barad's conceptualizations, there is a relational, differential apparatus by which mobility/immobility (or ray/particle) is marked. Barad's conceptualization of diffraction pushes this boundary marking farther to suggest that these marks are not just illusions but are ontological, material marks of mobility and immobility.

As Sharon Stevens and Katrina Powell and Pamela Takayoshi have shown us, diffraction (as Haraway and Barad explicate it) can be a useful orientation to specific methods for studying writing and rhetoric—and, I would argue, mobility work. Stevens (2004) draws on Haraway to articulate a diffractive ethnographic approach that has a goal of making a difference—not only in its impact, but also in the sense that the knowledge it makes is new, not a reflection of some preexisting reality. Powell and Takayoshi (2012) similarly acknowledge the potential of Barad's articulation of diffraction to push feminist epistemologies of reflexive practice even further by highlighting complicated relationships and specific material entanglements, as well as patterns of difference. While neither Stevens nor Powell and Takayoshi explicitly connect diffraction to mobility studies, their uptakes of diffraction highlight mobility work in acts of knowledge-making by attending to the differential and relational nature by which meanings are marked and mobilized in the work of researchers.

Like Powell and Takayoshi, I find diffraction a useful way to think about the active marking of boundaries that helps us attend not only to representation but also to interference, overlap, difference, and erasure. What diffraction helps me see is that a project that attends to boundary marking should attend not only to the markings of mobilities, bodies, and rhetorics, but also to the marking of the research(er) apparatus. This involves accounting for what matters and what is excluded from mattering in the intellectual lineages and concepts we construct (as Sano-Franchini advocates) and in our methodological approaches to the making of knowledge. Our findings in our research are entangled with our research apparatuses: the theoretical and methodological lineages we trace, the spaces and places we come from and research, the bodies and technologies we bring to research and the bodies and technologies we count in our research.

Therefore, as I engage with the robust conceptualizations of mobilities in the work of this collection and in the work of scholars like Adey and Barad, I also draw upon the work of scholars in our field who articulate indigenous approaches to relationality and difference-marking that can help us theorize and engage ethically in mobility work in acts of knowledge-making. Placing indigenous epistemologies in conversation with Western epistemologies is itself an act of boundary marking and mobilization in knowledge-making that takes up the "genuinely comparative approach" that Raúl Sánchez argues "is precisely what is needed if we want to theorize, study, and teach mark-making in a broader-than-merely alphabetic sense—that is, mark-making at the borders between Western Modernity and the Indigenous cultures of this hemisphere" (2017, 87).

Gabriela Ríos models indigenous approaches that center "embodied ways of knowing" and "land-based (or spatial) rather than temporal" meaning making (2015, 68). Ríos emphasizes the active, relational, co-constituting work of bodies and places in the creation and sharing of knowledge, reminding us that the relationality of mobility work is not only about relations among (human) bodies, but also among bodies, places, and spaces. Just as Adey argues that different relations among different bodies marks mobilities in different ways for different people, Ríos argues that different relations of bodies and spaces mark different possibilities for mobilities. Indeed, as Ríos explains, "Indigenous relationality recognizes that humans and the environment are in a relationship that is co-constituted and not just interdependent" (64). Like Barad, Ríos emphasizes that relationality is a co-constituting, ontological phenomenon. In other words, knowing and being take place in dynamic, nonlinear, spatial relations. This means that the accounts we create of acts of mobility are themselves acts of mobility. In other words, how we account for mobility work, including our own mobilities and mobilizations as researchers, is part of what Adey calls the differential, relational politics of mobility work, or what Barad calls diffraction, or what Ríos calls land-based rhetorics. Therefore, my own account of mobilities in a makerspace is informed by these onto-epistemologies of mobility work.

MAKING (AND) MOBILITY

I now turn to an illustration from my research, a multi-year ethnographic case study of a Seattle makerspace, where studying mobility and making presented me with methodological challenges that I seek to address by taking up the onto-epistemologies of mobility work I describe in the previous section. Makerspaces are warehouse-style spaces with traditional and emergent fabrication technologies such as sewing machines, woodworking and metalworking tools, laser cutters, 3D printers, computer-numerical control (CNC) routers, and small electronics. Also known as hackerspaces and fab labs, makerspaces are part of a maker movement that values creativity, entrepreneurship, collaboration, and democratizing access to technologies—and that (by its own account, as well as my own observations) is dominated, at least in the United States, by men (see Maker Movement 2020). Interest in making and makerspaces is growing in rhetoric, writing studies, the digital humanities, and professional and technical communication, evidenced in the work of scholars such as David Sheridan (2010); John Sherrill (2014); Jentery Sayers (2015); and Sarah Fox, Rachel Ulgado, and Daniela Rosner (2015). Makerspaces offer a fruitful site for examining the ways in which boundary marks, like what counts as "making" or "mobility" and who counts as "mobile" or "maker," make certain bodies and traditions matter at the exclusion of others, which in turn shapes what gets made, by whom, and for whom.

When I began my fieldwork, I noticed that it seemed like no one stood or sat still for long in the makerspace, and that they were often talking to me and each other while engaged in various forms of 3D making. Clearly, focusing only on words would not give us the whole picture of the dynamic making at play, and I came to understand my participatory interview-observation practices as "3D interviewing"—a name initially inspired by the movements of fabrication technologies, like 3D printers, on an XYZ axis—to help me describe my work to diffract bodies, movements, spatial relations, spoken and written words.[3] But my initial focus on mostly human movements (as I perceived and experienced them) changed as I got to know the people and processes in the space;

I eventually grew attuned as well to the movements of machines at work, the movements of constantly rearranged furniture, the movements of rhetoric and ideas through networks beyond the space.

And just as a commitment to difference and relationality in mobility work calls our attention not only to interferences and overlaps but also to erasures, I quickly came to realize that for all the bodies, machines, goals, and rhetorics that seemed to be moving and becoming, there were also bodies, machines, goals, and rhetorics that were *not* moving or becoming—or not even present. There were, for example, women who had been involved in founding the makerspace and whom I met at the beginning of my fieldwork, but who ended up leaving the space. And in a space where many of the practices privilege kinds of making associated with certain gendered, raced, or classed identities, I began to question the positive connotation afforded to mobility. Immobility may very well be an exclusion, but could it also be an alternative? After all, Adey argues that "there is never any absolute immobility, but only mobilities which we mistake for immobility" (2006, 83). In this volume, Rebecca Lorimer Leonard (chapter 4) reminds us, similarly, that immobility is constructed, and Carmen Kynard (chapter 5) shows us how immobility can be an act of resistance (in the case of an African American woman resisting her white male boss).

Furthermore, I found that the directions and rates of mobilities varied even in what seemed to be a shared space. There were times when a story I was tracing seemed to be not moving or moving backwards relative to other movement in the space, but when I zoomed out to the view from a year's time, I could see that movement differently. And, crucially, the tracing of these stories and movements is not a linear process, as both Barad and Ríos remind us. My own understandings change, so with every change in my own understanding and the understandings I share with participants and spaces, new past and present and future stories emerge. In other words, I have to account not only for the marking of mobility itself but also of the changing research apparatus and research space through which the boundaries of mobility are marked.

This means accounting for my own changing embodied relationship to the space. Indeed, I came to understand that despite the name "makerspace," neither "maker" nor "space" is a given. I worked to make space for myself, as an outsider to the local maker community, as a writing researcher studying a space where writing is not generally seen as making, as someone unfamiliar with the fabrication technologies I encountered there, as a woman in a space populated almost entirely by men during my fieldwork. The uneasiness I felt as I worked to make space for myself, to mark my own mobility in the space, was as much a part of my research(er) apparatus as the theoretical and methodological approach I was developing and my knowledge of writing, rhetoric, and communication as a practitioner and as a teacher. I do not have the space here to do justice to years of ongoing participatory research not only in the makerspace, but also in a collaborative partnership with one of the women who had initially been involved in the space and in a collaborative study with former students of a making-focused pedagogy in a class I taught during this research project. Instead, I will offer a brief account of how a mobility-marking moment early in my makerspace study both shaped and was shaped by my mobilities as a researcher.

The mobility-marking moment occurred in December 2015, eight months into my field work. Over those eight months, my own mobility in the space as a researcher had changed as I insinuated myself into the workplace culture and processes. At first, my movements were uncertain—I did not know where to put my bag, where to stand or sit, or what machines or objects I could touch. To return to Dolmage's point that spaces create and mark disability in the ways they normalize a certain kind of body, I am reminded that even though my relationship to the space and people in it was tentative at first, my able body still benefited from the ways in which the physical space and practices in the makerspace normalized bodies that move like mine. Still, I often felt overwhelmed by the unfamiliarity of the space, the machines, and the men in the space who did not know how to understand my presence in the space any more than I did. In the first few months, I tended to follow the CEO of the space, who was interested in my research from the beginning and brokered my entry into the space by narrating his actions and movements to me. But as I got to know the other regulars in the space, as well as the machines and processes, my mobility in the space became less tentative and more intentional. Following Ríos, I argue that this was not simply a function of linear time; the re-marking of my mobility was also a re-marking of my relationship to a space, a rehabituating of my own body to move with the bodies (human and machine) in the space. Or, as Ashanka Kumari (chapter 16) puts it in her insightful rereading of my mobility-marking moment in this volume, my mobility work as a researcher was (and is still) contingent and emergent. By December 2015, I had worked through what felt like the most difficult phase of making space for myself, and that re-marking of mobility over time led to another mobilization: incorporating video recording in my field work.

That December, I began using a small digital video camera—sometimes worn on a strap on my head, sometimes held at chest-level—as part of my recording techniques, which also included handwritten and hand-drawn notes, photographs and video taken on my iPhone, objects that I made and that were shared with me, and my embodied experiences and memories. The purpose of the video camera was not ethnographic filmmaking, but a means of accounting for mobility, bodies, knowledges, and rhetorics in the making—including the making of the research study through my active participation in the space. By that December, my mobility in the makerspace had been re-marked: I felt much more comfortable with the people, machines, and processes in the makerspace, and I felt comfortable asking their permission to video record parts of my participatory interactions, particularly since, by that point, there were web cameras installed throughout the space and on or in several machines so that the CEO and regulars could monitor activity. On that particular December day, as I recorded with the camera on my head, I moved throughout the makerspace, tracking conversations and making processes across spaces, machines, and bodies. I interacted with several of the regulars in the space, including Richard, a former graphic designer who helped found the makerspace and who is self-taught in every technology in the space.

On that particular day, Richard was moving, as he often does, among simultaneous projects: a small holiday wreath assembled from red and green pieces he was 3D printing and a plywood dress form to display an LED-enhanced costume he had designed. He was cutting the parts for the dress form on the industrial laser cutter, a machine that cuts through or etches a variety of materials, including wood, plastics, and textiles, with a powerful laser beam. I followed him over to the laser cutter to check on the progress of the cut, camera on my head and notebook and pencil in my hands. After a few seconds of watching the machine, Richard leaned over the machine and slid his right hand through a small opening in the front of the machine designed to create airflow across the cutting bed. With his fingertips, he pressed down the edge of the plywood as the laser beam passed nearby. Involuntarily, my eyes widened.

"Oh, is the board curving up?" I asked, calmly as I could, over the noise of the machine.

"Yeah, warping a bit," Richard replied, without looking up from the machine. As he continued to press down the plywood and watch the laser beam, I described the interaction in my handwritten notes, caught on camera as I tilted my head down to write. "Probably actually shouldn't be doing this," he added, "but . . ." His voice trailed off.

I laughed nervously. "Living on the edge, there," I offered.

Figure 2.1. Richard, a white man with a beard and brown hair (save for a pink ponytail) stands in front of an industrial laser cutter in a warehouse space with his left hand resting on the glass lid of the machine as he watches the machine cut. On the laser cutter bed is a sheet of pale plywood covered in curved lines (cuts for pieces). To the right of the machine is a computer monitor with the laser cutter's tool path and settings. Behind the laser cutter is an unfinished mural, predominantly in blue and yellow, of people working with tools. Access the video (and a transcript) on the Kairos PraxisWiki at http://praxis.technorhetoric .net/tiki-index.php?page=PraxisWiki%3A_%3A3D+Interviewing.

"Yeah, that's how it works sometimes," he said, still watching the machine's movements with his fingers pressing the warped plywood flat. After several seconds, he added, "What do they call that? A 'do as I say, not as I do'?" I laughed again and nodded.

The mobility-marking significance of this 36-second interaction—one of many in nearly two hours of footage from that day—unfolded not only in the moment, but also in relation to past and future interactions in the makerspace and in my analysis and writing. By that point, I had an understanding of the dangers associated with many of the powerful fabrication technologies in the space, and I had become fairly accustomed to observing risky actions, which were not infrequent. (Half an hour after the laser cutter interaction, Richard was using a mallet to force some of the interlocking dress form pieces together, and the heavy mallet head fell off the handle mid-swing. Fortunately, no fingers, toes, or equipment were harmed.) As I watched and edited the footage the next week—while also struggling with what I experienced as a steep learning curve for Adobe Premiere Pro—the laser cutter interaction caught my attention again, as the camera movements and footage prompted me to diffract—to draw on Barad's framework—the words and movements on camera with relationships, understandings, and experiences that happened off camera both before and during this moment.

I realized that just a few months earlier, I would not have understood laser cutting well enough to know that what Richard was doing was risky or to be able to hypothesize (in a question) why he might put his fingers in the machine while it was operating. I also realized that Richard's particular ethos in the space—as a cofounder, as someone with demonstrated competence with the machines, as someone who teaches others how to use the machines—afforded him the space to make that risky move. Just out of the camera frame was a group of regulars (all men), including the CEO, sitting at a conference table. They could see what Richard was doing, and no one stopped him or even remarked on his actions. By contrast, if I, or anyone else without Richard's ethos, had put my fingers on the laser cutter bed while the machine was operating, I would have been stopped immediately. Tellingly, as the camera frame reveals (being, as it was, positioned on my head to follow my gaze), I did not even look at the table group in anticipation of a reaction, because I knew there would be none. And even though I was nervous watching this risky maneuver, I did not intervene, out of deference to Richard's ethos. To put it in Adey's terms, the differential social relations in the space—specifically, the marking of maker ethos—means different movements and mobilities are possible for different bodies in the space. Therefore, instead of intervening in a risky maneuver, I merely sought confirmation of my hypothesis that he had put his fingers on the bed to press the warped board flat. I knew that Richard and his colleagues used scrap materials whenever possible (including warped plywood), and I also understood that the machine's settings were calibrated on the assumption of flat material, and that the laser beam might not cut accurately or completely through the warped section. Indeed, as Ashanka Kumari points out in her response in this volume, the warped plywood itself played an agentive role in the re-marking of mobility work in the space—both in Richard's work on his project and in my research work.

That 36-second interaction and accompanying video became the (nonlinear) starting point for a genealogical account of acts of making in the makerspace that traced both the past and future that unfolded from that moment: my own relationships and movements prior to and after that moment, Richard's relationships and movements prior to and after that moment, and the laser cutter's relationships and movements prior to and after that moment. In that interaction and in many subsequent interactions, I came to a different understanding of the "who" of mobility and making. Instead of marking Richard's human body as the "who" of that risky maneuver, I began to see such maneuvers as cyborg movements, where Richard's proprioception extended not only to his fingers but also to the laser beam. And Richard was not the only cyborg in that interaction: I was a human-camera-notebook cyborg myself. The head-mounted camera footage recorded and externalized not only what I was seeing and hearing, but also where I was looking (and not looking) and how my head and body moved—reminding me and the viewers of the clip that I am not passively gathering but actively co-constructing data, including the ongoing marking and re-marking of mobilities and bodies.

CONCLUSION

The significance of the laser cutter interaction is not that it was the most meaningful moment in my study in some absolute sense. Rather, the significance is the mobility work that it brought forth in and beyond the makerspace and my study, including not only my relationships and movements in the space, but also the insights that shaped my research, teaching, and practice outside of the space and the study. The story of this particular mobility-marking moment could have been told in many different ways, and different mobilities, bodies, and rhetorics could have been included and excluded. The point is that this moment was a way in, and I am accountable to it. Accounting for boundary marks—including the marking and re-marking of mobility in the research(er) apparatus—offers us a way to rework objectivity (or reliability or validity) in knowledge-making. Lucy Suchman, in troubling boundaries between technology design and technology use, advocates for a feminist approach that "reframes the locus of objectivity from an established body of knowledge not produced or owned by anyone, to knowledges in dynamic production, reproduction, and transformation, for which we are all responsible" (2002, 92). In accounting for boundary marks in the phenomena we study, including the concepts, traditions, and methods that form our research(er) apparatus, we mark the mobility and the located-ness of knowledges in the making.

As I noted at the beginning of this chapter, the mobility-marking apparatus I describe here comes from the intersections of theory, methodology, and practice, including the particulars of the makerspace and my relationship to it. As challenging as it was to study a space with completely unfamiliar technologies, where my difference (in terms of my expertise, experiences, and gender) was marked, and where my mobility in the space had to be brokered and negotiated over many months, I found the uneasiness to be a powerful reminder to account for shifting boundary marks. Furthermore, my lack of expertise in fabrication technologies made it not a choice but a necessity to share and acknowledge the locus of knowledge-making with participants. Indeed, as Janet Alsup advocates, sharing the locus of knowledge-making in this way moves beyond "member checks" as a validity measure at the end of qualitative, ethnographic data collection and analysis and toward a co-constructing of knowledge that accounts for the positionalities of the knowledge makers (2010). And a lack of expertise in what participants are doing certainly need not be the only impetus for shared knowledge-making.

In projects that have developed out of the makerspace study, I continue to cultivate shared responsibility for knowledge-making, especially in spaces that I inhabit more comfortably, like a writing classroom—where my whiteness, my education and expertise, and my able and cisgender body is not marked as different, and where my experience of the negotiations and markings of mobility is less acute. For me, this has meant not only inviting participants to be coauthors but co-constructing the data *and* the analytical apparatus with them and accounting for our positionalities and mobilities. And such accountability practices need not be limited to qualitative research; indeed, the reworking of objectivity in accounting for boundary marks in our research might also help us continue to trouble the boundary marks between "qualitative" and "quantitative" research (as Michael Williams and Brian Huot, 2012, have advocated). Whether our research is in classrooms, workplaces, digital spaces, corpora, or communities, we can share responsibility for the locus and making of knowledge, and we can account for the ongoing marking and re-marking of bodies, mobilities, and rhetorics.

NOTES

1. Though I mean "marked" in the sense of drawing boundary marks, I certainly think there is fruitful overlap with the linguistic sense of markedness that Christiane Donahue (this volume) highlights in her chapter.
2. I certainly acknowledge the work that many scholars in our field (including Kathleen Yancey 2016, as her most recent collection on reflection demonstrates) have done to reframe reflection as an active boundary-marking practice. I am not suggesting abandoning reflection, a powerful metaphor and practice in writing studies; I simply find diffraction to be a useful metaphor for accounting for the marking of difference within phenomena.
3. I offer an articulation of 3D interviewing as a method and give examples, including video footage filmed with a body-worn digital video camera, in my 2017 contribution to *Kairos* PraxisWiki (Shivers-McNair 2017).

REFERENCES

Adey, Peter. 2006. "If Mobility Is Everything, Then It is Nothing: Towards a Relational Politics of (Im)mobilities." *Mobilities* 1 (1): 75–94.

Alsup, Janet. 2010. "Beyond Member Checks: Toward Transformative Data Analysis." In *Change Matters: Critical Essays on Moving Social Justice Research from Theory to Policy*, edited by sj Miller and David Kirkland, 97–104. New York: Peter Lang.

Arola, Kristen. 2016. "Creative Repetition, Rhetorical Sovereignty, and the 'Electric Pow Wow.'" Presentation at the Thomas R. Watson Conference, Louisville, KY, October 20–22, 2016.

Barad, Karen. 2007. *Meeting the Universe Halfway: Quantum Physics and the Entanglement of Matter and Meaning*. Durham: Duke University Press.

Blommaert, Jan, and Bruce Horner. 2017. "Mobility and Academic Literacies: An Epistolary Conversation." *London Review of Education* 15 (1): 2–20.

Crowley, Sharon. 1999. "Afterword." In *Rhetorical Bodies*, edited by Jack Selzer and Sharon Crowley, 357–364. Madison: University of Wisconsin Press.

Cushman, Ellen. 2016. "Decolonial Rhetorics and Sequoyan." Presentation at the 50th Anniversary Dartmouth Conference, Hanover, NH, August 10–12, 2016.

Dolmage, Jay. 2009. "Disability, Usability, Universal Design." In *Rhetorically Rethinking Usability: Theories, Practices, and Methodologies*, edited by Susan Miller-Cochran and Rochelle Rodrigo, 167–190. New York: Hampton.

Fox, Sarah, Rachel Rose Ulgado, and Daniela K. Rosner. 2015. "Hacking Culture, Not Devices: Access and Recognition in Feminist Hackerspaces." *Proceedings of the 18th ACM Computer-Supported Cooperative Work & Social Computing*, Vancouver. https://dl.acm.org/doi/10.1145/2675133.2675223.

Haraway, Donna. 1991. *Simians, Cyborgs, and Women: The Re-Invention of Nature*. New York: Routledge.

Haraway, Donna. 1992. *The Promises of Monsters: A Regenerative Politics for Inappropriate/d Others*. New York: Routledge.

Kerschbaum, Stephanie. 2014. *Toward a New Rhetoric of Difference*. Urbana, IL: Conference on College Composition and Communication/National Council of Teachers of English.

Latour, Bruno. 1999. *Pandora's Hope: Essays on the Reality of Science Studies*. London: Harvard University Press.

Maker Movement. 2020. *Make: Community*. https://make.co/maker-movement/.

Powell, Katrina, and Pamela Takayoshi. 2012. *Practicing Research in Writing Studies: Reflexive and Ethically Responsible Research*. New York: Hampton.

Ríos, Gabriela. 2015. "Cultivating Land-Based Literacies and Rhetorics." *LiCS* 3 (1): 60–70.

Sánchez, Raúl. 2017. "Writing." In *Decolonizing Rhetoric and Composition Studies: New Latinx Keywords for Theory and Pedagogy*, edited by Iris Ruiz and Raúl Sánchez, 77–90. New York: Palgrave MacMillan.

Sano-Franchini, Jennifer. 2015. "Cultural Rhetorics and the Digital Humanities: Toward Cultural Reflexivity in Digital Making." In *Rhetoric and the Digital Humanities*, edited by Jim Ridolfo and William Hart-Davidson, 49–64. Chicago: University of Chicago Press.

Sayers, Jentery. 2015 "Making in the Academy: A Long View." *UVic Maker Lab*. http://www.maker.uvic.ca/union/.

Sheridan, David. 2010. "Fabricating Consent: Three-Dimensional Objects as Rhetorical Compositions." *Computers and Composition* 27: 249–265.

Sherrill, John. 2014. *Makers: Technical Communication in Post-Industrial Participatory Communities*. Thesis, Purdue University.

Shivers-McNair, Ann. 2017. "3D Interviewing with Researcher POV Video: Bodies and Knowledge in the Making." *Kairos: A Journal of Rhetoric, Technology, and Pedagogy* 21 (2). http://www.praxis.technorhetoric.net/tiki-index.php?page=PraxisWiki:_:3D%20Interviewing.

Stevens, Sharon. 2004. "Debating Ecology: Ethnographic Writing that 'Makes a Difference.'" *Ethnography Unbound: From Theory Shock to Critical Praxis*, edited by Stephen Brown and Sidney Dobrin, 157–180. New York: State University of New York Press.

Suchman, Lucy. 2002. "Located Accountabilities in Technology Production." *Scandinavian Journal of Information Systems* 14 (2): 91–105.

Williams, Michael, and Brian Huot. 2012. "A Modest Proposal for Common Ground and Language for Research in Writing." In *Practicing Research in Writing Studies: Reflexive and Ethically Responsible Research* edited by Katrina Powell and Pamela Takayoshi, 31–57. New York: Hampton.

Yancey, Kathleen, ed. 2016. *A Rhetoric of Reflection*. Logan: Utah State University Press.

3
SMALL M– TO BIG M–MOBILITIES
A Model

John Scenters-Zapico

People move: John's at School A and now he's moved to School B. We typically know fossilized outcomes of others' moves and know nothing about why and what happens when a move takes place. As a result, we end up treating professional moves as news, rather than the norm, despite their prevalence. Yet, from my first day in graduate school, I have wondered what my colleagues experience when they immerse themselves in a professional move. From an auto-ethnographic lens I use this chapter to explore my experiences moving, while proposing a small m–mobilities paradigm flexible enough for creating an informative approach to understanding our common and uncommon personal and professional experiences when we decide, or are forced, to move. The small m–mobilities model allows professionals a process to note reasons and patterns for moving; combined small m–mobilities narratives will help us make visible Big M–Mobilities narratives, which would serve as powerful insights into the conditions causing the movement of compositionists.

I spent thirteen of my fourteen years in various Writing Program Administrator (WPA) positions at the University of Texas, El Paso (UTEP), created and had approved by the Texas Board of Regents a highly successful PhD program in Rhetoric and Writing Studies (RWS), created one of the busiest writing centers in the country with successful Writing Across the Curriculum initiatives, was promoted from assistant to associate to full professor, was serving as dissertation and thesis advisor for more students than any other faculty member in the RWS program, and was a productive scholar. This may sound like a great setting and experience, but my successes were neither rewarded nor compensated. As a result, I left, taking a job at California State University, Long Beach (CSULB) as its inaugural WAC WPA in the fall of 2014. My move might appear as "free choice"; however, the reality is that my experience

DOI: 10.7330/9781646420209.c003

was more in line with what Richard Miller calls "constrained choice" (1999, 7), in that with such choices "we have no way of knowing for sure whether or not we've made the right choice at any given moment" (13). While many of us may have tenure, our work, programs, projects, etc., are too often treated by the university as temporary. From mobilities studies I came to realize that my experiences at UTEP represented something even more complex.

I begin my exploration by discussing some of the mobility research that informed this project, and then discuss and explore a small m–mobility paradigm, one I hope serves to build to a Big M–Mobility paradigm capable of informing the complexities of professional mobilities, from PhD students to veteran teachers and scholars. Finally, as an example of small m–mobility, I focus on my own professional and personal compounded "trip" moving from Texas to California. Here I examine how one small m–mobilities' analysis can help our understanding of professional experiences while explaining the affective as well as practical embodied experiences shaping the kind of movement—and stasis—that this writing program administrator experienced. I strive to build from Tim Cresswell's advice to avoid telling "stories to each other with no relevance beyond their own confines" (2006, 7). My goal is for my small m–mobilities to become part of many other small m–mobilities' narratives, which will lead to relevant Big M–Mobilities' insights into the why, how, and duration of being in mobility. As an auto-ethnographer I delved into my exterior physical engagements and interior thoughts, experiencing these within the changing social settings caused long before, during, and after my WPA move. By drawing from auto-ethnography's stress on self-reflection as a way of knowing and as an approach to understanding and explaining how we act and are acted upon, I share my personal experiences and evolving identity. As Hamilton, Smith, and Worthington state, I looked "inward at the vulnerable self that is moved, refracted, and resisted during the process" while also maintaining an "easily identifiable cultural component" (2008, 24; 22). Small m–moblities is squarely focused on cultural, social, political, and economic factors affecting the movement of labor within composition.

MOBILITIES, MOBILITIES, MOBILITIES

Two key conceptual terms are movement and mobility. Movement, Cresswell argues, is an abstracted form of mobility, a "general fact of displacement before the type, strategies, and social implications of that movement are considered" (2006, 3). While initially counterintuitive, Cresswell adds that movement is about place and location—because they are closely connected to how we interpret movement and mobility. When we use "location," this is ordinarily understood as static, objective, and impersonal. On the contrary, "place," when associated with mobility, is understood to be an active and personalized version, one we individualize—place is an event, "both the context for practice . . . and a product of practice" (Cresswell 2002, 26). A key difference between mobility and movement, then, is that mobility and place combine to make the flow between places personally experienced. We might say it is an existential way of being and describing our mobilities. The significant distinction here is that mobility is up close and personal, yet, at the same time, these qualities are difficult to grasp because people and things in mobility are often associated with things we do not understand, or even fear.

Mobility studies raises the argument that most of the disciplines from which it is derived take a "sedentarist" perspective, one assuming people and things are normally stationary rather than mobile. Any deviation from this view can be seen as something different, even dreaded. For example, people on the move, such as gypsies, compositionists, troubadours, vagabonds, rhetoricians, freeway flyers, hitchhikers, and hobos, to name a few, are "people without place, their status . . . tenuous at best" (Cresswell 2006, 11; also see George 1990 for a view of WPAs' experiences). The same critique is leveled at the social sciences' approach to seeing people "deterritorialized," left "nomadic and placeless in a frenetic and globalized existence. Mobilities looks at movements and the forces that drive, constrain and are produced by those movements" (Sheller and Urry 2006, 208). The argument here is that those who move or are in mobility undermine the norm of a sedentary, landed *status quo*. Within the terms of this sedentarist norm is also the notion that those on the move are on the lower end of the socioeconomic ladder. At the same time, we also know that those in higher social categories globetrot, work from multiple international locations, or, in the professoriate, hop jobs and take fellowships at desirable locations. Such individuals tend to have more control over their movements.

In "The Language of Exclusion," Mike Rose advances that the needs of students in writing classes are perceived as temporary, not part of the ordinary (normal) business of the university (1985). The logical conclusion of believing students' writing needs are temporary is that composition instruction (understood as performing a strictly remedial service) and its instructors are likewise temporary. These "itinerant" workers, often hired and paid as such, are not seen as part of the normal fabric of our institutions. They are, in short, not normal (or sedentary and static). On the one hand, some institutions seem to work very hard to keep us in stasis (per what we can accomplish institutionally), and on the other hand, by keeping us fixed, they can also create frictional working conditions. Stasis becomes the norm. The mobility shift alters that understanding, assuming movement as the norm. In my case, this conflict resulted in my delay in deciding to make any move. To explore why this was the case, I developed three conceptual tools to guide me in understanding my experiences.

In the next section I introduce three new concepts making up the small m–mobilities paradigm: 1. Mobility Stages, 2. Contingent and Emergent Places, and 3. Inertia Starters. Through these concepts I attempt to reveal how small m–mobilities can capture the dynamic movements causing mobility variables and notions that were once considered static. Mobility Stages, Contingent and Emergent Places, and Inertia Starters inductively came about as I sifted through my notes, emails, contracts, plans, and thoughts. Once developed, they helped me hone in on key issues and realize new understandings of my small m–mobilities experiences. In turn, these three key tools can serve to unite compositionists' experiences through our being able to finally see how, if we remain fragmented in the way we are treated, we are voiceless. If, however, we accumulate many compositionists' small m–mobilities' stories, we have a chance to turn our non-locations into healthy, valued, respected, and rewarded places.

1. Small m–mobility Stages

Small m–mobility stages are a means to document the approximate places and dates that we anticipate accomplishing or completing something during our periods of professional mobility. These can be differentiated from evolving and unpredictable variables as they appear, accounting for decisions causing possible alterations in course or even stasis. With mobility stages we are able to describe and document changing and altering mobilities while in motion or afterwards. In the case of a professional move like mine, I created some mobility stages ahead of time for two reasons. First, they served as a list of tasks I wanted to accomplish by specific dates. These stages underwent changes based on unseen, unpredictable circumstances or the needs of others who altered my own (e.g., family). Second, these stages are important in that they became blips on the radar for me to psychologically see I was "getting there," even though "there" was multiple and oftentimes evolving targets.

Mobility Stages are dynamic in that they can be planned, replanned, and unplanned. They can provide insights into how and where mobility subjects alter their trajectories. Like radar blips, Mobility Stages may not tell *why* mobility alterations take place, merely that they *do* take place.

2. Contingent and Emergent Events

Mobility Studies scholars have made it clear that they wish to disconnect from several disciplines that focus on static locations, people, and ideas, what Urry points out about sociology: It "views the social world as an array of separate 'societies', bounded entities or sedentary containers of geographical propinquity" (Sheller 2014, 793; Urry 2007; Urry 2000). As I studied my own mobilities, I realized that considering points or positions as static was not how I experienced them. I had to discover an alternative way to think of these points and positions, so I began considering our "to and from" points or positions as essential fluid mobility locations for several reasons.

First and simply, if we are studying mobilities we need points and positions; without them we could not focus on specific spaces of flows (Castells 1996) or one mobility space and not others. Mobility spaces, in order to be studied, need some form of visible or even defined unseen area of examination. For example, small m–mobilities are framed by local experiences such as job dissatisfaction and economic stagnation, and distant events such as a school's job call for a WPA, Rhetoric and Composition specialist, or composition adjunct. If we take these out of the space, we no longer have key architectural components for small m–mobilities.

Second, I began contemplating ways to capture the dynamism of what I experienced and perceived in my points or positions. I settled with Contingent and Emergent Events (CEE). Reflecting on it afterwards, I feel CEE captures the complexity of our to-and-from starting points, even if these are professional (administrative, political, lecturer, adjunct) positions like the one I was trying to hold onto at UTEP. While this auto-ethnography focuses on one person and his experiences, the angles that small m–mobilities ask us to examine could be helpful toward a better understanding of the movements of our large and growing body of contingent laborers within composition. It is a job in itself to have to work to keep hold of positions that are prone to being ignored or let go; but such experiences are yet another manifestation of our allegiance to a sedentarist framework for thinking of our work.

Most of our ostensibly static points, I argue, are made up of CEEs like our home and work locations. The insistence in mobility studies that we need to understand the mobilities between A and B is still accurate and needed, but in considering the space between A and B the only dynamic space, we negate the notion that A and B themselves are dynamic, fluid, in motion, perhaps even the space between wider sets of A and B—a canyon within a canyon.

Third, CEEs suggest an outer area, one constantly undergoing change. Our starting and destination points have the potential to be as dynamic as the mobility space we study. To overlook this results in not seeing an additional dynamic to our spaces of flows, and not realizing that our beginning and ending points, as part of the whole, are significant features for mobilities. Whenever a person or object begins, enters, or returns to a CEE, the person or object in the CEE experiences some form of friction, from people or objects in motion, or people or objects attempting to maintain their static positions.

Fourth, once we identify our key CEEs, and where people are part of the object of study, we need to recognize that they have some attachment (good, bad, or ambivalent) to the CEEs. This type of attachment I came to label as "Memorable Contingent and Emergent Events," ones that trigger notions of identity and place. Such attachments, for example, are how we actively "re-member" that which the attachment is in order to maintain and reproduce it, thereby transforming the attachment and our identity in relation to it (Tusting 2000). While Altman and Low (1992) have depicted place attachment as the ways that people and places become attached, Steele defines sense of place as "an experiential process created by the setting, combined with what a person brings to it" (Steele 1981, 9; also see Manzo 2003). Memorable Contingent and Emergent Events further clarify that they are composed of emotional attachments that, unless stated, would remain unknown to most people. In this way the concept of Memorable Contingent and Emergent Events is a strategy to bring out the ways in which places are ongoing constructions. From my experience I ended up seeing myself (in relation to UTEP and elsewhere) differently, too: I was someone who could leave, work elsewhere, was in demand, etc. Unfortunately, while this sounds like a great thing, we sacrifice much in being itinerant. Living in California now I see the contingent composition labor pool—Freeway Flyers—treated as throw-away, replaceable tools by the many universities hiring/firing/replacing them.

The components of CEEs are useful and practical. On one level they make us aware that locations are fluid. What makes Contingent and Emergent Events even more significant are the events we attribute to them or identify as these. For past, present, and future mobility professionals, CEEs will allow them to reflect and document what makes their locations more than static, fossilized settings. We begin to turn our gaze to positive or negative attachments and attributes that are distributed over oftentimes large swaths of geographical locations. From CEEs we will have two solid pieces of information. We will become aware of what types of geographical contact mobility professionals experience, while also becoming more sensitive to geographical psychological connections they have in their CEEs.

These first two stages set us up to delve into the third part of the small m–mobility paradigm. While stage 1 asks how we think about our movements, going beyond more than just the move itself, the second stage considers how fixed locations are actually mobile themselves, especially when we think about how places are constructed, and affective. Next, inertia starters give us the full picture of what activities and events actually create mobility and are key to understanding the why of movement.

3. Inertia Starters

Juxtaposed from CEEs, which evoke specific psychological attachments to events, the following discussion of Inertia Starters teases out and reveals personal, psychological (internal) experiences with (external) actions. Informed by Sheller and Urry's fourth theoretical influence, Inertia Starters concern "the recentering of the corporeal body as an affective vehicle through which we sense place and movement, and construct emotional geographies" (Sheller and Urry 2006, 216).

Why are the objects or people under study where they are, in the space of flows? In my quest to answer this question I arrived at a term I am adapting from physics and aircraft engines: Inertia is "that property of matter by virtue of which it continues in its existing state, whether of rest or of uniform motion in a straight line, unless that state is altered by an external force" (Oxford 2016a). An inertia starter is a device used on engines before electric starters were invented; these starters depended on a person to spin a motor out of its resting state to a firing state (Oxford 2016b). For mobility, I view inertia starters as the sum of a person's thoughts, experiences, and actions coalescing with enough energy to enact or alter movement. Two categories of inertia starters became apparent: external and internal.

Once CEEs were visible, I became aware that all mobilities need a reason to be, to come into presence mentally and physically. Watts asks, "When does a train journey begin? As an ethnographer it began with negotiating access and permission from the train operating company.

But it also began with imagining the journey, imagining some moment of arrival in sufficient clarity that I knew I would need to stay overnight near the final station-stop of Penzance . . ." (2008, 713). Watts's questions are what prompted me to dig wider and deeper in order to understand *why* mobilities begin and *what* inertia starters would look like. External inertia starters are what the object or person in mobility experiences from outside contacts; these might be positive or negative frictions (friction is necessary to both stasis and movement). Cresswell's definition of a mobilities approach additionally fuels my thinking into external inertia starters: "[A] mobilities approach considers all forms of movement from small-scale bodily movements, such as dance or walking, through infrastructural and transport aided movements to global flows of finance or labour. Understanding these things together adds up to more than the sum of the parts" (2010, 552). In seeking interconnections, ones that hinder or enable, I saw how these forces could actually serve as potential propellants. Likewise, I wondered what role musings and internal dialogue played. Internal Inertia Starters are generally psychological and unseen, yet they are experienced long before any movement takes place and, as I now see, are instrumental to movement.

Once the role of internal and external inertia starters became clear, I realized that Watts's journey had begun long before she accounted for it. I became aware that my own movements started before any visible movement took place as my understanding and insight into what I wanted personally and professionally became clearer. My inertia starters, while still in Contingent and Emergent Texas and UTEP, had internal and external inertia starters that would eventually determine and propel my mobility.

My professional dissatisfaction with UTEP administrators arose partly as a consequence of conflicting trajectories: I wanted a topnotch program; they, it seemed, wanted to keep the program in stasis—quiet, and in its place. My internal inertia starters derived from my experiences at Contingent and Emergent UTEP, and later in the process from Contingent and Emergent CSULB. There was jockeying from internal inertia starters manifested at UTEP that combined with external inertia starters (email and phone communications) from CSULB. These created an admixture of forces for *possible* mobilities. In my current location at CSULB, I am now among a large contingent composition labor force, and I am regularly saddened to hear and see their indifferent treatment. While many similarities to my small m–mobilities exist, their small m–mobilities' experiences, once told and documented, could unite into a Big M–Mobilities narrative, serving as inertia starters for humane and valued treatment. These admixtures show us how mobility studies can expand our thinking of "routine" moves and displacements for composition professionals.

In my present account, this also helps to explain my UTEP administrators' failures to respond to my funding requests for a documented need for additional tutors, online tutoring equipment, and staff training, to name a few. They may have imagined that the "needs" of the University Writing Center (UWC) were temporary and therefore could be ignored, unlike the need for, say, a medieval literature or accounting professor, since these (and the curriculum requiring courses in them) are believed to be stable, part of the enduring landscape of the institution and "higher" curriculum requiring courses in them. Perhaps more importantly from this mobility perspective, we can begin to make sense of why those of us in rhetoric and composition need to pay attention to mobility studies.

The sedentary-mobility dichotomy is further compounded by the view that people and things in mobility can also be categorized as immoral. Cresswell elaborates on this in the following way: "Mobility is experienced as *anachorism*—the spatial equivalent to *anachronism*. While anachronism is a logical category (a thing out of time), anachorism is a social and cultural category—a thing out of place or without place entirely. Insofar as place is a morally resonant thing-in-the world, mobility as anachorism is a threat to the moral world" (2006, 55). In my three decades in rhetoric and composition I have expressed concern over how much what we contribute to our institutions is simply ignored or is considered intimidating to administrators who are threatened by the fact that we are, contradictorily, two places at once; we are out of place while being a part of every place and discipline. Thinking of issues such as these became important in how I attempted to orient myself as I moved and, in hindsight, by studying my move and wondering how others' similar and dissimilar professional moves, our small m–mobilities, could possibly reveal Big M–Mobilities. What do some workplaces do to retain employees they have invested deeply in and others who seem indifferent to turnover and disruption? It is important to note that, like D'Mello and Sahay, I did not set off with or adopt an a priori methodology in making meaning of my collected and remembered information; as they suggest, "a set of themes was inductively evolved through an ongoing process of engagement with the data" (2007, 172). From my reflections, correspondence, conversations with friends both during and after the move, and my internal dialogues, I observed a set of themes inductively evolve into this small m–mobilities paradigm.

SMALL M–MOBILITIES OF A WRITING PROGRAM ADMINISTRATOR

In "The Art and Craft of Train Travel," Watts embarks upon a mobility narrative of a train journey, asking "how do links between places get made and broken whilst onboard a train carriage? What specific social and material relations and arrangements are involved?" (2008, 712). She shares snippets of observations via her notes, from sandy train seats and passenger types to mobile phones and bridges, what she calls "all the social and technological flotsam of train travel" (712). What struck me about Watts's study is her attention to detail; it is personal while also capturing the essences of her mobility experience. She notes where she seemingly morphs from auto-ethnographer to train passenger when she interacts with others on the train.

Watts provided me with ways to think about the complexity I was experiencing while on the move between Texas and California, morphing from researcher, observer, and ethnographer to passenger, memoirist, and subject. Cresswell's view that "[m]obility involves a displacement—the act of moving between locations [that] may be towns or cities, or they may be points a few centimeters apart" also accurately situated my journey (2006, 2). My experience in a professional move for twenty-one months opened up new reflections on my own professional mobility experiences. I became aware that other professionals on the move might have a lot in common, and we could learn from our shared mobility stories. These combined awarenesses, while "heady, and vertiginous . . . ," may also reveal "a more adequate rendering of the unsteady state in which we find ourselves" as compositionists (Horner et al., this volume, Introduction). What circumstances and documents come into play, and perhaps have in common, when we decide to explore the job market? As Bawarshi asks, does a genre mobilization cause "a redirection, a swerve or pivot move that opened[s] up new pathways and the possibility for new relations"? (Bawarshi, chapter 9). Johnson insightfully notes that such swerves and pivots make clear that "this lack of reciprocity was caused by changing spatial narratives," and "the small m–mobility model engages in the important work of providing tools for articulating micro-level concerns with professional and personal mobility" (chapter 12), and Epps's notion of being in non-places strikes an especially close and familiar sensation compositionists have experienced for decades (chapter 18).

The exploratory definition I arrived at for small m–mobilities rests on the following assumptions: First, mobility is by its very nature and terminology a social construct. This implies that it is composed of similar and shared experiences, ones that can allow us to interpret and understand possible inter/intra-movements and connections among small m–mobilities. Second, small m–mobilities exist in complicated interaction, and their movements are inherently some form of social interaction. The result is that their very mobility is dependent upon available and accessible mechanisms (transportation, courier, roads, jobs) and the ability of those (people, objects, ideas) experiencing small m–mobilities to locate, participate, interact, and react to them. When we recognize that small m–mobilities depend on such interactions, we can begin to make sense and create meaning from them. Third, the complex movement and interaction of people and objects in mobility stresses that each mobility is a distinct enactment. For example, if Watts repeated her train passage, she would have similar mobilities' notes as those included in her original essay. However, with a second trip she would also have many different variables, such as passengers, conductor, time of year (winter equals no sand on the seats, possibly).

INERTIA STARTERS IN TEXAS

In this section I analyze the clear conflict between the direction the UTEP program was heading and the direction I wanted and had believed I was working toward. These were directions that would never align.

The theory making up inertia starters helps answer Revill's call for a "theorisation of the role of infrastructure" in creating a desire to be mobile (2014, 506). UTEP administrators or other inter-/intra-institutional factors or actions create a complex interplay of external and internal inertia starters. While I believed I was creating small-scale changes at UTEP, aligned with Porter et al.'s work (2000) advocating achievable local action in order to create large-scale change, I came to realize that Johnson's institutional critique was more in line with what was transpiring: "Radical and disruptive change can lead to unpredictable and disturbing results, especially in institutions that have a long historical legacy, institutions like the modern university system" (2014, 382). Improvement based on documented successes and needs is not a guarantee for change, recognition, or equity.[1]

Several internal inertia starters were stirring me. On the one hand, the UWC at UTEP (enrollment 23,400) went from having approximately 5,200 student contacts per year when I started as director to over 12,000 per year in three years. Student and faculty assessment of our services was excellent; student writing was improving, and their view toward writing was positive. The same was true of our WAC/WID initiatives from the UWC, a separate innovative dissertation writing assistance program

62 SCENTERS-ZAPICO

Table 3.1. Delay as avoidance examples

I'll get back to you as soon as I can.
If I don't get back to you in a couple of weeks, contact me again.
I'll look into it.
I'll meet with the dean and get back to you.
I didn't have a chance to bring this up with the dean at our last meeting, but maybe next month. I promise.

for all PhD programs on campus and new, live, online tutoring. Despite more than doubling our numbers and our excellent assessments (at an open-admissions undergraduate school where informed writing tutoring is needed), the UWC's funding remained stagnant. This trend and treatment, sadly, are what many of my fellow WPAs experience nationwide.

I made countless visits to my chair, dean, and provost to seek increased funding to keep up with our demand. All were pleased with the results and data collection, but when it came to recognizing success for our students with an increased budget to hire more tutors to handle the demand and to open evenings and weekends, my campus bosses started ignoring my emails, or more commonly, they practiced "delay as avoidance" (table 3.1[2]). These responses and cancelled meetings kept me at bay for weeks, months, and finally, years. As a matter of fact, these replies became interchangeable on most subjects with administration.

As I see it now, my administrative superiors worked hard to maintain me in a state of professional stasis or inertia. It is easy to overlook the fact that it takes considerable effort and thought to keep people "in place" (and in limbo), despite conditions that would otherwise encourage them to leave. In my case, I was given (false) hope that the situation was in greater flux than it really was, whereas I was simply treading water. I experienced movement without mobility.

These responses, combined with other delay-as-avoidance tactics, created another step toward my small-m mobilities. While I would continue my request for equity, I took on another strategy: One afternoon I updated my résumé. This made me feel better, a shot of self-esteem from my hard work. Adey et al. perfectly capture this facet to inertia starters: "And in all these cases, becoming stuck, being bogged down, or being detected may also be a crucial event" to enacting mobilities (2014, 15). For me, my internal inertia starters were ones no one knew of, but they were the impetus for *any* possible future mobility. If I could not cause change locally, I would need an external inertia starter, like another institution looking for a WPA.

Small m– to Big M–Mobilities 63

Internal and external inertia starters are symbiotic variables in that one is irrelevant without the other. In this regard internal and external inertia starters are an ongoing dialogue shaping one's movements (including one's decision to stay in place). In February 2014, I flew to California for a campus visit and had a contract three days after I returned. I emailed my dean with the news that I had been extended an offer as full professor and WPA elsewhere and would like to meet with her. After a few days, she replied, "See [chair's name] about this." This response served to validate my sense of the need to be proactive and amenable to a move. In that same response, the dean cc'd my chair, so I decided I would let her contact me. If UTEP wanted to retain me under equitable circumstances, the chair would need to contact me this time. With two days remaining to sign my CSULB contract, my chair wrote to me: "We should probably get together and chat about this. Contact [my administrative assistant] to set up a meeting." I met with her the next morning, on the day before my contract was due.

My chair immediately stated she would hate to lose me, yet feared there was no funding available to compete with anyone. She next asked, "What are your needs?" While I was shocked that she mixed those two statements, I presented what I had been bringing to her attention for the last two years. Her immediate response was, "I don't think we can do anything. The budget is so tight, John. I can talk to [the dean], but I doubt she'll be able to do anything. I just don't think we have any money for the UWC or to compete."[3] At that moment I had the sad realization that I had invested fourteen years at UTEP; in colleagues, programs I started, students, and community friends. "After careful consideration," I succinctly wrote, "I feel the position at CSULB is the right one for me at this stage in my career." While there was no visible mobility yet, my mobility stage with a destination was now ready to be marked. A week too late the dean emailed me that we should talk about trying to come up with a counteroffer. Even though nothing had visibly moved, a combination of internal and external inertia starters had turned my movement motor on.

It became clear at this mobility stage that internal and external inertia starters are essential to understanding and studying mobility. Understanding that internal inertia starters inform possible movements and trajectories—but do not fully determine them—will guide us to better understandings of our more visible mobility: the movement between A and B. From this we can create awareness of a significant stage of mobilities, one beginning before any visible movement has started. The small m–mobilities paradigm can counter our disposition to misunderstand my experience at my former institution as a deviation from the norm rather than an ongoing effort by my supervisors to keep things working according to plan, as Johnson argues in his contribution to this collection. My supervisors had to work to maintain stasis, inertia, and status quo conditions.

MOVING FORWARD

This small m–mobile paradigm allows us to view our individual mobilities from several revealing angles. Cresswell laments that "Movement is rarely just movement; it carries with it the burden of meaning and it is this meaning that jumps scales. It is this issue of meaning that remains absent from accounts of mobility in general, and because it remains absent, important connections are not made" (2006, 6–7). The small m–mobility paradigm is the first component in a process to unburden some of the complex meaning-making evoked during our mobilities. Once the small m–mobility paradigm is applied to multiple types and forms of mobilities, our observations could prove useful for studying, interpreting, and connecting similar types of mobilities. For example, Watts could repeat her train journey at different times of the day or season, while others embark and study the "same" mobility. In this way the multiple experiences of these small m–mobilities would reveal commonalities of experience while also highlighting dissimilar qualities.

Horner teases out some important arguments causing the "to and from" that embattles our profession. Some of these include recognition "of students and of teachers with students—as also labor. . . . For to accept from the start a reductive definition and valuation of labor is to accept terms of negotiation set by capital, serving its interests" (2016, 93), and the "now well-documented 'feminization' of composition work—that is, its treatment as not real work, manifested in the relegation of much of the teaching of composition to contingent hires assigned low pay, no job security, and typically no benefits" (95). Contingent faculty, with histories at, more often than not, several institutions and online, are anything but "contingent." Most administrators feign care about quality education yet, as I've heard, look for someone with a pulse: no experience required to teach composition classes. We wonder why students struggle to write. Like Horner, whose passionate insights and arguments both rile up and intellectually stir, my aim is to bring out concrete small m–mobilities narratives, real life and real felt. Gathering small m–mobilities stories of how and why people move could show us more about the state of our field and our professional place within the academy at large. Arguing with an arsenal of many small m–mobilities' patterns will highlight the personal damage done, and the personal and institutional costs.

NOTES

1. This sentiment is also made clear in George (1990), Strickland and Gunner (2009), and McGee and Handa (2005).
2. Since I did not keep the emails, these and later samples are the types of responses I recall. I am certain most readers will recognize these types of responses.
3. By comparing my local UTEP Rhetoric and Composition salary with my peer full professors (and one associate professor), I had documented that my salary was between one-third to almost one-half less than theirs.

REFERENCES

Adey, Peter, David Bissell, Kevin Hannam, Peter Merriman, and Mimi Sheller, eds. 2014. *The Routledge Handbook of Mobilities.* London: Routledge.

Altman, Irwin, and Setha M. Low. 1992. "Place Attachment." In *Human Behavior and Environment: Advances in Theory and Research,* edited by Irwin Altman and Setha M. Low, 1–12. Boston: Springer.

Castells, Manuel. 1996. *The Rise of the Networked Society.* Oxford: Blackwell.

Cresswell, Tim. 2002. "Introduction: Theorizing Place." In *Mobilizing Place, Placing Mobility: The Politics of Representation in a Globalized World,* edited by Tim Cresswell and G. Verstraete, 11–32. Amsterdam: Rodopi.

Cresswell, Tim. 2006. *On the Move: Mobility in the Modern Western World.* New York: Routledge.

Cresswell, Tim. 2010. "Mobilities I: Catching up." *Progress in Human Geography* 35 (4): 550–558.

D'Mello, Marisa, and Sundeep Sahay. 2007. "'I Am Kind of a Nomad Where I Have to Go Places and Places' . . . Understanding Mobility, Place and Identity in Global Software Work from India." *Information and Organization* 17: 162–192.

George, Diana, ed. 1990. *Kitchen Cooks, Plate Twirlers & Troubadours: Writing Program Administrators Tell Their Stories.* Portsmouth, NH: Boynton/Cook.

Hamilton, Mary Lynn, Laura Smith, and Kristen Worthington. 2008. "Fitting the Methodology with the Research: An Exploration of Narrative, Self-Study and Auto-Ethnography." *Studying Teacher Education* 4 (1): 17–28. doi: 10.1080/17425960801976321.

Horner, Bruce. 2016. *Rewriting Composition: Terms of Exchange.* Carbondale: Southern Illinois University Press.

Johnson, Nathan R. 2014. "Protocological Rhetoric: Intervening in Institutions." *Journal of Technical Writing & Communication* 44 (4): 381–399.

Manzo, Lynne C. 2003. "Beyond House and Haven: Toward a Revisioning of Emotional Relationships with Places." *Journal of Environmental Psychology* 23: 47–61.

McGee, Sharon James and Carolyn Handa, eds. 2005. *Discord and Direction: The Postmodern Writing Program Administrator.* Logan: Utah State University Press.

Miller, Richard. 1999. "Critique's the Easy Part: Choice and the Scale of Relative Oppression." In *Kitchen Cooks, Plate Twirlers & Troubadours: Writing Program Administrators Tell Their Stories,* edited by Diana George, 3–13. Portsmouth, NH: Heinemann.

Oxford University. 2016a. "Inertia, n." *OED Online.* Oxford University Press. Accessed May 9, 2016.

Oxford University. 2016b. "Inertia Starter, n." *OED Online.* Oxford University Press. Accessed May 9, 2016.

Porter, James. E., Patricia A. Sullivan, Stuart Blythe, Jeffrey T. Grabill, and Libby Miles. 2000. "Institutional Critique: A Rhetorical Methodology for Change." *College Composition and Communication* 51 (4): 610–642.

Revill, George. 2014. "Histories." In *The Routledge Handbook of Mobilities,* edited by Peter Adey, David Bissell, Kevin Hannam, Peter Merriman, and Mimi Sheller, 506–516. London: Routledge.

Rose, Mike. 1985. "The Language of Exclusion: Writing Instruction at the University." *College English* 47 (4): 341–359.

Sheller, Mimi. 2014. "Sociology after the Mobilities Turn." In *The Routledge Handbook of Mobilities,* edited by Peter Adey, David Bissell, Kevin Hannam, Peter Merriman, and Mimi Sheller, 45–54. London: Routledge.

Sheller, Mimi, and John Urry. 2006. "The New Mobilities Paradigm." *Environment and Planning A* 38 (2): 207–226.

Steele, Fritz. 1981. *The Sense of Place.* Boston: CBI Publishing.

Strickland, Donna and Jeanne Gunner, eds. 2009. *The Writing Program Interrupted: Making Space for Critical Discourse.* Portsmouth, NH: Boynton/Cook.

Tusting, Karin. 2000. "New Literacy Studies and Time: An Exploration." In *Situated Literacies: Reading and Writing in Context,* edited by David Barton, Mary Hamilton, and Roz Ivanič, 35–51. New York: Routledge.

Urry, John. 2000. *Sociology Beyond Societies: Mobilities for the Twenty-first Century.* London: Routledge.

Urry, John. 2007. *Mobilities.* London: Polity.

Watts, Laura. 2008. "The Art and Craft of Train Travel." *Social & Cultural Geography* 9 (6): 711–726.

4
MANAGING WRITING ON THE MOVE

Rebecca Lorimer Leonard

I met Nimet when I tutored for a community literacy program in a city library. Every Saturday afternoon, I worked with whoever walked in the door on whatever writing project they brought with them. When Nimet started visiting regularly to work on a nursing school application, I wasn't surprised that we both brought valuable literacies to the table between us. But I was surprised by the conviction, good humor, and control with which Nimet passed literacies to me. While I shared my knowledge of US-based writing conventions, style, and academic practices, Nimet taught me Russian syntax, drew me maps of the Caucasus, and explained Soviet politics. The vast literate resources she called upon to conduct our exchanges led me to wonder about the extent of her multilingual literate repertoire; I wondered how she migrated between Azerbaijan and the US with her repertoire, and how it might have changed along the way.[1]

But during the time that Nimet and I met to work on her writing, her literacy development—in the English, Turkish/Azeri, and Russian she used—was both in and out of her control. Over the course of four years, we met for three planned hour-long interviews, several writing center sessions, three visits to her home, and various run-ins around campus. Together we worked on her writing assignments, applications to academic programs or for financial assistance, and business letters and emails, as well as her ongoing notetaking, reading, and timed writing practices. Throughout this process, she sometimes easily managed these practices and genres among her languages, and at other times felt her literacies were unfairly managed by unsupportive social or institutional agents.

In this chapter, I examine the management of literacy practices in Nimet's multilingual life. The chapter seeks to understand the nature of Nimet's literate struggle and success after immigration. What can four years of literacy experiences reveal about how a literate repertoire

---

DOI: 10.7330/9781646420209.c004

changes through movement? Beyond asking if Nimet's literacies do or do not move among her languages and the places she's lived in the world, this chapter focuses on the *how* and *why* of movement: the ways in which literacies move and the conditions and agents of that movement. In particular, I explore how one writer and several institutions attempt to control and benefit from literacies on the move. Following mobility studies' assumption that mobility is a norm rather than an aberration (introduction, this volume), and that "movement, itself, is a situation" in which literacy occurs (Lorimer Leonard 2013, 33), I show how Nimet's movements—across space, time, and repertoire—are managed by herself and by powerful others. I aim to pull apart the binary of fluidity and fixity by exploring mobility's full differentiation, especially through its shifting pace and direction.

In Nimet's experiences, literacy practices and materials are passed among people, organizations, and languages. Writers and institutions seek to manage the pace of literacy as it moves, expecting writing to be simultaneously fast (efficient) and slow (thoughtful). Institutions direct writers around bureaucratic labyrinths that often delay their educational or economic progress. In the end, literacy proves to be both sticky and slippery for multilingual migrants like Nimet and the institutions that seek to authorize literacy. This control is epitomic of writing in a mobile world, revealing the desire to slow literate change brought about by ever-diversifying writers and the literate repertoires they bring.

LITERATE MOBILITY AND INEQUALITY

I define mobility in terms of inequality: having the choice to move or stay put, to mobilize oneself or one's literacies, is a form of control that is economically and culturally advantageous. As noted in the introduction, mobility often is framed as a phenomenon of fluidity—flexible and flowing, across ever-loosening borders and boundaries—although the lived literacy experiences of multilingual writers are inflected with both struggle and success. Mobility studies has long foregrounded the relational qualities of movement, studying not presence or absence but the relations across a spectrum of mobilities (Adey 2006; Massey 1994). Migration scholars also suggest that forced movement maintains inequality, keeps workers available for exploitation, and seriously challenges claims about a free-flowing world (De Genova 2010; Freitag and von Oppen 2010; Manderscheid 2009) just as literacy and language scholars argue for literacy's unstable movement under globalization (Hernández-Zamora 2010; Hesford 2006; Jacquemet 2005; Prendergast

2008; Reynolds 2000; Warriner 2007). In other words, "regimes of mobility" (Glick Schiller and Salazar 2013; Shamir 2005) benefit from not only stopping movement but also keeping things in motion. Regimes of mobility maintain programs of border control, refugee camps, temporary worker visas, and waves of deportation or immigrant detention. In the context of literacy, regimes enact language and literacy tests or maintain professed standards of certification and credentialing. They suppress as well as propel literacy.

In this chapter, I focus on the relationship between literate and geographic mobility and the agents who benefit from moving literacy around.[2] Nimet's literate experiences demonstrate the complex mobility of multilingual literacies. Although Nimet has skillfully managed her literate practices nearly her entire life, she also has found her literacies under the management of others in the US, often to the detriment of the literate development that would grant the social and personal goals she imagined migrating for in the first place. This chapter's organization highlights this contrast in individual and institutional understandings of literacy management. I first describe how Nimet sees herself as a writer—an established multilingual professional nimbly controlling her literacy—and then how schools see her—an accented immigrant writer who endangers the quality control of their certifications and credentials. This dissonance characterizes Nimet's simultaneous struggle and success with writing.

ONE WRITER MANAGING MOVEMENT

In Azerbaijan and in the US, Nimet has managed the movement of her literacies in several ways, including passing pedagogies among people and sending materials transnationally. In these experiences, Nimet adeptly controls the pace—speeding it up or slowing it down—and direction—to what person or location it is headed—of her literate repertoire for personal, professional, and intellectual gain.

Passing Pedagogies

Before migrating to the US and attending nursing school, Nimet taught English to students and English teachers in Azerbaijan. She also taught Azeri to English-speaking teachers and volunteers working in the country. Early on in her career as a teacher, she saw how pedagogy was managed by the political system that regulated schools. For example, she said that writing instruction was designed to respond to the correspondence of "Karl Marx, Friedrich Engels, Lenin" as well as to "communism, socialism . . . the history of the Soviet Union [which] they emphasize everywhere, it doesn't matter your major." Pedagogy was also designed around the materials and practices available under that political system:

> During my time, the Soviet Union education system focus on reading and writing, never listening, speaking, never ever. We have only one DVD or something. We used to go the lab and they put you on wait list because limit equipment and more students. . . . When I was a teacher I saw that if you teach the language you have to take this four skills together. Otherwise you cannot learn language.

In her experience, the Soviet system endorsed reading and writing over speaking and listening by limiting the equipment for learning in those modes. By extension, Nimet understood the Soviet system, then, to want to keep these skills separate—she believed the Soviet education system didn't want people to learn how to listen and speak in English but didn't explicitly speculate as to why.

Because she found the politically endorsed pedagogies ineffective—her teaching experience showed her that the separation of skills inhibited her students' English language learning—she passed alternative pedagogies among language teachers, working around government-mandated curricula and collaborating with other teachers to create different kinds of literacy teaching.

> We founded Azerbaijani English Teachers Association with one of my friend, she uses perfect British English because she worked at American embassy. . . . So we just make this one association and the high school and university people come and apply ourselves . . . to this organization, Azerbaijan English Teachers Association (AzETA). Yeah, we just contact the British Council and the American ambassador, American Council Education and Soros Foundation. They all have branch in my country. We go and ask, just let's involve this organization, help us with a book. We finish the book and we write it ourselves, not our government, government doesn't care. And we saw the result. . . . We begin just twelve people. Now we have eight hundred members.

Nimet's work with this organization was mainly motivated by the desire to share more effective language pedagogy. Nimet and her colleagues were the agents of this literacy movement—they were the ones organizing, teaching, appealing for funding, creating their own materials, and passing on practices. Because the "government doesn't care," they worked around pedagogy that emphasized only reading and writing, integrating all language-learning skills into a book that they wrote themselves, which produced results in teaching and learning in Azerbaijan.

Nimet describes the AzETA hosting conferences of two hundred people from ten regions around the country, "preparing teachers to give workshop," which they then used to "give workshop to other people." Members of the organization would travel to schools around the country, sometimes supported by British or American embassy funds for buses, food, or materials printing, to "kind of spread the new teaching techniques." Nimet explains, "we need to help—we wanted not just needed—we wanted to help the secondary school and the university to teach effectively because they don't know what to do." Nimet and the AzETA went on the road, managing the proliferation of a teacher-created literacy curriculum. Her geographic movement transformed both language learning curriculum as well as language teacher collaborations.

Nimet extended this movement when she used these pedagogies to teach Azeri to English-speaking volunteers working in Azerbaijan:

> I used to teach Azerbaijan language to the Peace Corps volunteers in my country. For example, we make the domino, you know the domino? We write the words on the domino and just word by word we make that. . . . First it's hard, and then people that needs it, bring here all the visual aids, put in. Share. And if you want you can go and make yourself. Yeah, this is usually most of the things we learn. . . . I learned in Peace Corps, teach them, experience and bring here and give the workshop all the [AzETA] members of here. Step by step.

Nimet used integrative language teaching strategies to create "step by step" the movement of literacy around the country. She modeled the collaboration of the AzETA, encouraging volunteers to bring visual aids to the classes, sharing them and passing them around, which in turn informed the workshops Nimet gave back to the AzETA. While starting and growing such a teaching network is indicative of Nimet's bustling personal and educational activism, it also emphasizes the lateral global reach of literacy management. In these three successive accounts, Nimet saw a pedagogical lack created by certain political conditions, acted with others to respond to it, appealed to global organizations for funding, and set into motion literacy practices that spread better language pedagogy around the country. Although it is important to grant the powerful presence of British and American funders in this sequence of events, the teachers nevertheless powerfully directed how English language literacy moved.

Sending Materials

Nimet also manages the movement of literacy materials. When asked to recall if she carried out any transnational correspondence as a migrant,

Nimet relayed a story about the complicated literacy path of a single laptop she sent to a friend in Azerbaijan.

> Last year I wrote a letter to send back to my friend [in Azerbaijan]. I just write a letter, put inside a laptop and then just wrap. Yeah, this is a present. I wrote in English . . . the communication must be in English to understand both side. I could write also in Turkish but her English is better than her Turkish. Also it is easier for me to write it in English than Turkish. . . . She is from Finland but she works in Turkey as a travel agent. . . . [She] takes this one to Turkey, and my friend [from Azerbaijan] comes to Istanbul to pick up laptop.

Essentially, Nimet sent a laptop from the US to Azerbaijan via a Finnish travel agent who works in Turkey. She wrote a letter in English to be read by both the Finnish and Azeri friends and folded it inside the laptop. Nimet moved both of these literacy materials, one folded inside the other, along a transnational path, sending as a gift contemporary literacy technology explained by an ancient literacy genre. Nimet's literacy management contains layers of literate and material mobility: she manages materials among multiple readers in multiple locations even as she considers how to compose the accompanied writing among the writer's and readers' multiple languages. She ultimately chooses English as a lingua franca even though it is not her most fluent language because it is the language in which she is most comfortable composing the specific genre of the letter.

As the laptop and the letter are put into motion, their meaning changes. Far from a machine and a piece of paper, the literacy materials become educationally and economically significant to their senders and receivers in multiple locations (Vieira 2016). The moving laptop becomes an opportunity to practice a kind of global audience awareness: Nimet muses about which language will be most effective to helping her readers understand what the laptop is for and where it should go. The moving letter becomes an opportunity to "prevail with English writing": Nimet finds the informality of friendly correspondence in particular helps her to not "care about the sentence," while the structure of the genre gives her a way to "organize your ideas, your thoughts in a good way, or grammatically." Nimet says that when she writes a letter

> you are thinking a different way. . . . you start you know "Dear something" or finish "sincerely something" official. Sometimes the verb, it's not right there; you have to use a specific verb to express. When I write, something is wrong, this word is not right here. I just go google and just put the synonym. . . . But in writing it is just there. If you miss something you see that something wrong. You have to write everything in its place.

In a way, Nimet is contrasting the ephemeral quality of orality which "automatically comes and we don't pay attention to grammar." But she is also talking about the literacy learning affordances of a letter in particular, a genre that, as Nimet says, "makes a journey" or is made to move. Thus, managing the transnational movement of literate materials provides Nimet the opportunity to develop specific literacy practices in English, subtly transforming her literate repertoire. In this literacy event, Nimet controlled several layers of mobility at once, sending a gift to a friend, staying in touch with another friend, thinking among her languages, and intentionally composing only in English.

SCHOOLS MANAGING MOVEMENT

While much of her literate repertoire has been under her control for most of her life, Nimet's literacies also have been managed by powerful institutions, especially after her immigration to the US. The institutions she has encountered—a community college, a language school, and a university nursing program—speed up and slow down the movement of her literacy when it suits them; they engage in bureaucratic misdirection, sending Nimet through a maze of classes and certifications in pursuit of (assumed to be academic, unaccented) literacy standards. In fact, when schools are in charge, Nimet's multilingual literacies appear to be slowed down or stuck, even when they are still on the move. Viewing Nimet's seemingly immobile literacies as still mobile points away from literacy lack and toward literacy management—the agents and conditions that benefit from controlling the kinds of mobility Nimet experiences.

Pacing Literacy

The classroom literacy experiences Nimet describes are run through with cultural and gendered dynamics that shape the pace of her literate mobility. Speaking of composing essays in a college general education course, Nimet defines a writing process managed by the expectations of others.

> That's why it is hard for us. Not hard, I cannot say it's only hard. But also take our time more. If you write this one page—one hour. This page I can spend sometime five, six hours. My teacher she asked me how many hours you spend for that? I said 12 hours. She is surprised. I said, I don't think so; this is not surprising. . . . It is the other; sometimes we think in our own language and then convert in our brain to the other. Sometimes it's the

cultural clash. You can't use it, you won't, you don't, you cannot express the sentence. And you stuck there, how can I express? I want to tell this idea. You want to say that this is this. This is that. But again, takes time.

Nimet describes her writing process on an hourly scale, emphasizing the material practicalities of having to "convert in [one's] brain to the other" language while writing. But when she slides out to a cultural scale, placing composing in a context of cultural difference, Nimet reveals that being stuck among languages is not just a matter of staring at a screen, but also a matter of converting one's identity. This takes time. It is no wonder, then, that what looks like stalled writing production on paper is the product of a shifting, often teacher-imposed "cultural clash" that expects quick, efficient, and error-free writing.

Specifically, Nimet attributes her negative experiences with writing in her nursing program courses in the US to the pressure to write quickly and to call on English-based writing skills that she has not yet developed. As a nursing student in a clinical setting, the pressure to quickly write care plans and reflective journals is high, and Nimet and other nursing participants in the larger study from which Nimet's case is drawn expressed shutting down under what they identified as US-based classroom expectations for production. She explains that in the clinical setting she is "kind of frozen" as she "just [sits] there" thinking, "I cannot do this now. I cannot write this one because I have no idea." Nimet's feeling of being frozen seems to stem from having "no idea" what to write about as well as lacking what she calls the "word phrases" and "sentence structure" that would help her quickly express those ideas when they come. In other words, Nimet's stalled production is influenced by cultural context, misunderstanding of or low interest in content, and elusive academic English resources. These pressures are both common—many monolingual, nonmigrant college writers would describe their writer's block similarly—but also unique, as the multiplication of these pressures causes Nimet to feel frozen as she attempts to compose among her languages.

Thus, what looks like Nimet's writer's block might also be a kind of institution block, in which slowed-down writing stems not just from language learning in process but also from uninformed readers' expectations or ideologies (Davila 2016; Hinds 1987; Matsuda and Cox 2009). Further, what appears to be a classroom context shutting a writer down is also a classroom context speeding a writer up—because Nimet does not write efficiently, she is deemed too slow, not fast enough. Nimet cannot win in this contradictory pacing of literacy management.

Directing Literacy

Nimet's literate mobility also is managed by institutional agents beyond the classroom. Under the control of program advisors and mentors, Nimet's multilingual literacies remain hidden as she is directed toward literacy support that misdirects her progress. For example, both Nimet and her fellow nursing student Paj describe the management of Nimet's literacies by advisors and staff as particularly frustrating to Nimet's educational and economic mobility.[3] As the undergraduate representative to a nursing school advisory committee, Paj was able to participate in committee conversations about its multilingual nursing students. According to Paj, the committee used Nimet (presumably without name) as an example of problematic multilingual students, suggesting students should be "kicked out" or "take an English course on the side" if they "are not competent enough in their English." In this meeting, Paj suggested that "the application process for nursing school should be good enough to determine whether we're sufficient in English, in our writing skills," attempting to intervene in what she heard as uninformed views of English and writing competence. Although committee members' claims were often couched in worries about student success or future patient safety, Paj interpreted the committee's deliberations as willfully impeding the progress of students who had already been deemed qualified. Paj was witness to the creation of a bureaucratic process meant to misdirect multilingual writers' energies. As writers attempted to move forward and up in the program, the program attempted to move writers to the sidelines or out, pointing them toward additional requirements.

For her part, Nimet had attempted to respond to an instructor's ultimatum to take a "separate English course on the side" or else "not go on" in the nursing program. In following this instructor's demand to get extra support, and because she also wished to improve her English-language skills, Nimet tried registering for a course at a local private English language school whose director said she didn't need the courses they provided: "She told me that you don't need . . . yeah don't waste your money; you are the university student." Further, she had already passed the full ESL sequence at the local community college, so she resorted to an (expensive) additional ESL course at the university where she was a nursing student called "advanced communication skills." Nimet explains, "The name is deceiving (laughing) . . . sometimes in group work, it is hard to understand because almost 12 was from China, 1 from Japan, some Thailand, and me and one from Peru. Yeah it just pronunciation, repeat after us something. Yeah just pronounce." Although the class was pitched exactly for Nimet's needs, the instructor relied on outdated audiolingual methods, and Nimet found that her academic English, which she felt she desperately needed to stay on track in nursing school, did not improve. She said, "Yeah I wanted to critique but I said no, I pay already." Taking this one extra course turned her two-year nursing degree into a three-year degree to accommodate the demands of one nursing instructor and the implied threat of expulsion.

Thus, both Paj and Nimet suspected the school's literate management was motivated by something other than an "English problem." Paj describes the course as "completely useless to her because she already understands English." Paj also notes that "the native speakers are having problems with the medical terminology, so of course us who are not native speakers are gonna have problems with that also, and that doesn't mean we have English problem." When asked why she thought she and other multilingual nurses felt pressure about their communication skills, Nimet said quite plainly, "It's not an English problem, not an English problem. It's the environment." As savvy multilingual writers, both Paj and Nimet know that the misdirected movement they encounter in their program doesn't always stem from their own competence, but also from the "environment" of the program—the values and beliefs about "English problems" held by faculty, staff, and students, and fostered in the program itself.

STRUGGLE AND SUCCESS IN LITERATE MOBILITY

What does the management of literacy reveal about literate struggle and success? What does it suggest about how mobility changes literacy? The accounts above show how writers and schools differently benefit from managing mobile literacy. When Nimet controls how her literacies move, among colleagues and friends, among the pieces of languages that comprise her literate repertoire, she participates in language—she is an active literacy innovator, expanding her own repertoire and metalinguistic awareness. She identifies as a writer, teacher, and leader. She takes pride in what she can do with writing. When institutions control the pace and direction of Nimet's literate movement, they maintain a literate power structure that grants their authority to keep writers in and out of their classrooms and, sometimes, the country. This control seems an attempt to push against the tide of literate change brought about by ever-diversifying writers and the literate repertoires they bring. These inconsistent and elusive attempts to create and control change are definitive of modern mobile literacies: The nature of literate agency under mobility is slippery and highly contingent on the conditions that greet mobile literacy upon arrival.

Nimet's literacy experiences complicate conventional assumptions about agency in mobile literacies. Her experiences show how both writers and institutions move literacy among locations and languages, passing practices and materials among writers and languages, slowing literacy down, speeding it up, pushing it in different directions. Nimet's literate repertoire is not simply shut down by powerful others. Rather, she and institutional agents act together as literacy managers to set the pace and direction of literate movement. For example, Nimet's literate experiences in Azerbaijan position her in a bureaucratic role as she manages the geographic, economic, and literate mobility of herself and other teachers in the AzETA. As managers, both Nimet and institutional agents move literacy practices and materials for a variety of reasons, including exerting control over language change or maintaining perceived cultural or linguistic standards. Such management also seems to be an attempt to control the contingency of literacy's value under globalization. To these ends migrant writers like Nimet take a pragmatic stance, managing the literate practices that serve them best. Indeed, for Nimet, ambivalence is a more accurate reaction to the power of schools to manage her writing, perhaps because she has taken on managerial roles herself, creating alternative bureaucracies around existing ones in Azerbaijan.

But after migration to the US, institutional procedures—including transfer credit, degree requirements, and language tests—take control of much of what Nimet can accomplish with her rich repertoire. Although Nimet controlled her literate mobility in Azerbaijan, in the US slow literacy was not necessarily a speed she could afford. Just as slow food movements can appear bourgeois at times, so can the slow literacy movement be considered a luxury. As an immigrant with a student visa, Nimet needed to get a move on: graduate, get a job, provide for her family, send money home, feel successful. She did not necessarily have time to slow down and appreciate her own admittedly fascinating literate repertoire. So, while Nimet does wield agency as she manages how her literacies move, this is an agency that runs up against the power of institutions to move her writing around after immigration. This is an issue of pace: Nimet turns out to accomplish her literacy goals—she finishes her nursing program—but she does so a year behind her cohort and with additional accrued expenses to satisfy the desires of faculty and staff.

Further, the management of mobile literacies is very much shaped by issues of race, class, and gender. Nimet's literacy experiences show

how even the same writer can experience differentiated mobility as a member of a more or less powerful group. As Doreen Massey (1994) argues, the condition of late capitalism differently disempowers subjects in that "different social groups, and different individuals, are placed in very distinct ways in relation to these flows and interconnections" (149). As a multilingual teacher trainer in Azerbaijan, Nimet manages her and others' mobile practices in English. As a multilingual nursing student in the US, her multilingual and English languages skills will possibly never satisfy her teachers. The role of multilingualism in Nimet's accounts is particularly illuminating of this predicament as it is endorsed as both a personal and professional asset before migration to the US, and condemned as a racial or cultural deficit afterward. In Nimet's descriptions of reactions toward her accent, multilingual literacy finds itself in social disfavor, with her oral or written evidence of other languages treated as violating an assumed English-only norm.

In fact, this is knowledge passed among the multilingual migrants who increasingly comprise the nursing programs and staff of hospitals in the US. Nimet shares the warning of colleagues who point toward other kinds of literate management: "just keep an eye, or keep a good ear or listen with them, careful of misunderstanding." Nimet continues,

> I know everything [in English] related to RN and I say I won't have any problem. But I have a friend who graduated high school here, and she said we will have a problem. She had really good English but some people they don't like you, some people don't like diversity. . . . Also one thing they say is if something is going wrong, right away they suspect it's the non-native speakers . . . because of the English making misunderstanding. They proved that no, after investigation the root of the reason is totally different. But some people make assumption or judgment directly of you when you maybe didn't understand, but in a rude way.

The powerful actors in Nimet's nursing work and school environment set out to manage her literacy no matter her kind or level of English mastery. Teachers and advisors seem to be acting on the promises of autonomous literacy—that a course or test will bequeath the literacy knowledge Nimet needs to move—which in practice become roadblocks. From Nimet's point of view, this management was motivated not by her need to learn the academic English to do well, but by deepset linguistic discrimination, willful misunderstanding of difference, and suspicion of nonwhite others in work or school settings. Together, Paj and Nimet agreed that the nursing faculty most of all seemed not "happy with [Nimet's] accent" even though, according to Paj, "she knows everything" about nursing. While clinical settings may assume

English-language intelligibility to be a matter of success and safety, claims that accents are liabilities might be excuses for discrimination under the guise of safety. While it is true that clinical contexts educate amidst real patient pain and suffering and thus justifiably demand the highest of nursing communication skills, actual English proficiency is but one factor conditioning the literate practices of nurses (Leki 2003, 84, 86). So, although Nimet and Paj grant the program's gate-keeping as potentially supporting patient safety, Paj says, "if we need to work on our oral skills, like our accents, that something that we might not be able to fix!"

The sticking point of accent as aural or written evidence of multilingualism is especially susceptible to institutional management. Both Paj and Nimet provide examples of the willful misunderstanding of listeners and readers to spoken and written accent. As Paj observes, "a lot of the doctors have accents . . . but you don't hear nurses telling them or the preceptors telling them like you need to take an English course. So, it's like, no. You know they're knowledgeable; the accent doesn't mean anything." Here, both status and gender drive this management. Multilingual writers (as doctors often are) who already maintain a level of professional or class prestige are forgiven for their accent, while those striving to earn or gain prestige are granted no favors. Rarely was an assumption of knowledge granted to nursing students like Paj or Nimet, who were instead cautioned in teacher feedback or directed to pronunciation courses that set them back a semester in degree progress. This is misunderstanding on purpose, an institution or individual putting the impetus for legibility on certain writers and using their struggle to measure up as evidence of their literate ineligibility.

In the end, foregrounding the management of literacy shows how mobile literacies can simultaneously empower and disempower writers like Nimet. As powerful institutional actors manage writers' repertoires, they often ignore multilingual capacities, focusing on accent as proof that writers are intellectually or professionally incapable. In Nimet's case, the nursing school not only slowed down and misdirected her literacies, it also kept her moving, sending her to seek extra support she did not need in a roundabout hunt for native-like English proficiency. This forced movement was distracting both to her progress in the standard academic English she sought as well as the maintenance of her multilingual literate repertoire as a whole. But foregrounding management also reveals the promise of literacies that move. Acknowledging that Nimet's literate repertoire comes from somewhere, that it has a personal, political, and geographic history, illuminates the depth and

80 LEONARD

complexity of what Nimet can do with language and what she brings with her to the US.

NOTES

1. I use "repertoire" to mean "biographically organized complexes of resources" learned in formal and informal contexts rather than static containers of competence (Blommaert and Backus 2012, 8). Thus, what appears to be an incomplete, or "truncated" repertoire (Blommaert 2010), might actually be a lived repertoire in process.

2. Here, geographic mobility means the forced or chosen movements of immigrants, the back and forth travel of international students or labor migrants, or the cross-border travel of literacy materials, with or without writers. Literate mobility is the cross-border maintenance of reading and writing traditions after immigration, the transfer of writing practices among languages, and the persistence of literate identities in new contexts.

3. Nimet and Paj knew I had interviewed both of them but did not know that they each had described each other's similar experiences. In data analysis I was able to recognize the identical events in each of their narratives. Nevertheless, their interviews still remained confidential to each other and to their other nursing school colleagues.

REFERENCES

Adey, Peter. 2006. "If Mobility is Everything Then it is Nothing: Towards a Relational Politics of (Im)mobilities." *Mobilities* 1 (1): 75–94.

Blommaert, Jan. 2010. *The Sociolinguistics of Globalization*. Cambridge: Cambridge University Press.

Blommaert, Jan, and Ad Backus. 2012. "Superdiverse Repertoires and the Individual." *Tilburg Papers in Culture Studies*, Paper 24.

Davila, Bethany. 2016. "The Inevitability of 'Standard' English: Discursive Constructions of Standard Language Ideologies." *Written Communication* 33 (2): 127–148.

De Genova, Nicholas. 2010. "The Deportation Regime: Sovereignty, Space, and the Freedom of Movement." In *The Deportation Regime: Sovereignty, Space, and the Freedom of Movement*, edited by Nicholas de Genova and Nathalie Peutz, 93–112. Durham: Duke University Press.

Freitag, Ulrike, and Achim von Oppen, eds. 2010. *Translocality: The Study of Globalising Processes from a Southern Perspective*. Leiden, Netherlands: Brill.

Glick Schiller, Nina, and Noel B. Salazar. 2013. "Regimes of Mobility Across the Globe." *Journal of Ethnic and Migration Studies* 39 (2): 183–200.

Hernández-Zamora, Gregorio. 2010. *Decolonizing Literacy: Mexican Lives in the Era of Global Capitalism*. Clevedon, UK: Multilingual Matters.

Hesford, Wendy. 2006. "Global Turns and Cautions in Rhetoric and Composition Studies." *PMLA* 121 (3): 787–801.

Hinds, John. 1987. "Reader vs. Writer Responsibility: A New Typology." In *Writing Across Languages: Analysis of L2 Text*, edited by Ulla Connor and Robert Kaplan, 141–152. Reading, MA: Addison-Wesley.

Jacquemet, Marco. 2005. "Transidiomatic Practices: Language and Power in the Age of Globalization." *Language and Communication* 25 (3): 257–277.

Leki, Ilona. 2003. "Living Through College Literacy: Nursing in a Second Language." *Written Communication* 20 (1): 81–98.

Lorimer Leonard, Rebecca. 2013. "Traveling Literacies: Multilingual Writing on the Move." *Research in the Teaching of English* 48 (1): 13–39.

Manderscheid, Katharina. 2009. "Unequal Mobilities." In *Mobilities and Inequality*, edited by Timo Ohnmacht, Hanja Maksim, and Manfred Max Bergman, 27–50. Burlington, VT: Ashgate.

Massey, Doreen. 1994. *Space, Place, and Gender*. Minneapolis: University of Minnesota Press.

Matsuda, Paul Kei, and Michelle Cox. 2009. "Reading an ESL Writer's Text." In *ESL Writers: A Guide for Writing Center Tutors*. 2nd ed. Edited by Shanti Bruce and Ben Rafoth, 39–47. Portsmouth, NH: Boynton/Cook.

Prendergast, Catherine. 2008. *Buying into English: Language and Investment in the New Capitalist World*. Pittsburgh: University of Pittsburgh Press.

Reynolds, Nedra. 2000. "Who's Going to Cross this Border? Travel Metaphors, Material Conditions, and Contested Places." *JAC* 20 (3): 541–564.

Shamir, Ronen. 2005. "Without Borders? Notes on Globalization as a Mobility Regime." *Sociological Theory* 23 (2): 197–217.

Vieira, Kate. 2016. "Writing Remittances: Migration-Driven Literacy Learning in a Brazilian Homeland." *Research in the Teaching of English* 50 (4): 422–449.

Warriner, Doris S. 2007. "Transnational Literacies: Immigration, Language Learning, and Identity." *Linguistics and Education* 18 (3): 201–214.

5

"PRETTY FOR A BLACK GIRL"
AfroDigital Black Feminisms and the Critical Context of "Mobile Black Security"

Carmen Kynard

RACE, PLACE, AND BLACK GIRL MIGRATIONS IN COLOR CASTE SYSTEMS: THE NARRATIVE BEGINS

There has been no single semester in my years of teaching undergraduate courses, which I began in 1998, where hair and skin color as endemic to a racial caste system have not been politicized in both classroom discussions and course assignments by black female college students. It's not all of them, but it's always some of them, whether that is an explicit part of the course or not. By color caste system, I mean a racialized hierarchy that maps out "good hair," "bad hair," "light skin," and "dark skin"—what I think of as an arsenal of body politics functioning as societal discourses that divide, differentiate, and lead to unjust social practices for black women (Glenn 2009). I am using the terminology of a caste system explicitly here. While the beauty-industrial-complex certainly oppresses all women with its compulsory white femininity and hegemonic masculinity, the issues that black women face are unique in this beauty-industrial-complex (Gill 2008). Beauty and aesthetics are thus part of "controlling images" (Collins 1990) that link global, symbolic violence with the elevation of whiteness and denigration of all else (Banks 2000; Caldwell 1991; Rooks 1996). I borrow from Tim Cresswell and treat colorism as an intricate part of the "microgeographies" of black life where power, white aesthetics, and black identities pattern space and access (2011, 551).

To give a better sense of my classrooms, one specific example can give a glimpse into these polemics. Every semester, for sixteen years, there has always been that one brave white student—usually male—who wants to boldly go where no other has gone before and so says something along the lines of: "Why is this color stuff important? Aren't they [black women] all the same and look alike anyway?" In

---

DOI: 10.7330/9781646420209.c005

one particular class, this comment came from the one white male student amongst twenty-one black women and nine black men. This is an extreme example only because it represents a classroom of thirty-one students where thirty are black, but this is what the last sixteen years of my teaching life have looked like. I am not exaggerating, and I am exhausted.

In a moment like this, I don't respond at first. Unlike some other teachers, I don't fret too much that a fistfight will jump off. I also make sure that I do not perform white bourgeois liberal politeness, comfort, and racial-tension-cleansing. Instead, I like to sing a little song in my head at these moments to calm my own nerves and in my mind's ear, I sound really good. If I am feeling a little old school and nostalgic on that day, I will sing, in my head, Michael Jackson's "Rock with You" (1979) in its classic 1980s soul vibe: *Girl, close your eyes/ Let that rhythm get into you/ Don't try to fight it/ There ain't nuthin that you can do.* If I am feeling a bit more earthy, I take it to the Bronx and hum myself a little Fat Joe (2004), and, in my mind's eye, I do the rockaway: *Said my [ninjas] don't dance/we just pull up our pants/And do the rockaway/now lean back, lean back, lean back.* That's right. Unlike the bourgeois, corporate-esque white feminism of Sheryl Sandberg (2013), I don't attempt to lean in. Instead, I *lean back.*

I am not suggesting that these are comical or funny moments in the classroom, because they certainly are not. My point is not to humor myself but to simply get myself through the class and, hopefully, through the day, because when it all falls down, these kinds of conversations about race in the college classroom will be more aggressively penalized for someone like me than for a white teacher. White students are almost always more vocal in their complaints against faculty of color, especially black female faculty—who, as black women, are seen as angry and aggressive anyway (Weitz and Gordon 1993). My point here is to really convey the weight and risk of the last sixteen years of my teaching when I mobilize young black women's specific concerns in classrooms to more fully contextualize the impact of the student I will describe next.

SPACE-MAKING AND AN AFRODIGITAL BLACK VERNACULAR

In February 2014, Andrene, a young black woman in one of my first-year writing classes, created a website that collected her writings from the course, a requirement in my courses. Andrene's website is called "Pretty for a Black Girl," and with that bold move, my pedagogical history has been altered.[1] After this moment, no student has ever again loudly proclaimed that color caste systems are unimportant.

"Pretty for a Black Girl" and its cultural practices of AfroDigital black feminisms complicates both the politics of knowledge and mobility from the social imaginaries of black women in and out of the academy. As the late Barbara Christian always argued, changes in knowledge production are the precondition for greater representation of black communities—and for black women in particular—in the academy (1994). I am most interested in linking Andrene's black feminist digital design and mobility studies in a way that can illuminate Fred Moten's notion of a "mobile black sociality" (Harney and Moten 2013; Critical Resistance 2015). Moten reminds us that the police officer Darren Wilson, who murdered Michael Brown in Ferguson, Missouri, was not attempting to violate Brown's individual personhood but was, instead, shooting at "mobile black sociality." Brown's black body represented an insurgent black life, even though he was merely walking down the street, by a state apparatus that sanctioned the white identity of Wilson as someone who could only perceive Brown as a profound threat to a white social order. Moten's notion of "mobile black sociality" thus moves us away from simplistic narratives of space, place, time, and mobilities in a racialized western academy (Harney and Moten 2013). "Mobile black sociality" imbues conversations about digital technologies with a unique set of "social imaginaries," to borrow from Charles Taylor, where ideas, identities, and experiences in a racist world are always in *practice*, constrained and enabled simultaneously (2003). Andrene's rewriting of my classrooms emanates from a digital space that she designed from what I call an AfroDigital black vernacular that is critically shaping what I now call (and will define here as): cultural-spatial contouring, multimedia blackscapes, and black navigational messaging as ethos, all of which result in its own critical cartography.

Cultural-spatial contouring

The very naming of Andrene's website, built on the university's ePortfolio platform, challenges white standards of beauty. Her phrase constitutes the "microgeographies" of colorism in her life and encompasses the "macrogeographies" of skin color caste systems at the same time. She uses her header and background to visually target her specific location of "pretty black girlness": Her header features a woman shrouded in an afro and hues of purple, while her background shows striations of purple (that lead to other hues) in her attempt to contest a pejorative, racial expression that shaped her childhood: "so black that you are purple." Her deliberate color scheme and image selections (alongside her customization of the HTML in her main container) for her header, footer, and background all communicate a decidedly black female space, what I am calling *cultural-spatial contouring*.

Multimedia blackscapes

Andrene's website collects a series of multimedia texts to complement this *cultural-spatial contouring*: (1) short, personal narratives with race-conscious images curated from the internet; (2) stories and images from African American female college students across the country about their experiences in college; (3) research using website, video, and print sources related to black women's gendered/raced discrimination of their hair; and (4) artifacts, videos, and images that relay what she calls "the politics of othering." Thus, Andrene designs a black-visual digital space, what I am calling a *multimedia blackscape* (remixing the notions and forms of e-scape and landscape). Her *multimedia blackscape* serves as a way to mediate the race-gendered relations that her body encounters in the multiple worlds in which she interacts, where she moves through communities of school, work, home, friends, classroom, neighborhood, and media continually othered as black and female and kinky-haired and *browner-skinned*.

Black navigational messaging as ethos

The content and visual design, all of which require CSS customization, however, are not the only vessels that carry Andrene's meanings. Black navigational messaging sits at the core of how you move across and within the multiple sections of the website. The naming of her main sections and subsections—namely top-navigation tabs and left-navigation tabs—work to achieve what I see as a black rhetorical place and aesthetic space. One section, called "Burning through the Cerebral Cortex," collects short synopses of articles, videos, and websites that she has examined that relate to discriminatory histories and current practices related to black women who wear their hair in its natural state. Hair and skin color thus carry literacy into social spaces such that these specific body politics have their own story to tell, stories that young black women are always reading.

The terms, now clickable since they are sections of the website, stand as gateways to Andrene's black womanist space. The section title

"Burning through the Cerebral Cortex" is a concept that has circulated widely amongst black women since Oprah Winfrey used this phrase to describe black women's oppressive relationships with the history of hair straightening, both mentally and physically, a cultural trope that many black women will immediately recognize. Popular culture is thus an obvious flow in the social/digital space that Andrene creates but still operates in a way that is not immediately recognizable to a mainstreamed everyone; her site still addresses black women invested in alternative conversations and processes of beauty and race. Thus, part of the unique rhetorical purposing that Andrene manifests with this website comes from a quite deliberate investment in a black female audience. As a website, Andrene's work is thereby "positioned in a nexus of relations" to the other black female locales in which she makes meaning, acts, and lives out her life (Leander et al. 2015, 336).

One of Andrene's top tabs, perhaps my favorite, presents various components of what she learned about legal cases related to black hair. She calls that section: What If I Was My Hair? Note that this is not a grammatical mistake: *what if I were my hair* does not mean the same thing as *what if I wuzzzz* in the cultural practices of African American Language. Andrene's question is really not a question. It is a threat, as in, come get some because I. Am. Ready. For. You. When she is talking to non-like-minded audiences on this website, she is not using the polite, demure, subservient-apprentice etiquette that students are always expected to perform—a performance we sometimes mistakenly label "academic discourse." Instead, she mobilizes the discursive styles of African American Language via her strategic use of direct address. This is a conscious departure from the demands of school-based white linguistic etiquette, which is especially hurled at students of color who are still often hopelessly rendered as people who have not mastered the master code yet and can therefore justify all manner of dumbed-down, basic-skills teaching.

As if anticipating critiques that she is haphazardly making design and rhetorical decisions in a way that exceed the possibility of her intentionality, Andrene punctuates her website with a footer that remains static for every click you make at this site. The footer is a quote from Audre Lorde: "If we do not define ourselves for ourselves, we will be defined by others—for their use and to our detriment" (1984, 45). Thus, across Andrene's website, she uses iconic figures of African descent, a black lexicon, and the morphosyntactic structures of African American Language to name the spaces of her site and mobilize black vernacular culture towards her digital rhetorics.

Critical cartographies

Andrene's cultural-spatial contouring, multimedia blackscapes, and black navigational messaging represent black women's vernacular technological creativity. As a critical cartographer, Katherine McKittrick reminds us that black women's lives are enmeshed with traditional geographic arrangements where different ways of knowing and writing constantly contest the ways that space is (re)produced in dominant culture and empire (2006). Taking inspiration from McKittrick, I situate this technological creativity in classrooms as a central site of geographic struggle (Brock et al. 2010; Hall 2011). McKittrick's scholarship as a cultural geographer compels us to relate critical black feminist cartographies to the ways we (re)read digital work by young black women like Andrene in classrooms as a *spacial* intervention in whiteness, neoliberal imperatives, and racist boundaries/binaries calculatingly maintained by the twenty-first century neoliberal university (McDowell 1999). Thus, young black women in classrooms serve as "geographic subjects" who offer critical "clues as to how more humanly workable geographies might be imagined" (McKittrick 2006, xxiii).

AUDIENCE-MAKING AND BLACK TECHNOCULTURAL CREATIVITY

Instead of marking Andrene's black vernacular creativity as merely a set of departures from an imagined (yet standardized) norm, I treat her black vernacular movements as a totemic system such that the very digital space that Andrene has created acts with and through black vernacular in both visual, alphabetic, sonic, and epistemological ways (Richardson 2003). A seemingly incessant focus on morphosyntactic structures as the sole marker of African American Language outside of the critical contexts in which that language finds meaning inhibits the fuller experience of the range of black vernacular creativity that a space like Andrene's website both dynamically represents and relies on.

By July 2014, Andrene's website had more than 5,000 visits. When you look at ePortfolios across the country, you see a distinct difference between Andrene's ePortfolio and other students' works. Students with the most views on this platform (spanning colleges across the country) are those who have created very uber-professionalized websites of seemingly three variations: (1) ePortfolios designed specifically for national accreditation systems; (2) ePortfolios designed specifically for professional jobs (teaching, public administration, business); and (3) ePortfolios designed as digital resumés. Unsurprisingly, these ePorfolios, for the most part, all look and sound the same across the country with little to almost no re-mixing of the platform's CSS template, design, and multimedia possibilities. Like with all forms of new media branding (Marwick 2013), these neoliberal formulas for students' ePortfolios are made to look as if they allow students a degree of agency and self-actualization when, in actuality, the overdetermined, institutional goals of these ePortfolios to perform and secure students' careerism merely markets a pre-professional, discursively cloned, collegiate self, defined solely by commercial and capital interests. Andrene's view count then also indicates the ways that black insurgency intervenes and innovates on some of the most corporatized literacy practices sustained by higher education. Her explicit political messaging also moves past the "micro-celebrity status" mongering (Marwick 2013) offered to many black female social media icons. Pretty for a Black Girl thus uses black insurgency to change the game on a national scale for what is possible for something as seemingly innocuous as ePortfolios.

Andrene's accumulation of visitors and classroom fans further mark the current time-space of my classroom in a specific way now. Ever since Andrene's website went public, there has been no instance of a student suggesting—in print or aloud—that the issue of a color caste system is irrelevant. Students might still think it, but with the digital audience that Andrene and her website command, with a following unsurpassed by any other student, their comments are not credible enough to be audible in my classrooms anymore. And it's quite palpable. The very speed and rhythm of this change in my classroom for what I once considered routine social language/practice are what I am marking as new "cultural flow" or "liquid life" (Appadurai 1996; Bauman 2005). The dominant construct of the "classroom-as-container" and main "geography of education" holds little sway here (Leander et al. 2015). The very directionality of learning and its processes are altered. Andrene is not talking to her faculty (or most of the folk who teach composition rhetoric) with her website, and the fierce impetus behind its origins does not come from me either. To borrow from Leander et al., the online and offline spaces in which Andrene has formed her ideas and identities interrupt "the spatiotemporal contours" of her life and, in turn, do the same for my classrooms (2015, 330).

NEW BLACK DIGITAL MIGRATIONS IN CURRICULUM AND DESIGN

It's not uncommon to walk into the computer lab today when I teach students web design and see black and AfroLatina women with Andrene's website nested as one of their open tabs as they design their own web pages, often clicking back and forth between their own web pages and Andrene's web pages. In fact, a new grammatical construct has also become quite popular and it goes something like this: Professor Carmen, can I _____ (enter an action verb) like "Pretty for a Black Girl"? Initially, these questions were perplexing for me because students would often ask a question, using Andrene's website as an example, about the very demonstration they had just experienced. For instance, during the demonstration of where to add the footer text and how to code for its opacity, border, font, and color design, a student has often asked: "Can I add a quote like 'Pretty for a Black Girl'?" This seemed like a strange question since the entire demonstration at that moment was about adding a quote and building its meaning simultaneously with digital design elements allowed by the platform. But I then realized that these questions were querying the political allowances of cultural rhetoric in digital spaces. The query works more as a kind of roll call for students who are often shouting out the authors, artists, and activists they have selected—literally yelling the names across the computer lab—as if to encourage, center, and incite the explicit cultural politic that each student/designer is constructing. The same kind of querying has happened in classroom dialogues about headers and background designs each semester in the computer lab.[2]

None of the students who talk about Andrene's ePortfolio has ever called her Andrene like I do; they reference Andrene's person and her web space the same way: as "Pretty for a Black Girl." She has thus destabilized the space of my classroom where black women's pain and repression were once rendered irrelevant and illogical, despite my own vocal disagreements, by (usually white) students' dismissals of black women's experiences. New movements of ideas and bodies are difficult to sustain, generally speaking, but so far, at least when it comes to discussions of color caste systems in my classroom, it's all good in the hood. The repeated expressions of Andrene's language by young women of color in my classes, no longer arguing their case, but highlighting a successful case in Andrene, allows a new uptake of political positions. AfroDigital design is thus a kind of "transition movement" in my classrooms where students use other digital spaces to push the limits of their social imaginaries and beingness in the world. I would argue here that the black women in my classes use a media space such as Andrene's website in the same way that they use digital spaces to teach themselves to transition to, care for, and politicize the relevance of their natural hair, the topic of Andrene's website. Just as they are radicalizing the design of their transitions to alternative hair aesthetics, they are also radicalizing the function and design of their digital projects in my classes.

"PHONE DOWN": MOBILE PHONES/MOBILE BLACK SOCIALITY

Theories related to technocultural capital (Brock et al. 2010), African American/ethnic rhetoric in a multimedia age (Banks 2005, 2011), and decolonized technologies (Fouché 2006, 2012) arrive at a different understanding of Andrene's competencies. While histories of technology often omit marginalized communities, scholarship committed to racial counter-narratives of technology use in racially marginalized communities offers theories and methodologies for examining the technocultural capital of racially subordinated groups (Everett 2002; Fouché 2006). The needs, histories, circumstances, and desires of communities of color continually point out the ways technological innovation, rather than just invention, configures new critical and alternative realities (Sinclair 2004).

It may be obvious that, as a writer/designer, Andrene achieved something beyond simply getting an A in a college writing class. What might not, however, be as obvious is that Andrene did not enter the classroom with any web design background, had never been introduced to HTML/CSS, and does not have broadband at home. In fact, Andrene, a commuter student, did not own a computer. As is the case for many racially/economically subordinated groups, Andrene's handheld device is her primary connection to all things digital (Pew Research Internet Project 2019). In the context of mobilities and mobility studies, mobile phones and the mobile internet function as more than just tools for negotiating everyday life; they also function as a critical support for the practices and meanings where people reimagine their social surroundings. As Goggin (2010, 2015) reminds us, the mobile internet takes shape in differing social and cultural contexts for a variety of users, compelling us to see how hair and skin politics for black female mobile users constitutes its own universe, set of sharing practices, and the movements therein.

Meanwhile, Andrene is the "kind of student" who many faculty at my university imagine to be so challenged and overwhelmed by a curriculum nested in digital cultures that the scholarship related to the "fifth canon" has often been publicly called irrelevant in this setting (Lunsford 2006; Selber 2004; Hawisher and Selfe 1999; Writing in Digital Environments 2005; Yancey 2006). In contrast, Andrene's technocultural competence derives not from white-controlled and designed machines but from a deep desire for critically raced/gendered networks of participation nested in her own cultural rhetorics that are expressed verbally, visually, sonically, and spatially. Stuck in a narrow web 1.0 focus about the digital divide, many faculty members seem sure that working-class/working poor, first-generation, racially subjugated masses are alienated by digital technologies. Though the physical availability of digital media is no insignificant matter, the sociotechnical factors related to how and why poor / of color people access technology, including the limited opportunities that their teachers provide them given the over-reliance on computer-based drill practice, offer the most meaningful discussions of access today (Warschauer and Matuchniak 2010). Those discussions, however, must still be tempered by two facts, the first representing recent, general data and the second representing my own classrooms: (1) As of April 2015, African American youth use the internet more than any other youth group in the United States; (2) in my own classrooms, the most visually dynamic and interactive digital projects with the most viewers come from working class and/or students of color and not the privileged/white students with the most expensive computers and regular broadband access (Wright 2005).

#BLACKLIVESMATTER HERE AND EVERYWHERE

With Andrene as a guiding symbol, I mark her vernacular technocultural expressivity within a specific set of possibilities set in motion by three dynamics:

1. Shifting racial demographics at urban, public colleges (first most notably achieved in the 1970s where, for instance, for the first time in US educational history, as many black students attended white colleges as HBCUs).

2. A black protest movement that innovates and relies on the newest, most available technologies in order to push forth alternative sites of knowledge, cultural rhetorics, new authoring, and media productions.

3. New temporalities for cross-spatial, non-classroom-contained learning where our students' connections to justice and aesthetics are centrally and critically informed by cultural, popular, and community movements outside of our classrooms.

Andrene's revocabularization of rhetorical possibility, media production, and content for my classrooms is, of course, not without a historical context and precedence. When we think back to black freedom struggles of the 1960s and 1970s, college writing classrooms were also respatialized with these same three dynamics towards new radical pedagogies that were in communication with the literate and activist worlds of black student protests and black arts movements, all of which I regard as technologies (Kynard 2013; Baker 1993). My point in looking at this history of the 1960s and 1970s, albeit briefly, is to recognize that classrooms in white universities have rarely represented, corralled, or organized the local black movements all around them and the most available modes of communication and persuasion those movements exploit. I present this history as a reminder of Ruth Wilson Gilmore's argument about the danger of disentangling struggles for social change from larger movements and social histories, what she calls a disarticulation (1993, 2002) that only works to reproduce a multiculturalized professional managerial class that Andrene's ePortfolio is contesting.

The power structure never accomplishes its ultimate goal of unidirectionality and never leaves black women mute in our "geographies of engagement" (Peake and Kobayashi 2002, 55). The academy and all of its constituents obviously reinforce social privileges and hierarchies, but it can also be used to destabilize these racial hierarchies via both a relentless critique of its mechanisms and a displacement/replacement of its most glorified, discursive constructs. Andrene's stamp at the bottom of her website, a borrowing from Audre Lorde, perhaps bears the most critical reminder: "If we do not define ourselves for ourselves, we will be defined by others—for their use and to our detriment."

My essay drew its inspiration from a case study of one student, Andrene, in an attempt to follow the vision she mobilized for my classes with "Pretty for a Black Girl." I hope to achieve something that goes beyond the mainstream academy's tendency to do what Hortense Spillers calls using black people just as the "raw material" for a "note of inspiration" and never as a specific history that can be explained in theoretical terms, generates its own discourse, and frames a vocabulary necessitating black women's inclusion in the conversation (2007, 300). Andrene's digital work thus highlights the ways that a black feminist cartography of struggle respatializes multiple domains: (1) the ongoing violence against and marginalization of black students in college today; (2) multiple locations of legitimate knowledge-making and intellectual content; and (3) dominant understandings of educational technologies and young women of color's digital productions. AfroDigital black feminisms in the critical context of "mobile black sociality" offers us one *blackscape* where we can see what it might mean and look like for students to design and learn in a way that canvases their own humanity from the deeply storied and historied spaces in which they make meaning of the world.

NOTES

1. Please see bitly.com/andrene.
2. This essay/case study represents half of a more fully developed chapter in my forthcoming book project called *Young Black Women Writing/Righting the Word: Sites of Recursive Memory.*

REFERENCES

Appadurai, Arjun. 1996. *Modernity at Large: Cultural Dimensions of Globalization*. Minneapolis: University of Minnesota Press.

Baker, Houston A., Jr. 1993. *Black Studies, Rap, and the Academy*. Chicago: University of Chicago Press.

Banks, Adam J. 2005. *Race, Rhetoric, and Technology: Searching for Higher Ground*. Mahwah, NJ: Lawrence Erlbaum Associates.

Banks, Adam J. 2011. *Digital Griots: African American Rhetoric in a Multimedia Age*. Carbondale: Southern Illinois Press.

Banks, Ingrid. 2000. *Hair Matters: Beauty, Power and Black Women's Consciousness*. New York: New York University Press.

Bauman, Zygmunt. 2005. *Liquid Life*. Cambridge: Polity Press.

Brock, André, Lynette Kvasny, and Kayla Hales. 2010. "Cultural Appropriations of Technical Capital: Black Women, Weblogs, and the Digital Divide." *Information, Communication & Society* 13 (7): 1040–1059.

Caldwell, Paulette M. 1991. "A Hair Piece: Perspectives on the Intersection of Race and Gender." *Duke Law Journal* 40 (2): 365–396.

Christian, Barbara. 1994. "Diminishing Returns: Can Black Feminisms Survive the Academy?" In *Multiculturalism: A Critical Reader*, edited by David Theo Goldberg, 168–174. Boston: Blackwell Publishers.

Collins, Patricia Hill. 1990. *Black Feminist Thought: Knowledge, Consciousness, and the Politics of Empowerment*. Boston: Unwin Hyman.

Cresswell, Tim. 2011. "Mobilities I: Catching Up." *Progress in Human Geography* 35 (4): 550–558.

Critical Resistance. 2015. "Do Black Lives Matter? Robin D.G. Kelley and Fred Moten in Conversation." https://vimeo.com/116111740.

Everett, Anna. 2002. "The Revolution Will Be Digitized: Afrocentricity and the Digital Public Sphere." *Social Text* 20 (2): 125–146.

Fat Joe. 2004. "Lean Back." *True Story*. Terror Squad. Rifkind.

Fouché, Rayvon. 2006. "Say It loud, I'm Black and I'm Proud: African Americans, American Artifactual Culture, and Black Vernacular Technological Creativity." *American Quarterly* 58 (3): 639–661.

Fouché, Rayvon. 2012. "From Black Inventors to One Laptop Per Child: Exporting a Racial Politics of Technology." In *Race After the Internet*, edited by Lisa Nakamura and Peter Chow-White, 61–84. New York: Routledge.

Gill, Rosalind. 2008. "Culture and Subjectivity in Neoliberal and Postfeminist Times." *Subjectivity* 25: 432–445.

Gilmore, Ruth Wilson. 1993. "Public Enemies and Private Intellectuals: Apartheid USA." *Race & Class* 35: 69–78.

Gilmore, Ruth Wilson. 2002. "Fatal Couplings of Power and Difference: Notes on Racism and Geography." *The Professional Geographer* 54 (1), 15–24.

Glenn, Evelyn Nakano, ed. 2009. *Shades of Difference: Why Skin Color Matters*. Stanford: Stanford University Press.

Goggin, Gerard. 2010. *Global Mobile Media*. New York: Routledge.

Goggin, Gerard. 2015. "Mobile Web 2.0: New Imaginaries of Mobile Internet." In *Theories of the Mobile Internet: Materialities and Imaginaries*, edited by Andrew Herman, Jan Hadlaw, and Thom Swiss, 134–148. New York: Routledge.

Hall, Ted. 2011. "Designing from Their Own Social Worlds: The Digital Story of Three African American Young Women." *English Teaching: Practice and Critique* 10 (1): 7–20.

Harney, Stefano, and Fred Moten. 2013. *The Undercommons: Fugitive Planning and Black Study*. Brooklyn, NY: Autonomedia.

Hawisher, Gail E., and Cynthia L. Selfe, eds. 1999. *Passions, Pedagogies, and 21st Century Technologies*. Logan: Utah State University Press.

Kynard, Carmen. 2013. *Vernacular Insurrections: Race, Black Protest, and the New Century in Composition-Literacies Studies.* Albany: State University of New York Press.

Jackson, Michael. 1979. "Rock with You." Rod Temperton, composer. *Off the Wall.* Epic Records.

Leander, Kevin M., Nathan C. Phillips, and Katherine Headrick Taylor. 2015. "The Changing Social Spaces of Learning: Mapping New Mobilities." *Review of Research in Education* 34: 329–394.

Lorde, Audre. 1984. *Sister Outsider.* Freedom, CA: Crossing Press.

Lunsford, Andrea A. 2006. "Writing, Technologies, and the Fifth Canon." *Computers and Composition* 23 (2): 169–177.

Marwick, Alice E. 2013. *Status Update: Celebrity, Publicity, and Branding in the Social Media Age.* New Haven: Yale University Press.

McDowell, Linda. 1999. *Gender, Identity, and Place: Understanding Feminist Geographies.* Minneapolis: University of Minnesota Press.

McKittrick, Katherine. 2006. *Demonic Grounds: Black Women and the Cartographies of Struggle.* Minneapolis: University of Minnesota Press.

Peake, Linda, and Audrey Kobayashi. 2002. "Policies and Practices for an Antiracist Geography at the Millennium." *The Professional Geographer* 54 (1): 50–61.

Pew Research Internet Project. 2019. "Mobile Fact Sheet." Pew Research Center. June 12, 2019. https://www.pewresearch.org/internet/fact-sheet/mobile/#who-is-smartphone -dependent.

Richardson, Elaine. 2003. *African American Literacies.* New York: Routledge.

Rooks, Noliwe M. 1996. *Hair Raising: Beauty, Culture, and African American Women.* New Brunswick: Rutgers University Press.

Sandberg, Sheryl. 2013. *Lean In: Women, Work, and the Will to Lead.* New York: Alfred A. Knopf.

Selber, Stuart A. 2004. *Multiliteracies for a Digital Age.* Carbondale: Southern Illinois University Press.

Sinclair, Bruce. 2004. *Technology and the African-American Experience: Needs and Opportunities for Study.* Cambridge, MA: MIT Press.

Spillers, Hortense. 2007. "'Whatcha Gonna Do?': Revisiting 'Mama's Baby, Papa's Maybe: An American Grammar Book': A Conversation with Hortense Spillers, Saidiya Hartman, Farah Jasmine Griffin, Shelly Eversley, and Jennifer L. Morgan." *Women's Studies Quarterly* 35 (1/2): 299–309.

Taylor, Charles. 2003. *Modern Social Imaginaries.* Durham: Duke University Press.

Warschauer, Mark, and Tina Matuchniak. 2010. "New Technology and Digital Worlds: Analyzing Evidence of Equity in Access, Use, and Outcomes." *Review of Research in Education* 34: 179–225.

Weitz, Rose, and Leonard Gordon. 1993. "Images of Black Women Among Anglo College Students." *Sex Roles* 28 (1/2): 19–34.

Wright, Michelle M. 2005. "Finding a Place in Cyberspace: Black Women, Technology, and Identity." *Frontiers* 26 (1): 48–59.

Writing in Digital Environments (WIDE) Research Center Collective. 2005. "Why Teach Digital Writing?" *Kairos* 10 (1). http://kairos.technorhetoric.net/10.1/binder2.html ?coverweb/wide/index.html.

Yancey, Kathleen Blake, ed. 2006. *Delivering College Composition: The Fifth Canon.* Portsmouth, NH: Boynton/Cook.

6

COMPOSING TO MOBILIZE KNOWLEDGE
Lessons from a Design-Thinking-Based Writing Course

Scott Wible

At its core, design thinking is a theory and method aimed at defining and solving problems through direct, regular engagement with people. Design thinkers observe people and interview them about their experiences within their communities, and they use this knowledge to create solutions to the communities' problems, testing prototypes of these solutions with community members to get immediate feedback on how they fit the users' values, contexts, and needs. Mobility is a key part of this design practice, as design thinkers believe they can't understand a community's problem and create innovative solutions simply by sitting in an office, relying on market research, focus groups, or even their own perceptions of a particular problem or a fitting solution; instead, design thinkers emphasize the need to "get out of the building" in order to talk with and learn from stakeholders and potential users (Blank 2014). Physical mobility gains meaning within this methodology, then, as design thinkers believe that meeting with stakeholders, listening to their stories, and observing their day-to-day experiences help them to make meaning about user needs and to transform that knowledge into solutions that fit the contexts of their lives.

In this chapter, however, I examine not how design thinkers prioritize physical mobility—getting "out of the building" as a research priority—but rather how they mobilize knowledge through and for field research. I focus in particular on how specific textual practices in design work facilitate both the creation of knowledge and the transformation of this knowledge as it circulates among and gets used by different groups to develop a context-specific solution. Toward these ends, I describe my multi-semester teaching collaboration with the University of Maryland's Academy for Innovation and Entrepreneurship, analyzing how, through the design thinking process, my professional writing students learn to

DOI: 10.7330/9781646420209.c006

shape their problem definitions and solution ideas in ways that allow community members to interact with, respond to, and even reshape this knowledge. Design thinking pedagogy and practice, then, helps us to understand how knowledge can be mobilized to foster co-generation of both problem definitions and creative solutions that fit with a community's worldviews and everyday practices.

Through this analysis, I deepen our collective examination of mobility frameworks by considering how design thinking adds important nuance to conceptions of knowledge mobilization and how, by extension, it might inform approaches to teaching research and invention in rhetoric and writing studies. At the same time, I use writing studies theory both to add a critical dimension to design thinking methodology as well as to foster a more collaborative conception of knowledge mobilization.

SITUATING DESIGN THINKING IN THE PROFESSIONAL WRITING COURSE

Design thinking's emphasis on problem-solving initially drew me to the University of Maryland's Academy for Innovation and Entrepreneurship, which promotes the integration of design thinking methods across all departments on campus. Our upper-division general education professional writing courses, at their core, emphasize students' learning how to use writing to solve real-world problems, but I knew we did a better job of teaching students how to write proposals in support of their solutions than we did teaching students how to actually discover and design those solutions in the first place. Integrating design thinking methodology into my professional writing course has helped me to address this concern.

As it has been developed and promulgated by Stanford University's d.School, design thinking is a methodology that people use to approach and solve complex, multi-dimensional problems, such as those related to public health (e.g., "How might we create a safer environment for pedestrians in downtown College Park?") and human resources (e.g., "How might we help first-year faculty transition to professional and personal life at the University of Maryland?"). As Richard Marback explains, these are "wicked problems" in that they are contextualized, value-laden, and solvable in more than one way (2009, W400). Design thinkers embrace this wickedness by taking a human-centered approach, working to deeply understand people's values by listening to stories about their experiences and to create solutions that meet their needs and fit the contexts of their lives. Specifically, design thinkers work iteratively through these five stages:

1. Empathy Mode, which involves getting out of the building and immersing oneself in a particular context, conducting ethnographic-style research such as observations and interviews in order to understand how people act, think, and feel in their daily lives.

2. Define Mode, when the designer synthesizes this empathy research and crafts a meaningful, actionable problem statement, one that defines the design challenge she will work to solve.

3. Ideate Mode, which involves concentrated, semi-structured brainstorming focused on generating a wide range of ideas for possible solutions and then selecting those possibilities that have the greatest potential to solve the problem.

4. Prototype Mode, when the designer creates artifacts that invite users to experience critical aspects of the solution idea.

5. Test Phase, in which the designer allows users to engage with the prototype, generating valuable information and insights about how users experience, interact with, and respond to the prototype as well as key elements of the overall solution design.

This entire design thinking process is purposefully recursive, with students looping back to previous modes at key moments to deepen their understanding of the community context and the users they are designing solutions for. When working in the define mode, for example, a designer might determine that she needs to conduct more empathy research. While testing a prototype, meanwhile, designers conduct another form of empathy research as they watch users interact with a solution. And designers work through multiple stages of prototyping and testing, developing different or more refined prototypes along the way. From a pedagogical perspective, design thinking helps students learn to become more flexible, innovative problem-solvers as they learn processes and methods for moving into and engaging with local communities as a means to analyze and define problems and invent, develop, and refine solutions.

DEFINING KNOWLEDGE MOBILITY FOR THE DESIGN THINKING WRITING COURSE

In this essay I use "mobility" as a way to think through how specific material acts of composing shape knowledge into forms that propel the problem-defining and problem-solving work at the heart of design thinking. The concept of "knowledge mobility" emerges from education research in the Canadian, UK, and Australian traditions concerned with improving how knowledge gets put to use in policy and practice. As education scholars Tara Fenwick and Lesley Farrell explain, "knowledge mobility" prompts us to focus not simply on the creation of knowledge but also on the "activities of moving and sustaining applications of the knowledge" (2012, 3). Knowledge can be mobilized by and between communities, they explain, because knowledge itself is "able to be . . . mobilized as language" (3). A critical practice for scholars, then, is composing "[t]exts [that] make knowledge portable" (3).

Significantly, the term "knowledge mobilization" emerged as a way to move beyond terms such as "knowledge transfer" and "knowledge translation" that suggest a one-way exchange from researcher to practitioner, with researchers creating evidence-based "knowledge" and then practitioners (e.g., policymakers, citizen groups) simply putting that knowledge to use. "Knowledge mobilization," on the other hand, envisions the process as one in which *both* researchers "make knowledge portable" by composing texts that help non-expert audiences to understand and put evidence-based research to use *and* practitioners make decisions and initiate actions that transform this knowledge (Community Engaged Scholarship Institute n.d.). In this way, knowledge mobilization scholars recognize that knowledge is situated, such that it "cannot avoid [being] . . . reconstituted with differently inflected meanings as [it] circulates[s] through new locations" (Fenwick and Farrell 2012, 3), particularly as policymakers, civic groups, and other organizations and individuals use and reshape this knowledge within the contexts of their own lived experience.

Knowledge mobilization serves as a useful frame for considering design thinking research methods. While the definition of writing as a "knowledge-making activity" is central to the discipline of rhetoric and composition studies (Estrem 2015, 19), a mobilities framework brings into sharper relief how design thinkers generate knowledge through engagement with communities: engaging with stakeholders and user groups in order to hear stories about their experiences and to analyze these stories toward the end of defining the problem to solve. Design-thinking-based writing pedagogy presents a substantive example of how students compose in genres that both "make knowledge portable" and prompt students and users to reshape this knowledge as it circulates through iterative cycles of prototyping and testing. In the sections that follow, I analyze how several textual genres central to design thinking prompt students to compose in ways that facilitate knowledge mobilization, circulating ideas in forms that can be reshaped by project teammates as well as community members.

MOBILIZING KNOWLEDGE TO FOSTER
COLLABORATIVE SOLUTION DESIGN

In this section I use knowledge mobilization as a frame to analyze my writing students' work through the design thinking process—empathetically researching, defining, ideating, prototyping, and testing—in order to illustrate how shaping knowledge into portable, textual forms promotes collaborative syntheses of field research and the generative, iterative development of solutions.

Composing Questions to Enable Empathetic Travel

While design thinkers talk about empathy research in terms of physical movement—"getting out of the building," in Steve Blank's words (Blank 2014)—it requires even more so a kind of metaphysical mobility. Essayist Leslie Jamison explains, "Empathy comes from the Greek *empatheia—em* (into) and *pathos* (feeling)—a penetration, a kind of travel. It suggests you enter another person's pain as you'd enter another country, through immigration and customs, border crossing by way of query" (Jamison 2014, 6). In my most recent professional writing course, students worked on a project commissioned by the Office of Faculty Affairs: design a way to improve some aspect of new faculty's transition to professional life at the University of Maryland. In their empathy research, then, students asked questions that helped them to travel along with faculty members through their first year at Maryland, drawing out faculty members' stories about their experiences as a way of more deeply understanding not only what professors do but also how they feel about their professional lives. In their empathy interview questions, though, students did not ask questions like "What has been the hardest aspect of your transition to Maryland?" or "What could have helped you the most in your first semester at Maryland?" both of which put the onus on the faculty themselves to identify the source of their struggles and successes. Instead, students attempted to evoke detail-rich stories about faculty members' experiences with prompts such as "Describe a moment from your first year when you felt frustrated in your transition to Maryland" and "Tell me about a time when you left campus feeling energized and thinking, 'I love working here.'" Other students used a stack of cards that included several concerns common to first-year professors—getting to know the area, learning campus culture, improving teaching, balancing life stuff, starting research, accessing campus resources, identifying growth opportunities, building relationships—and asked faculty to rank them in order of how they prioritized or spent their time in their first

100   WIBLE

semester; more significant than how they were specifically sorted, these cards helped to prompt conversations that revealed first-year faculty members' values and needs to students.

The types of questions students ask facilitate this type of empathetic travel into the value-laden contexts of the people and communities they work with. As Jamison contends, "Empathy isn't just listening, it's asking the questions whose answers need to be listened to" (2014, 5). Rather than having students start the project by imagining what professors' lives are like and by asking themselves what they think professors need to improve their transition to life at Maryland, students met and talked with faculty in their research labs, in their offices, and in their classrooms in order to begin to see how their professors envision and carry out their professional lives. Indeed, as Jamison suggests, "Empathy requires inquiry as much as imagination. Empathy requires knowing you know nothing. Empathy means acknowledging a horizon of context that extends perpetually beyond what you can see" (5). Many students, in the reflective writing they did throughout the course, acknowledged that asking for and listening to professors' stories stripped away many conceptions they had about faculty lives and helped them to "cros[s] by way of query" (6) into the spaces and moments where faculty experienced frustrations and joys in their first semesters on campus.

Composing to Synthesize Research and Define User Problems

As student teams interviewed and observed people connected to their topic, they shaped and articulated the meaning of their research in the define mode through two specific written genres: user empathy maps and point-of-view (POV) statements. After conducting empathy interviews in pairs, students came back to class and joined together in smaller groups; they took turns reading their detailed interview notes—not simply summarizing those interviews, but reading their notes line-by-line—while their teammates used Post-it notes and markers to jot down key words, phrases, and quotes from the interview notes. Students wrote just one item per Post-it note. As they recomposed their empathy research notes in this way, students reshaped faculty members' lived experiences into textual forms that could be analyzed and synthesized in different ways.

Having made "knowledge portable" on Post-it notes, students created user empathy maps to help them visualize and identify relationships between faculty members' actions, words, emotions, and needs. Specifically, students arranged their Post-it notes on a type of "map" (see

USER EMPATHY MAP			
NEEDS Use & Usability	SAY Quotes & Defining Words	THINK Thoughts & Beliefs	NEEDS Deeper Meaning
	DO (or Say They Do) Actions & Behaviors	FEEL Feelings & Emotions	

Figure 6.1.

figure 6.1). The analytical benefits of the user empathy map became clearer as students layered notes from several different interviews onto it, for they began to see clusters of similar thoughts and feelings emerging in the lived experiences of faculty members. For example, first-year faculty in STEM disciplines expressed feelings of "academic loneliness" as they faced the time- and energy-intensive work of creating their own research teams for the first time, while several humanities faculty members felt both hopefulness and trepidation about wanting to integrate issues of diversity and inclusion into their courses, but not feeling like they knew how best to do it.

As students arranged those small, portable texts on their user empathy maps, they reshaped knowledge about users' values and experiences into a sharply focused POV statement, which takes a templated shape (see figure 6.2). This genre forces students to synthesize their empathy research. In so doing, they necessarily leave out some of the experiences and problems they learned that community members face. This narrower focus might seem to discourage truly "innovative" problem-solving, but the POV's attention to easily overlooked or often-ignored insights gained through empathy research concentrates designers' subsequent invention activity in ways that can generate potential breakthrough

POINT OF VIEW STATEMENT

(Description of User)

needs a way to

(User's Need)

because, surprisingly,

(Insight from User Empathy Map)

.

Figure 6.2.

solutions. The team working on the science faculty starting a research lab, for example, composed a POV statement that explained how Nathalie, a first-semester biology professor starting up a research lab for the first time, needs a way to feel connection and companionship with other researchers on campus because she has experienced "academic loneliness" since stepping on campus and not immediately joining an already vibrant communal research team. As this example suggests, the POV statement genre contains an insight or perspective about the user that teams discovered through their empathy research and crystallized through their user empathy map analysis. Admittedly, I give students significant feedback through several drafts of these POV statements, both as students try out several POVs that emerge from different clusters of Post-it notes on their user empathy maps and as they try to articulate the need and the insight in concise yet not-too-narrow ways. This particular insight focuses the team on meeting not simply some surface-level need but rather a deeper underlying issue, and the POV statement guides teams' invention activity and shapes their solution designs as they work through the rest of the design thinking process.

Composing to Mobilize Knowledge 103

To culminate the problem definition phase of this course, students textualized their knowledge into research posters that showcased their POV statements, relevant clusters from their user empathy maps, and revealing quotes from their empathy interviews. Students presented these posters to Office of Faculty Affairs staff; textualizing their knowledge this way drew out stories from the OFA staff's own experiences with faculty, stories that in some cases resonated with and enriched students' POVs and in other instances prompted students to revise or reshape their definition of the problem. These analytical techniques and texts in design thinking's define mode, then, reinforce for students the idea that problem definition emerges through interaction between writers and readers or between designers and users, and it encourages students to pursue a deeper, more nuanced understanding of how their users experience and make meaning about particular aspects of their daily lives.

Composing Texts to Spark Collaborative Invention

Ideation involves a semi-structured, team-based approach to brainstorming solutions, and two writing practices in particular enable designers and students to mobilize knowledge from their problem definition stage and propel it through early invention work. First, students compose How Might We (HMW) questions, which energize and focus students' brainstorming work. To compose HMW questions, students slightly reframe the needs and insights in their team's POV statements, aiming to compose questions that are broad enough to draw forth a wide range of solutions yet narrow enough that they focus the team on inventing solutions that meet a specific goal. The team working on STEM faculty, for example, crafted HMW questions like "HMW make creating the research team the most exciting part of the first year?" and "HMW build camaraderie among faculty creating new research teams?" As they composed HMW questions, then, students mobilized the knowledge embedded in their POV statements, particularly those empathetic insights about people's thoughts and emotions, and reshaped these into an actionable question that could launch their idea creation.

After teams selected three HMW questions to use as brainstorming prompts, they set up their brainstorming space, with butcher paper on the wall and Post-it notes and Sharpies in hand. These HMW questions propelled invention over the next ten to fifteen minutes, pushing students to think in imaginative yet structured ways about the problem and solutions, and to generate kernels of ideas that could later be developed into full-fledged solutions. Indeed, the aim here is quantity. Students are encouraged to defer judgment, to build on each other's ideas, to be visual, and to "headline"—that is, to jot down a phrase or draw a quick picture, slap the Post-it on the board, quickly explain it, and move on.

Indeed, composing on Post-it notes during this brainstorming session keeps students focused on generating lots of ideas and building on one another's ideas. Many design thinkers see the Post-it note's restricted space as critically important for innovation, as it prompts collaborators to get more ideas in the open rather than trying to flesh out lots of details and elements of any one idea before sharing it. This use of Post-it notes reflects design thinking's focus "less on making decisions" and more on "creating options from which to choose" (Osterwalder and Pignaur 2010, 143). This ideation stage presents a moment and space for teams to amplify their physical and mental energy toward generating a greater quantity of ideas to develop in the first place.

Ideation, then, prompts us to consider the forms in which students create and mobilize knowledge during invention processes. Marback suggests that wicked problems, since they are so context-bound and value-laden, demand "inventing a solution" rather than simply "discovering an answer" (2009, W400)—that is, designing a solution that embodies knowledge about the constraints and potentials of a particular context rather than searching for and importing a solution from some other time, space, and community. The HMW question genre keeps students focused on these contexts—particularly users' values and needs—and directs their energy toward generating many solution ideas. After teams vote on the ideas that have the greatest potential to delight users or to make the biggest breakthrough in addressing a problem, they move that idea forward in the design thinking process and reshape this knowledge into prototypes that will facilitate user engagement.

Composing Multimodally to Reshape Knowledge with Stakeholders

In our typical professional writing courses, students spend several weeks "discovering an answer" (Marback 2009, W400) to the problem they've identified and articulating their proposal in full. At that point, students present their solution with the aim of persuading stakeholders to support it. Since they have already invested so much time in creating the solution in detail, students are less open to changing parts of it or scrapping it completely and moving in a new direction in the face of stakeholders' questions, concerns, or critiques.

Design thinking methods instead urge teams to create their solution iteratively, roughly crafting prototypes that both mobilize knowledge about how the solution meets user needs and that promote this knowledge being reshaped in subsequent stages of solution design. Mobilizing knowledge in this way enables students to continue learning and reshaping their solution designs to fit the specific contexts of users' lives. Here students make significant decisions about the forms through which they communicate their developing solution ideas, for these genres influence potential users' engagement with the solution idea and, in turn, the ways user knowledge can be reshaped into further solution designs.

Given this emphasis on iteratively developing a solution through user feedback, the critical work in prototyping and testing is deciding how to "make knowledge portable" (Fenwick and Farrell 2012, 3). Having created empathetic knowledge about the contexts of users' lives and generated the kernel of an idea about how to address their needs, students need to shape that knowledge in a way that both helps users to experience how the solution would fit into their lives and, significantly, remains permeable and malleable to new knowledge that emerges from the prototype testing itself. Toward that end, student teams in my public health writing classes, who worked to redesign different aspects of students' on-campus health experiences, created one of four different types of multimodal prototypes:

- Annotated sketches that highlight key features of a solution. One team, for example, drew several screens of a web page aimed at helping students to understand and access the full range of mental health resources on campus and in the surrounding community.

- A storyboard, in which teams create a series of sketches or photos to outline a sequence of events or highlight specific details of an activity. One team created an eight-panel storyboard that walked users through a mental health education module designed for first-year orientation.

- Role-play prototyping, in which the team creates key props and then has users role-play through an experience. One team, for instance, had users play the role of hungry, rushed students visiting a free breakfast shack on campus in order to determine what modes of educational messaging might best reach these students.

- "Works Like/Feels Like" prototyping, in which the team creates a very basic physical object that gives users the opportunity to see, hold, play, and work with that object or virtually walk through a space. For example, one team designing an annex to the student health center created a rough physical model of the space using cardboard, markers, and yarn.

Again, in the design thinking process, the emphasis is on creating a simple artifact or activity that helps the designer to walk users through the new experience they're trying to create with the solution. Testing the prototype generates new knowledge about users' values and experiences and about how specific aspects of the solution do or don't meet their needs and desires, knowledge that the students spin forward into subsequent prototype designs as they continue working to create a tight fit between their solution design and community needs.

This iterative process of developing solution ideas accentuates several key aspects of knowledge mobilization. The design thinking process requires students to make their solution ideas both "portable" and "transformable," such that they are able to generate new knowledge from user interaction with the prototype and to shape that knowledge into subsequent, ever more developed prototypes and solution designs. Teaching prototyping genres—annotated sketches, storyboards, role playing, and "works like/feels like" objects—accentuated how multimodal composing does not simply support or stimulate students' and community members' collaborative invention, but rather is part of the knowledge-making activity itself. Indeed, prototype testing in design thinking operates as a form of distributed cognition, which Dorothy Winsor, via Edwin Hutchins, describes as a phenomenon in which "people and their tools ac[t] in concert . . . to accomplish a kind of cognition that no individual could achieve separately" (Winsor 2003, 6). Winsor, writing specifically about engineers, explains the value of distributed cognition this way: "[A]cting jointly . . . a group of engineers can maintain a variety of theories that contribute to their design work, whereas an individual would have trouble seeing from a similar multiplicity of perspectives at once" (Winsor 2003, 6). Design thinkers carry out prototype testing in this same spirit of seeing the solution idea from multiple perspectives at once—including, critically, the perspectives of people for whose lives the solution has been designed.

The aim of creating and testing prototypes, in other words, is not to seek confirmation about a solution idea but rather to bring designers together with users to think with and through the prototype—to generate new knowledge about users' experiences that didn't emerge through earlier empathy research and about how the solution could best fit the contexts of users' lives. As Winsor explains when defining engineering as knowledge work, "[A]lthough the goal of engineering may be to produce useful objects, engineers do not construct such objects themselves. Rather, they aim to generate knowledge that will allow such objects to be built" (Winsor 1996, 5). Similarly, within my professional writing courses, the goal was not for students to have a product or solution ready to "launch" at semester's end but rather for them to learn how to generate and reshape knowledge that helps them to design a solution that fits a user's context-specific need. Through their multiple rounds of prototyping and testing, students identified specific aspects of their solution ideas they wanted to learn more about, and they composed their prototype genres in a way that would likely draw out user feedback. Over subsequent rounds of prototype composition and testing, the solution design comes to embody the knowledge generated in this distributed fashion among designers, users, and prototype tools.

MOBILIZING WRITING STUDIES KNOWLEDGE TO RESHAPE DESIGN THINKING METHODOLOGIES

Attention to how students mobilize knowledge through the design thinking process underscores key strategies we might usefully integrate into our approaches for teaching research in the writing course, particularly strategies that influence how students engage in processes of defining problems and developing solutions. Filtering through interview transcripts and observation notes and paring down those insights into a POV statement challenges students to see problem definitions as contingent statements reflective of a particular stakeholder's point of view. These robust yet tightly focused POV statements in turn create productive constraints on students' intellectual activity in brainstorming sessions, while the lean prototyping and testing cycle encourages students to compose solution ideas in ways that make the ideas portable yet pliable, able to be shaped by users as they engage with them.

This attention to student mobility through the research process, however, also highlights critical ways in which design thinking can benefit from deep, sustained engagement with writing studies. No doubt many readers will see parallels between design thinking's empathy mode and ethnographic approaches to teaching research and writing represented in texts such as Bonnie Stone Sunstein and Elizabeth Chiseri-Strater's (2011) *FieldWorking*, while professional writing scholars and teachers will recognize the usability testing and user experience methods they teach in design thinking's prototype and testing modes (Redish and Barnum 2011). Moreover, writing scholars invested in service-learning and community engagement projects, such as those outlined in Thomas Deans's (2002) *Writing and Community Action* textbook, Eli Goldblatt and Temple University's partnership with Tree House Books, and David Jolliffe's Arkansas Delta Oral History Project will see much resonance with design thinking's human-centered orientation toward solving local, community-defined problems (Goldblatt and Jolliffe 2014). I myself have taught all three of these types of writing courses—ethnography-based, usability-focused, and service learning-oriented—and those experiences facilitated both my initial conversations and ongoing work with the Academy for Innovation and Entrepreneurship. The academy's leaders now recognize writing studies as a discipline on campus that in critical ways "speaks the same language" (their words, not mine) as entrepreneurship and innovation scholars and practitioners. These similarities in approaches are significant, I believe, because they help us to gain deeper insight into how entrepreneurship and innovation are at least partly grounded in an epistemology that we share in writing studies, namely, a belief in the social nature of knowledge and the collaborative nature of knowledge construction. Just as design thinkers assume that physical, intellectual, and emotional mobility can generate knowledge, as designers engage with potential consumers and communities who experience the problem in need of solving, many writing studies scholars teach students to make meaning through movement within their communities—engaging, interacting, and communicating with stakeholders to transform local contexts through writing.

While design thinking promotes composition that mobilizes problem definitions and solution ideas, the way it narrows students' focus on specific user groups' needs highlights opportunities to introduce other modes of humanistic research into the design process. The design thinking process as conceived in the Stanford University d.School and as taught at institutions such as the University of Maryland is propelled by ethnographic research. As historian Peter N. Miller suggests in a *Chronicle of Higher Education* article, however, design thinking research "is all conducted in the present tense, with no sense that the past matters to the present. . . . Libraries, archives, museums, the great repositories of the human past are rarely called upon for help" (2015). Design thinking's approach, Miller argues, reveals a significant contradiction in its claim to be a human-centered practice, for it seemingly ignores how the past shapes and lives on in a particular community's present life. Students may indeed create sharp, focused POV statements that reveal deeper, often unacknowledged insights about a person's experience, but they also potentially strip away some of the social, cultural, and political complexity of human behavior. For example, student teams in my public health writing courses heard many fascinating stories about people's experiences that revealed their perspectives on and action (or inaction) toward specific mental health behaviors, but as they worked to make sense of those stories and sharpen them into POV statements, my students did not consider broader economic and social changes

Composing to Mobilize Knowledge   109

that might contribute to the increasing percentage of college students experiencing mental health issues. Design thinking research methods do prompt students to dive more deeply into the cultural community they are working with, but this deep dive should also include the types of humanistic and social research that happen through reading, watching, and listening to the wide range of cultural artifacts produced by and for a community. I could design my Writing for the Health Professions course, for example, in a way that prompts student-designers to more deeply understand the cultural influences on community members' attitudes toward health, medicine, nutrition, and wellness, while students in the course focused on first-year faculty's transition to Maryland could engage with sociological and psychological examinations, or perhaps even literary representations of faculty experiences in higher education.

This attention to social and cultural dimensions of health also points to an equally significant blind spot in design thinking pedagogy, and it's one that our present focus on mobility draws into greater focus: the politics of mobility and how it influences designers' identification of communities to engage and problems to pursue. We can encourage students to reflect on how they imagine the local "public" when they begin to consider a "community" issue they want to explore. For example, what local spaces do they imagine when they envision the local "public" and what groups live there? Is "the public" they envision monolingual or linguistically diverse? Racially diverse? Ethnically diverse? Socioeconomically diverse? And what types of issues become relevant when one considers these questions and broadens the spatial contexts where one considers it to be important to work?

Here we can prompt student reflection on the spaces where they see themselves working to solve particular types of problems and to examine the larger historical, social, and cultural perspectives that lead them to attend to some locations and communities but not others. Composition scholars with expertise in service-learning and community-based pedagogies in particular have much to offer design thinking and lean startup educators, as they have developed specific approaches for teaching rhetorical, policy, and historical analysis; intercultural inquiry; stakeholder and community engagement; and self-reflection that can help students to take up and carry out research and writing in ways that benefit both their learning and the academic and community institutions and members involved (Carter and Conrad 2012; Coogan 2006; Himley 2004; see also Hartline, chapter 14).

Equally as important, this reflection on our students' physical and intellectual mobility in defining the "community" also carries important implications for considerations of knowledge mobilization. Fenwick and Farrell's reminder that knowledge "cannot avoid [being] . . . reconstituted with differently inflected meanings as [it] circulates[s] through new locations" (2012, 3) prompts us to consider the importance of engaging historically marginalized communities with design thinking projects, for both empathy and prototype testing research create opportunities for these groups to use their experiences, values, and worldviews to reshape too-often reified knowledge about their needs and potential solutions to address them. By critically engaging with design thinking methods as knowledge mobilization work—teaching students to engage in empathetic inquiry as a means to "acknowledg[e] a horizon of context that extends perpetually beyond what you can see" (Jamison 2014, 5) and teaching them to compose and test multimodal prototypes not to confirm their own ideas but to co-generate knowledge with users and embed it into solution designs—writing studies scholars can expand our understanding of how colleges and universities work in, serve, and—most important—are transformed by the cultural and social knowledge of their local communities.

REFERENCES

Blank, Steve. 2014. Address. Startup Shell. University of Maryland, College Park, Maryland. December 11, 2014.

Carter, Shannon, and James H. Conrad. 2012. "In Possession of Community: Toward a More Sustainable Local." *College Composition and Communication* 64 (1): 82–106.

Community Engaged Scholarship Institute, University of Guelph. n.d. "About Knowledge Mobilization." http://www.cesinstitute.ca/cesi/knowledge-mobilization/about-knowledge-mobilization/.

Coogan, David. 2006. "Service Learning and Social Change: The Case for Materialist Rhetoric." *College Composition and Communication* 57 (4): 667–693.

Deans, Thomas. 2002. *Writing and Community Action: A Service-Learning Rhetoric with Readings.* New York: Longman.

Estrem, Heidi. 2015. "Writing is a Knowledge-Making Activity." In *Naming What We Know: Threshold Concepts of Writing Studies,* edited by Linda Adler-Kassner and Elizabeth Wardle, 19–20. Logan: Utah State University Press.

Fenwick, Tara, and Lesley Farrell. 2012. "Knowledge Mobilization: The New Research Imperative." In *Knowledge Mobilization and Educational Research: Politics, Languages, and Responsibilities,* edited by Tara Fenwick and Lesley Farrell, 1–13. London: Routledge.

Goldblatt, Eli, and David A. Jolliffe. 2014. "The Unintended Consequences of Literacy Sponsorship." In *Literacy, Economy, and Power: Writing and Research after Literacy in American Lives,* edited by John Duffy, Julie Nelson Christoph, Eli Goldblatt, Nelson Graff, Rebecca S. Nowacek, and Bryan Trabold, 127–135. Carbondale: Southern Illinois University Press.

Himley, Margaret. 2004. "Facing (Up to) 'the Stranger' in Community Service Learning." *College Composition and Communication* 55 (3): 416–438.

Jamison, Leslie. 2014. *The Empathy Exams.* Minneapolis, MN: Graywolf.

Marback, Richard. 2009. "Embracing Wicked Problems: The Turn to Design in Composition Studies." *College Composition and Communication* 61 (2): W397-W419.

Miller, Peter N. 2015. "Is 'Design Thinking' the New Liberal Arts?" *Chronicle of Higher Education*, March 26, 2015. http://www.chronicle.com/article/Is-Design-Thinking-the-New/228779.

Osterwalder, Alexander, and Yves Pignaur. 2010. *Business Model Generation.* New York: Wiley.

Redish, Ginny, and Carol Barnum. 2011. "Overlap, Influence, Intertwining: The Interplay of UX and Technical Communication." *Journal of Usability Studies* 6 (3): 90–101.

Sunstein, Bonnie Stone, and Elizabeth Chiseri-Strater. 2011. *FieldWorking: Reading and Writing Research.* 4th ed. Boston: Bedford/St. Martin's.

Winsor, Dorothy. 1996. *Writing Like an Engineer: A Rhetorical Education.* New York: Routledge.

Winsor, Dorothy. 2003. *Writing Power: Communication in an Engineering Center.* Albany: State University of New York Press.

7

RETHINKING PAST, PRESENT, PRESENCE
On the Process of Mobilizing Other People's Lives

Jody Shipka

*Mobility involves a fragile entanglement of physical movement, repre-
sentations, and practices. . . . Constellations from the past can break
through into the present in surprising ways.*

—Tim Cresswell (2010)

On April 2, 2011 I attended a yard sale where I purchased six boxes of
materials once belonging to a couple named Dorothy and Fred. The
boxes contained, among other things, photo albums, trip diaries, and
fifteen scrapbooks, the latter covering a span of thirty-one years—from
1950, two years after the couple married, to 1981, the year that Dorothy
died. Questions about the various ways in which, times at which, and
spaces through which the collection moved during Dorothy and Fred's
lifetime and in the years since their deaths leave much room for specu-
lation. Yet this does not mean that the items in the collection prove
entirely indecipherable. Many items contain traces, or "footprints"
(Adey 2010, 43), of the couple's movement and clues about how these
items might have moved, the routes they might have taken, and the purposes they may have served. The travel diaries and scrapbooks in particular provide details about where and how the couple moved, as well as the
kinds of things they were *moved by.* For instance, Dorothy's travel diaries
and scrapbooks often reference and/or visually depict people, locations,
landscapes, events, and even meals that the couple found particularly
interesting, enjoyable, or, conversely, troubling.

The items in the collection bear still other evidence of movement
and transformation—postmarks on envelopes, images of Fred working
in the garden, last rides in cars, handwritten sketches for designing
flower beds, medical reports, death certificates, insurance claims for

---

DOI: 10.7330/9781646420209.c007

stolen property, and even a diagram for booby-trapping the garage. Another aspect of the collection's mobility has to do with its materiality, specifically, its age, increasing fragility and ongoing decay. With time, glue loses its hold, photos fade, and the pages of the scrapbooks and items contained within become increasingly brittle, some tearing or crumbling at the touch, others falling entirely out of order. Put simply, while physically engaging with these materials it becomes difficult to ignore how this collection of seemingly still/stilled images and artifacts continues, in fact, to move, (d)evolve, and transform.

While the contents of the collection itself coupled with their increasingly fragile condition hold much potential for thinking about varieties of movement and transformation, I'd underscore here a point made by many mobility scholars, namely, that it is not, nor can it be, all about movement (see especially Bissell 2007; Bissell and Fuller 2011; Urry 2007). Put otherwise, "'moorings' are often as important as 'mobilities'" (Cresswell 2010, 18). As Hahn and Weiss have argued, the movement of things may "well include extended periods of inertness and stasis in the sense of *not being used* or *being buried*—things may appear on the horizon of perception, and they may recede" (2013, 9, emphasis in original).

Some of the earliest scrapbooks and photo albums document the time Dorothy and Fred spent living in Germany, where Fred was stationed with the army. While the bulk of the collection focuses on their life in Baltimore, I mention these representations of their time abroad because of the emphasis Dorothy appears to have placed on stabilizing—likely in order to help others see, and vicariously experience, the day-to-dayness of their lives there—what they did, what they saw, and how they used and even moved through these spaces. The way these still photos, these thin slices of life, have been annotated (e.g., "My favorite corner," "Our favorite spot. Couch is dark blue," "The last laundry in Europe"), suggest that they functioned, not only as a way for the couple to better remember places where they lived, but as a way of helping others orient themselves to, and share in, the couple's lives and travels in Europe. One photo album opens with handwritten notes from Dorothy and another from Fred, the content of which suggests the album was, in fact, created in order to be sent to family or friends back home. The note begins in Dorothy's hand and is juxtaposed with an image of Dorothy sitting in a chair next to a bookcase: "Hello Everybody! I certainly wish I could talk to each of you as you look through this." The message continues in Fred's hand and is juxtaposed with an image of Fred, dressed in his uniform, writing at a desk: "Since you have not visited us thus far,

114   SHIPKA

[Dorothy] prepared this booklet of snapshots to show you our home, our Heidelberg, and some scenes from our travels in Europe."

COLLABORATING WITH THE DEAD

In her study of scrapbooks, Jessica Helfand has noted that "to spend any time at all with scrapbooks is to fall a little bit in love with the people who created them," adding that the "more you familiarize yourself with the stories, the more you want to know—sometimes forging a path that takes you beyond the scrapbook itself" (2008, 176). While working with these strangers' artifacts, I, like Helfand, have been struck and at times overwhelmed by the texture, complexity, and mystery of the traces left by these "bodies long gone" (Lutz 2015, xxi). As often as I have had occasion to move these artifacts themselves (i.e., from one residence to another, from one scholarly project to another), I have also found myself "*moved by*" (Adey 2010, 162) them—intellectually, imaginatively, emotionally, and physically.

Dorothy's travel diaries in particular have afforded me opportunities to forge a path beyond the paper, ink, and glue-based nature of the collection and to use space and location as a way of collaborating with the dead—a collaboration motivated by my desire to try to understand something of these strangers' lives, relationship, and experiences while adding to and reflecting on my own. In the video project "49 Years/849 Miles," I share with viewers my attempts (along with my partner) to retrace a trip Dorothy and Fred made from Baltimore to St. Louis in the summer of 1963. While my partner and I based our movements on those of strangers, we inevitably transformed that trip, making it our own—populating it with our own rhythms, histories, and intentions. In this way, their experiences, practices, and memories became folded into, and thus transformed, our own. Curiously enough, at some point while videotaping the trip we began directing our comments to strangers—not just Dorothy and Fred but an audience also comprised of the unborn, the not-yet-born. A discernable shift occurred as our conversations and the choices I made while taping were geared to the potential of future collaborators, those who might someday acquire the details of this particular journey—our attempt to collaborate with the dead—and make it their own, resulting in something of a double, or even triple, collaboration with the dead.

Having spent a good amount of time over the past few years working with the materials in the collection (see for instance, Shipka 2011a, 2012a, 2012b, 2016), I have grown increasingly eager to learn how others might engage with them. Part of this, I suspect, has to do with how the movement and potential of these items—and my understanding of them—has slowed, thickened, hardened, and therefore stabilized over time. Put otherwise, having forged certain connections, however speculative, between these items, I began wondering, following Hahn and Weiss, about the potentials for difference, movement, meaning, and transformation that I had overlooked, buried, or rendered unnecessarily still as a result of my increasing familiarity with them.

The "Inhabiting Dorothy" project was inspired in part by this desire to remobilize the potentials of this collection—to understand Dorothy and her world in ways other than what had become my habit. And it was inspired, in part, by projects where people restage or reenact their own family photos. Unlike those projects, however, this one asks people to recreate, respond to, or otherwise attempt to inhabit (to mobilize and, as a result, transform) materials belonging to people they have never met.

Much as I imagine Dorothy did when assembling the scrapbook containing select images of their time abroad to share with others, I selected and digitized 63 images from the collection. After uploading them to Flickr, I began soliciting participants for the project. With a mind toward the distinction Tim Ingold makes between *objects* (solid, intact, finished, stable) and *materials* (fluid, porous, active, emergent, transformable) (2013, 19), I encouraged participants to treat the images as materials, to make them their own, to "join forces" with them, "bringing them together or splitting them apart, synthesizing and distilling, in anticipation of what might emerge" (Ingold 2013, 21). Just as my partner and I made Dorothy and Fred's 1963 journey to St. Louis our own, I wanted participants to explore what Jason Stanyek and Benjamin Piekut refer to as the "sedimented pasts *and possible futures*" (2010, 19, my emphasis) of these materials.

Put simply, the project invites participants to engage in *intermundane collaborations*—arrangements of "interpenetration between the worlds of the living and dead" (Stanyek and Piekut 2010, 14). Following Stanyek and Piekut, it invites an arrangement or juxtaposition of technologies, bodies, and spaces that is "less about preservation than it is about complex forms of rearticulation" (16). Like Erin Anderson's work in particular, the project explores possibilities of enlisting and mobilizing the dead—these traces of lives lived, "as active participants in the composition of the new" (2012 n.p.). In short, I was curious to learn how the past might "break through into the present in surprising ways" (Cresswell 2010, 19) and vice versa.

To date, approximately forty people have participated in the project. In "The Things They Left Behind: The Estate Sale as Archive," I find myself again attempting to still or stabilize the meaning potentials of these materials by grouping the final products shared with me into seven categories: (1) the creation of a new photographic image that replicates or updates an image in the collection; (2) the creation of a hybrid image that merges the old and new—often created with Photoshop, PowerPoint, or another photo-based application; (3) the creation of an original piece of artwork inspired by an image in the collection; (4) choosing from one's old family photos that resembled or resonated with the images in the collection; (5) the creation of text-based/alphabetic inhabitations (a poem, a meditation, definitional "musings" on the couple's names); (6) the creation of video inhabitations; and (7) the creation of audio-only inhabitations.

In his critique of photographic theory, Jonas Larsen argues that the complex and highly distributed networks of humans and nonhumans associated with the practice of photographing itself are absent from most scholarship, as the tendency has been to jump straight from a consideration of photography to photographs themselves. When, Larsen contends, scholars "go directly to the representational worlds of photographs and skip over their production, movement and circulation . . . the diverse hybrid practices and flows of photography are rendered invisible" (2008, 143). In a similar vein, Tim Ingold expresses concern with how, in the fields of material and visual culture, the focus has also been on finished objects and how these seemingly stable objects become caught up in life histories and social interactions. "What is lost," Ingold argues, "is the creativity of the productive processes that bring the artefacts themselves into being: on the one hand in the generative currents of the materials of which they are made; on the other in the sensory awareness of practitioners" (2013, 7). Thus, for both Larsen and Ingold, the concern is that the variously embodied and highly distributed processes of making—and to this, we might add, processes of distribution, circulation, reception, and valuation—are rendered invisible, "swallowed up in objects made; processes of seeing in images seen" (Ingold 2013, 7).

Beyond being interested in the final products resulting from participants' attempts to inhabit Dorothy's materials, I was eager to learn more about how people felt, and what they did, why, and how as they engaged these materials. As Cresswell reminds, "understanding physical movement is one aspect of mobility. But this says nothing about what these mobilities are made to mean or how they are practiced" (2010, 19). In an attempt to better understand participants' embodied experiences,

I asked them to provide me with a brief process narrative. Here, I was primarily interested in why people chose the image(s) they did, why they inhabited the materials as they did, and how it felt to inhabit these materials. With an interest in mobilizing conceptions of agency that may well include, but are not strictly bound to or limited by a consideration of the human, I sought to learn about the role(s) nonhumans played in their overall process and how they helped shape the overall process and realization of the final product. Finally, I was interested in the potential "stickiness" of the experience itself—a kind of movement I take to be located between the here and now and the not-quite-here-and-now. Put otherwise, I wanted to understand if participants experienced connections to other times, places, people, and activities throughout the real-time process of mobilizing these materials, and if so, how.

* * *

When asked about how and why they chose the images they did, many participants reported choosing images that "moved" them—whether emotionally, intellectually, creatively, or imaginatively. Many underscored wanting or needing to work with something they could identify with—something often described in terms of specific images that "spoke to" or "jumped out" at them, resonating with their own memories and lived experience. As one participant explained, "I searched until I found something relatable, something in which I could already see myself. A concept, a place, an image, an activity maybe—wherein I already was present."

For others, choosing images had more to do with those they found intriguing, curious, or perplexing. As one participant explained: "It intrigued me that Dorothy included a TV with a blank screen in among all the other artifacts of her life. There is an encapsulated duality in that image, for me, of extreme randomness (the blank screen, the corner of the room . . . the electrical cord), all rescued from the void of randomness by her label 'Jan16th/Inauguration Day'—so specific." Another participant chose to inhabit a picture Dorothy took of her kitchen by taking a picture of her own kitchen, explaining that she felt it important to do so because domestic spaces such as "kitchens and living rooms are often overlooked, not remembered." Explaining the inspiration behind his poem titled "We Look Like This" (a line Dorothy used as one of her image captions), Christopher Allen Varlack said the images in the collection made him wonder about the kinds of things Dorothy did and did not document. As he explained, "The starting place [for the poem] was with her captions—more vivid in the early years. Because these captions reveal less of her voice and her character as time progressed, that seemed significant—a transformation or descent into silence, a voice in need of recovery."

In his discussion of tourist activity, Adey maintains that "it's the whole of the body and not just the eyes that see, experience and compose tourist activity . . . one could imagine a host of embodiments associated with the tourist experience from smells and touches to excitations, thrills and fears" (2010, 154). Some participants reported engaging with, and being moved by, the images in the collection in a more fully embodied or visceral way. One participant talked about how her process involved waiting for her "gut brain to establish a connection" to the materials—a connection that, in turn, provided her with inspiration and, so, a place to start. Describing her process for working with both digital and nondigital forms of composition, Lauren Goldstein wrote: "Much of what I do . . . is intuitive—I trust the inclinations that rise up when something 'feels' complete or feels like it would work well together . . . [I've learned] to just 'go with it' when I recognize those feelings and emotions." And as Jen Michaels recalled: "I'd actually looked at the [Flickr album] several times, rarely getting more than a few photos in before clicking out. I loved the project concept, but didn't feel 'pulled' toward any of the photos." It wasn't until later that she thought to browse the album again and came across the image of the cake decorated to read, "Happy Birthday Dear! 1957." "I immediately sat up and leaned closer to my iPhone," Michaels recalled. "My mind started calculating—that was it. My gears were turning."

I will have more to say about Michaels's process shortly, but I wanted to touch briefly on some of the humans and nonhumans identified in the process narratives. Beyond Dorothy herself, the items in the collection, and various humans and nonhumans pictured there, people identified a diverse range of human and nonhuman supports. In addition to various programs and apps—Photoshop, PowerPoint, iMovie, Pic Stitch, and Camera360—people mentioned various kinds of cameras, acrylic and watercolor paint, music, advertisements, smart phones, glue, collaging materials, books, pets, spouses and partners, automobiles, music, postings on Facebook, memories, personal photos, and other kinds of ephemera and memorabilia. Some of these participants became part of, and so are evidenced in, the inhabitations themselves (acrylic paint, smart phones, pets, and memorabilia), while others remained to varying degrees invisible—behind-the-scenes, absent-present participants in action.

Many participants reported that once they found something they wanted or were able to do, they "stuck" with that idea, thereby working to stabilize or solidify their approaches to the project, and in so doing, necessarily closing down or rendering still other potentials for

Rethinking Past, Present, Presence   119

transforming the materials in the collection. Jackie Bach's process, by contrast, was striking for the way it kept moving, transforming and evolving over time—how one way of attempting to engage the materials invariably (and often after some sort of perceived failure) led to other ideas. Bach's "original concept" was to create a modernized version of the images in the collection. "I took one photo, [but the concept] quickly fell apart as most of the photos needed people, and I just didn't have the people readily available, nor did I want to be in them myself. I wanted to be the photographer." As she began to think about other ways to inhabit the photos, she was struck by how Dorothy often provided color references to things depicted in the black and white photos ("couch is dark blue," or "chair is dark blue"). "How neat would it be," Bach wondered, "to colorize these photos?!" She then began the time-intensive, tedious process of digitally colorizing images from the collection. Although she would only colorize a handful of the images before changing directions once more, Bach's comments about the colorization process suggest something of the imaginative travel and affective engagement afforded by the images and her process of engaging with them: "You really learn to live in the photos when you are thinking about what colors things may have been."

Bach goes on to state how seeing the "Dorothy selfie" (a black and white self-portrait Dorothy made while standing in front of a mirror) "made way for a new idea—Instagram. I mean what is Instagram after all?" Bach writes, "It's a program that takes current photos and adds filters to make them look old! And a place [for people] to post a massive amount of filtered selfies." She then set about creating an Instagram account for Dorothy, filtering, cropping, and altering select images in the collection in order to make them appear more contemporary. She explained that she "did the last half [of the photos] via phone, which [she thought] really modernizes the whole process. Who would have thought," Bach continued, "when she took these black and white photos that someday a little hand-held device would so easily be able to manipulate the photos and post them for everyone to see. Crazy!"

In attempting to better understand participants' processes, I've relied on brief, text-based, retrospectively authored accounts. Like Alan Latham (2003), Nigel Thrift (2008), Peter Adey (2010), and others, I am concerned about what might be left out, un- or under-represented when asking people to reflect verbally or in writing about their experiences with mobility, or in this case, about their processes of inhabiting Dorothy's materials. Indeed, if we accept that dimensions of these experiences and processes are noncognitive/nonverbal, the problem remains of how to attend to these dimensions in our research. How, in other words, might "we get beyond the matter of *talk*?" (Adey 2010, 156, emphasis in original), thereby mobilizing a richer understanding of the role that other senses and communicative modes play in knowing, communicating, and being.

In documenting her process, Jen Michaels provided me a way of moving beyond retrospective, text/talk-based accounts of process by submitting a written process narrative and links to a wide assortment of still and moving images and a half dozen additional audio files that captured some of the sounds associated with her process.

In so doing, Michaels provided me with ways of reading about as well as seeing and hearing dimensions of the processes she employed while recreating the black and white image of a cake decorated to read "Happy Birthday Dear! 1957." (Note: For her inhabitation, Michaels recreated both the cake itself as well as the image.) Some of the humans and non-humans Michaels represented as playing a role in her process included her iPhone 6, an assortment of apps, her mother's 1996 Honda Accord EX with Sirius XM Radio (tuned to the station "50s on 5"), a KitchenAid Pro 600 mixer and wall oven, and a LeapPad Word Whammer toy used to distract her infant son while she worked.

Michaels' account was particularly striking for the ways it highlighted the "stickiness" associated with this experience, revealing connections to other times, places, people, and activities she experienced while recreating the "Dorothy cake." As she reflects in her process narrative:

> It's only much later, standing in the grocery store aisle in front of a sea of cake mixes, that I'll realize what attracted me to the [1957 cake]. I had just stepped back from the shelves, and whipped my iPhone 6 out of a jacket pocket. I felt compelled to Google 'cake mix popularity 1950s' to see which cake mix brand, if any, would most closely approximate the original cake. At that moment, I thought, "This is what it's about for me, not just today but most days. It's about trying to replicate some food photo that I saw online. Trying to use what I know, and learn new things, to bring into existence a physical, 3D, edible thing that looked delicious in the pictures."

Michaels goes on to describe some of her own embodied practices as a baker and the role that baking has played and continues to play in her life. For Michaels, self-taught baker and cook, baking is an act of "love and caring," a practice that makes her feel "in control and confident," one that yields "legible results" that are appreciated by family members—one that allows her, within an hour or two, to determine whether she's been successful.

MAKING WAVES: DISRUPTION, VISIBILITY, AND INTENTIONAL DISPARITY

To illustrate how "our mobilities make waves," Peter Adey offers readers a simple thought experiment (2010, 19). One is asked to imagine oneself sitting beside a perfectly still pond on a hot day. Motivated by the desire of cooling off, one places one's feet in the water, thereby initiating a series of changes in the pond itself and, with this, for the experiences, actions, and interactions it affords. "For the water beetle," Adey notes, "crossing the pond is now a rather different proposition. For someone passing by, observing their reflections in the glassy surface of the pond, we have disrupted their stare" (2010, 20). Insofar as these examples suggest movement-as-disruption/distortion (in both instances, it seems, having the surface of the water remain still would be preferable given the goals of the humans and nonhumans mentioned here), they bring to mind portions of Jen Michaels' process narrative where she reflects upon her attempts to forge connections with Dorothy in hopes of better understanding something of the textures of her world:

> It seems silly now, in retrospect, that I went into this thinking that I'd be inhabiting *Dorothy*. Instead, every attempt I made to get closer to the original cake reinforced the distance between us. I soon realized that even calling it "the Dorothy cake" was silly because I didn't know for sure whether Dorothy made the cake, nor for whom the cake was intended (other than someone called "Dear," which is written on the cake).

Michaels continues:

> In some ways, I felt close to Dorothy. I brought my groceries home to a 1959 split-level home that I have purposely *not* renovated to have an open floor plan. In that sense, too, Dorothy and I probably had similar cooking experiences. But other than that, I could constantly feel Dorothy slipping beyond my reach.

To be fair, the point of the "Inhabiting Dorothy" project was never about asking people to connect with, or to provide me with a way of connecting with Dorothy and the "truth" of her world, though some seemed eerily able to conjure her in ways I'd not anticipated—whether by replicating her handwriting or colorizing her world. What I did hope to learn was how these traces of strangers' lives and my increasingly static understandings of their potentials might be remobilized, reanimated, and reimagined with and by other bodies, spaces, intentions, and potentials. With a mind toward Adey's example of those hoping to see their reflections in the glassy surface of the pond, the project was designed to occasion disruption, distortion, and with this, transformation. Put otherwise, it was not about seeing clearly the past in ways approximating how Dorothy might have lived, perceived, or understood it, *but of engaging with the past as it moves through the present always already on its way to becoming something, sometime, and somewhere else.* So while the project has certainly rendered Dorothy and her world a little more distant, absent, unknowable—reminding me again of its irretrievability, underscoring the fact of her death and all that has been left unknown and unknowable, this deadness, this absence, need not be something to mourn, but rather something to celebrate as we engage with it and attempt to enliven it differently. Put still otherwise, the deadness, the absence, is something with which, around which, and through which we might move and be moved on our way to becoming something, somewhere, or someplace else.

In his discussion of representations of mobility—and by "representations" he refers to how mobilities assume meanings in particular socio-historical contexts—Cresswell gives the example of walking, suggesting that it has been associated with narratives of "worthiness, morality, and aesthetics that constantly contrast it with more mechanized forms of movement which are presented as less authentic, less worthy, less ethical" (2010, 20). In inviting participants to inhabit Dorothy's materials, I attempted to underscore the emergent, transformative, and celebratory spirit in which the project was initially conceived and always intended. Following arguments made by some Rhetoric and Composition scholars (see Glenn and Enoch 2010; Sharer 1999; and Johnson 2010), the project represents a way of "letting go of the disciplinary ideal of the kinds of materials that constitute primary and archival material" and to explore what other, "lower-case-*a* archives" might hold—archives that don't immediately promise insights into the practices or histories of our field (Glenn and Enoch 2010, 15). Similarly, in keeping with some film and cinema studies scholars, I believe strongly in the value of working with orphaned artifacts that help to foreground the "experiences of everyday people" and that document the "practices and discourses of everyday lived relations" (Zimmerman 2008, 3). Put simply, this project represents a kind of remediation—one that, following Bolter and Grusin's definition, offers participants an opportunity to "honor" these traces of strangers' lives even as they work to "rival and revise" (2000, 15) their "intended" or "original" (read: unknowable, irretrievable, always already transformed) meanings or associations.

While most of those who participated in the project seemed to recognize, if not appreciate, the emergent, transformative, and celebratory nature of the project, I am aware that not everyone shares, or will share, this response. With a mind toward the distinction Cresswell made between representations of walking, some may see the mobilizations associated with this project as somehow unworthy, inauthentic, or even unethical. Some, like those in Adey's pond example, might prefer the kind of reflection afforded by a still pond, and, as a result, find discomforting the various kinds and degrees of distortion or disruption that these mobilizations, these waves of transformation, make possible. Others might be discomforted by issues related to consent or permission, something that is often difficult, if not impossible, to obtain when working with found, abandoned, or orphaned artifacts. Still others might find discomforting what Jaimie Baron has termed the experience of "intentional disparity" (2014, 89). In her work on found footage and appropriation films, Baron distinguishes between the temporal and intentional disparity often experienced by those encountering strangers' home movies, videos, and snapshots. While the experience of temporal disparity can be inviting and pleasing (e.g., while watching other people's home movies, we recognize the texture of daily life, and are able to reflect on its similarities and differences to our own place, position, and time), it is the experience of intentional disparity that can prove unsettling for some. Not only are we not likely a part of the intended audience, but insofar as these materials are appropriated into other texts/contexts and given new life and meaning, this involves a change, not only in the audience but also the function of these materials.

And so, the question becomes one of weighing risks over benefits. In choosing to purchase Dorothy's collection, I felt it important to keep everything, all six boxes, together. While cognizant that in attempting to keep the collection together, I was foreclosing opportunities for it to move and transform in still other ways, my concern was that the collection, this life, would be split apart by collectors or antique dealers, with the more valuable portions sold off separately for a profit. Another consideration: That the whole of the collection, or the parts deemed less valuable and so left behind, would be disposed of at the end of the sale. In the end, choosing to keep the collection together in the hopes of sharing as much of Dorothy's life as I could with others, seemed like it was (not-so-simply) the more appropriate thing to do.

CONCLUSION: ON THE VARIETIES AND TEXTURES OF STILLNESS

While Composition, as both a discipline and course, has a history of attending to and researching composing processes, the focus has primarily been on human agency/intention and the production of print-based, alphabetic (and often times scholarly, academic, or workplace) texts to the exclusion of other kinds of texts, artifacts, and processes of making (for some recent exceptions, see Micciche 2014; Prior and Hengst 2010; Roozen 2010; Shipka 2011b). I have argued here for an increasingly dynamic focus for composition research, theory, and practice, one that conceptualizes research and composing processes as heterogeneous, complexly-layered arrangements of humans and nonhumans, and that treats agency, action, and collaboration not as the special province of the human, the living, but rather, as distributed amongst various kinds of entities—human and nonhuman—all possessing different potentials, intentions, capabilities, lifespans, and potentials for movement. I have underscored as well the importance of attending to the way written texts as well as those comprised of a mix of modes represent mobility, are variously mobilized (i.e., produced, circulated, consumed, and valued) while simultaneously providing opportunities for movement (physical, intellectual, imaginative) and affective engagement.

Importantly, as I've also attempted to demonstrate here, matters of movement and stillness (or action and inaction, moorings and mobilities) are relative, relational, and differentially accessed. As Cresswell notes: "One person's speed is another person's slowness. Some move in such a way that others get fixed in place" (2010, 21). Prior to coming into my possession, Dorothy's collection had been stored (and, so, as I understand, unused, buried, or stilled) in the house of Fred's brother until the time of his (the brother's) death. Further, it is the collection's relative stability/durability or stillness (it is, after all, comprised of still photographs, handwritten text, and other print-based artifacts affixed to the pages of the scrapbook—contents that I purchased after having made the conscious choice of trying to keep these various pieces of Dorothy's life together, stabilized, held in one place) that has allowed me to handle, sort, analyze, and digitize it, placing select components into new networks of circulation so they might in turn be distributed, reinhabited, mobilized, reanimated, and transformed.

Given the marked difference between the kind of waiting or stillness experienced by the participant who reported having to wait for her "gut brain" to establish a connection to the materials, and the "dissonance between representation and practice" (Cresswell 2010, 20) reported by Michaels (who admitted turning away from the project when she didn't feel "pulled toward" any of the photos), our scholarship needs to begin attending to instances when people, ideas, and things, appear not to move; when they wait, resist, hesitate, stabilize, or harden. Put otherwise, we need to begin tracing various kinds and degrees of movement *as well as* forms and degrees of stillness, hesitancy, inaction, stuckness, and waiting. We need to consider how "stillness is thoroughly incorporated into the practices of movement" (Cresswell 2012, 648), how it also allows us to "create spaces and stories" (Cresswell and Merriman 2011, 5). How it too is everywhere.

REFERENCES

Adey, Peter. 2010. *Mobility*. New York: Routledge.

Anderson, Erin. 2012. "An Unlikely Conversation: Oral History as/and Composition." Presentation at the Conference on College Composition and Communication, St. Louis, Missouri, March 21–24, 2012.

Baron, Jaimie. 2014. *The Archive Effect: Found Footage and the Audiovisual Experience of History*. New York: Routledge.

Bissell, David. 2007. "Animating Suspension: Waiting for Mobilities." *Mobilities* 2 (2): 277–298.

Bissell, David, and Gillian Fuller, eds. 2011. *Stillness in a Mobile World*. New York: Routledge.

Bolter, Jay David, and Richard Grusin. 2000. *Remediation: Understanding New Media*. Cambridge, MA: MIT Press.

Cresswell, Tim. 2010. "Toward a Politics of Mobility." *Environment and Planning D: Society and Space* 28: 17–31.

Cresswell, Tim. 2012. "Mobilities II: Still." *Progress in Human Geography* 36 (5): 645–653.

Cresswell, Tim, and Peter Merriman. 2011. "Introduction: Geographies of Mobilities: Practices, Spaces, Subjects." In *Geographies of Mobilities: Practices, Spaces, Subjects*, edited by Tim Cresswell and Peter Merriman, 1–18. Burlington: Ashgate.

Glenn, Cheryl, and Jessica Enoch. 2010. "Invigorating Historiographic Practices in Rhetoric and Composition Studies." In *Working in the Archives: Practical Research Methods for Rhetoric and Composition*, edited by Alexis B. Ramsey, Wendy B. Sharer, Barbara L'Eplattenier, and Lisa S. Mastrangelo, 11–27. Carbondale: Southern Illinois University Press.

Hahn, Hans Peter, and Hadas Weiss. 2013. "Introduction: Biographies, Travel and Itineraries of Things." In *Mobility, Meaning and Transformations of Things: Shifting Contexts of Material Culture through Time and Space*, edited by Hans Peter Hahn and Hadas Weiss, 1–14. Oxford: Oxbow.

Helfand, Jessica. 2008. *Scrapbooks: An American History*. New Haven: Yale University Press.

Ingold, Tim. 2013. *Making: Anthropology, Archaeology, Art and Architecture*. New York: Routledge.

Johnson, Nan. 2010. "Autobiography of an Archivist." In *Working in the Archives: Practical Research Methods for Rhetoric and Composition*, edited by Alexis B. Ramsey, Wendy B. Sharer, Barbara L'Eplattenier, and Lisa S. Mastrangelo, 290–302. Carbondale: Southern Illinois University Press.

Larsen, Jonas. 2008. "Practices and Flows of Digital Photography: An Ethnographic Framework." *Mobilities* 3 (1): 141–160.

Latham, Alan. 2003. "Research, Performance, and Doing Human Geography: Some Reflections on the Diary-photograph, Diary-interview Method." *Environment and Planning A* 35: 1993–2017.

Lutz, Deborah. 2015. *The Bronte Cabinet: Three Lives in Nine Objects*. New York: Norton.

Micciche, Laura R. 2014. "Writing Material." *College English* 76 (6): 488–505.

Prior, Paul A., and Julie A. Hengst, eds. 2010. *Exploring Semiotic Remediation as Discourse Practice*. New York: Palgrave Macmillan.

Roozen, Kevin. 2010. "Tracing Trajectories of Practice: Repurposing in One Student's Developing Disciplinary Writing Processes." *Written Communication* 27 (3): 318–354.

Sharer, Wendy B. 1999. "Disintegrating Bodies of Knowledge: Historical Material and Revisionary Histories of Rhetoric." In *Rhetorical Bodies*, edited by Jack Selzer and Sharon Crowley, 120–142. Madison: University of Wisconsin Press.

Shipka, Jody. 2011a. "Other People's Lives: A Projection." In "Master Hands, A Video Mashup Round Table," edited by James J. Brown Jr. and Richard Marback. *Enculturation* 11. http://enculturation.net/master-hands-video-mashup-round-table.

Shipka, Jody. 2011b. *Toward a Composition Made Whole*. Pittsburgh: University of Pittsburgh Press.

Shipka, Jody. 2012a. "49 Years/849 Miles." Presentation at the Thomas R. Watson Conference, Louisville, Kentucky, October 18–20, 2012.

Shipka, Jody. 2012b. "To Preserve, Digitize and Project: On the Process of Composing Other People's Lives." *Enculturation* 14. http://enculturation.net/preserve-digitize -project.

Shipka, Jody. 2016. "The Things They Left Behind" and "The Making of the Things They Left Behind." In *Provocations: Reconstructing the Archive*, featuring the work of Erin R. Anderson, Trisha N. Campbell, Alexander Hidalgo, and Jody Shipka, edited by Patrick W. Berry, Gail E. Hawisher, and Cynthia L. Selfe. Logan: Computers and Composition Digital Press and Utah State University Press. http://ccdigitalpress.org /reconstructingthearchive/shipka.html.

Stanyek, Jason, and Benjamin Piekut. 2010. "Deadness: Technologies of the Intermundane." *The Drama Review* 54 (1): 14–38.

Thrift, Nigel. 2008. *Non-Representational Theory: Space, Politics, Affect*. New York: Routledge.

Urry, John. 2007. *Mobilities*. Cambridge: Polity.

Zimmerman, Patricia R. 2008. "The Home Movie Movement: Excavations, Artifacts, Minings." In *Mining the Home Movie: Excavations in Histories and Memories*, edited by Karen L. Ishizuka and Patricia R. Zimmerman, 1–28. Berkeley: University of California Press.

8

IMAGINE A SCHOOLYARD
Mobilizing Urban Literacy Sponsorship Networks

Eli Goldblatt

The term "mobility" can describe a variety of actions shaped or limited by literacy. Mobility can apply to the movement of documented or undocumented immigrants across national borders; the fluidity of official or rogue information across the Web on multiple platforms; and most certainly the flow of regulated and illicit capital in and out of profit centers, tax shelters, and government-sponsored projects. Schools hold back or promote students by their performance on exams designed, for better or worse, to assess the learners' facility with dominant discourse. Jobs are open to people holding certain degrees and closed to others without them, no matter what the people themselves know or can do. Literacy comprises, enforces, defies, and compromises the laws governing every action and transaction within any transit system. The definition, glory, and violence of literacy emerge from the way symbol systems encourage, enact, and restrict human movement.

In this chapter, I narrow my focus to consider the possibilities, pitfalls, and commitments associated with a single project that invites an analysis of both mobility as well as networks of literacy sponsorship at one moment in a single urban location. The case I present here involves the redevelopment of school grounds in one of the most economically stressed neighborhoods of Philadelphia.[1] This project is neither a model nor a cautionary tale but rather an instance of action that dramatizes mobility within relationships among a variety of literacy actors on an urban stage. Some of the players represent traditionally powerful institutions, while others represent disenfranchised groups and communities. Their shifting roles and relations illustrate to me this collection editors' assertion in the introduction that a "mobility paradigm" more accurately tracks "the unsteady state in which we find ourselves" (see introduction, this volume). I think their observation that mobility and not stability is the constant state becomes particularly telling when we are looking

DOI: 10.7330/9781646420209.c008

128   GOLDBLATT

at the complexities of oppression and neglect in underfunded and undervalued systems that serve primarily black and brown people in American cities.

CECIL B. MOORE SCHOOL

Cecil B. Moore School is located in North Philadelphia, within two blocks of the dormitories on Temple University's northern edge. According to school district figures,[2] Moore enrolls approximately 600 children in grades K–8. In 2012, before three nearby schools were closed by the school district, only about 200 students attended Moore, but now the school is filled beyond capacity. One hundred percent of the students are categorized as economically disadvantaged and eligible for free breakfast and lunch under a federally funded program. The student population is 93 percent African-American and 2.4 percent Latino, with less than 1 percent English language learners, 10.3 percent identified as having some disability, and none categorized as "mentally gifted." Test scores have been extremely low in recent years, with 2014 math scores across the grades below 25 percent for proficient and only slightly higher for reading in some grades.[3] On the other hand, serious incidents in the classroom—such as assault, theft, and drug offenses—have decreased significantly since a new principal and vice principal took over in 2014. Principal Stein, a white man in his late thirties, and Vice Principal Green, an African American man of about the same age, came into the school as a team from a disciplinary school elsewhere in the district that they had turned around in the previous five years. Students at Moore were running the halls wildly the year before they arrived; now the halls are quiet, students in classrooms pay attention and respond to their teachers. Children in all grades work at their desks or move around the room in a cheerful and engaged manner, sing or play in their music classes, participate in gym classes. Many fewer fights take place after school outside the immediate school property as far as administrators and teachers can tell.

No fully functioning parent association has existed at Moore for at least the last five years, but the beginnings of a small group have formed around Denise, a parent who runs an after-school dance/drill team and shows enthusiasm for various other school initiatives. When Mr. Stein first arrived at the school, parent gatherings brought only a handful of adults, but attendance was higher in his second year. Adults face great challenges in the area around the school. According to 2015 data reported by the *Philadelphia Inquirer*, unemployment in the portion of

Imagine a Schoolyard   129

North Central Philadelphia, west of Temple University—home to about 59,000 people—is 20.6 percent, and the poverty rate is 47.9 percent. Of the area's adult population, 25.8 percent have no high school education and fewer than half (46.3 percent) graduated high school. Of the fifty-five neighborhoods in the city, the police district is ranked tenth highest in violent crimes and twelfth in property crimes in June 2016 ("Crime in Philadelphia" 2016).

The budget for the school is extremely minimal, affording the staff a meager supply of paper, pencils, and books. The long-time art teacher hasn't had a budget for many years and regularly buys materials for her class out of her own pocket. Moore School had a science room in the past but lost the teacher to a suburban school. That teacher wasn't replaced, the room became a regular classroom, and all its specialized equipment fell into disuse and disrepair. Moore did recently receive over thirty used computers from Temple; one teacher maintains a computer lab, mostly serving children in grades 5–8. In short, classes continue under difficult circumstances, teachers can teach in a way they could not when the school first became so overcrowded, and there is hope that students will learn more effectively now. However, it's a school where odds are against both students and teachers.

Given the greater need students and parents have for remedial education, learning support, social services, and violence prevention programs, one would think schools like Moore should receive greater state and city funding to address educational needs, but inequities persist. The Philadelphia School District spent $13,549 per student in 2013–14. Nearby suburban school district Lower Merion spent $27,421 that year (ranked third in the state in expenditures), and the relatively more working-class suburban district Ben Salem spent $18,905 per pupil the same year ("School Spending" 2016). The extent of poverty in the city, where 80% of students are eligible for free lunch compared to 43% statewide, results in a much lower contribution from local sources to the public-school budget (Jablow 2015). The city school district ranks in the lower half of all districts, far lower even than Pennsylvania's other large city, Pittsburgh, which spent $21,754 per pupil in 2013–14. Funding thus pools and eddies unequally in the state's educational resource flow. Some will blame a state legislature dominated by white and nonurban career politicians who have been consistently unresponsive to the needs of poor and minority urban populations.[4] For our purposes, we can surely say that financial resources are seldom mobilized for the sake of children in Philadelphia who most need attention.

MOORE SCHOOLYARD REDEVELOPMENT PLAN

In 2014, I began to look around for a way to turn a vacant lot near Moore School into a garden. My focus at that moment was not on Moore but on Tree House Books, a nonprofit after-school and summer literacy center for students ages six to thirteen and their parents in the neighborhood around Moore School (see Luetzow, Macaluso, and Goldblatt 2014). The organization's double storefront home is three blocks from the northern edge of the Temple campus, and as many as twenty-five Temple students have volunteered there each semester over the last ten years. As a founding board member and a consultant to the executive director, I hoped to find a place near Tree House where kids could investigate plants and animals as a way of motivating and grounding them in both academic and imaginative reading and writing. I had my eye on a lot almost a block long that stood empty and littered behind Tree House and across the street from Moore.

One afternoon in February 2014, I ran into a young man I had coached in baseball around my Philadelphia home when he and my son were schoolmates. He was working for the Pennsylvania Horticultural Society, and I realized he might know how I could discover who owned that vacant lot. He told me I should contact the Water Department. "They always know who owns what," he said. As it happened, I had a former student who was then a deputy chief of staff to the Water Department commissioner. I contacted her, and she set up a meeting for me with a group of people interested in storm water recovery, a city-wide project funded largely by the federal government to redevelop urban pavement in order to increase rain absorption and prevent sewers from overflowing and polluting the neighborhoods.

The Water Department group showed real interest in the idea of redeveloping pavement in that neighborhood, but over the course of a few weeks it became clear that they were less excited by a one-block stretch of weeds and trash behind Tree House and more by the relatively vast amount of pavement surrounding nearby Moore School on the other side of 15th Street. Once I discovered that a nonprofit developer called Neighborhood Improvements had bought up the lot and intended to build low-income housing there, I shifted my attention across the street to Moore. With help from the Water Department, the principal and other interested parties were able to apply for and receive a planning grant from the Community Design Collaborative (CDC), a nonprofit that recruits architects to work *pro bono* on first drafts of renovation plans for schools and other civic organizations contemplating construction projects for which they must eventually seek outside funding. This process required public discussions and coordination with the school administration, a job mostly squired through by CDC volunteer architects, Water Department environmental scientist and planner Beth, and Alex, the co-executive director of a small urban farm/community-organizing group called Philadelphia Urban Creators (PUC) and a recent graduate from Temple.[5] Those initial draft plans became available in October 2015 and then began a thorough intensive discussion in local subcommittees connected to the school. The rapidity of movement among the various players in 2014–15 seems to me another illustration that, unless considerable energy holds a system in stasis (especially one under tremendous stress), mobility is the norm. New and serendipitous relationships can form quickly. This is a challenge and a hope for literacy organizers who are looking for ways to spark productive change.

The Water Department group suggested early in this planning process that I contact Lois Brink, a landscape architecture professor from University of Colorado Denver, who had been instrumental in greening schools in her home city. She and her husband Jake Gaffigan had recently moved their environmental design organization, The Big SandBox, to Philadelphia.[6] They had started a partnership with the Water Department and the Philadelphia School District to redevelop yards around selected city schools under an initiative called the Philadelphia Green School Alliance. The idea of using storm water recovery money to improve and green school properties had not been tried at large scale in other cities. I connected Lois with a few small organizations I knew in North Philadelphia as well as interested faculty and staff at Temple. Once we had the CDC draft plans, Lois went about developing subcommittees with a variety of interests in the grounds (see figure 8.1, a "snowflake" chart of participants she developed with her landscape architecture class at CU Denver). In the closing months of 2015, she held meetings at Moore with representatives from neighborhood organizations, sports activists, local churches, civic groups, developers, and democratic ward leaders. With the advice of a range of stakeholders, Lois and her students clumped the participants into these interest groups:

- Higher education
- Temple University—literacy, teacher preparation, and science education
- CU Denver—landscape architecture and city planning
- Community infrastructure and jobs
- Neighborhood improvements—nonprofit builders of neighborhood low-income housing

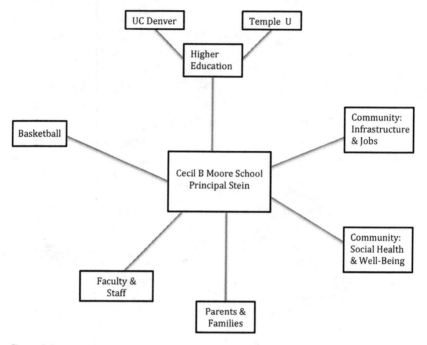

Figure 8.1.

- Water Department
- North Lives and other local economic development agencies
- Community social health and well-being
- Churches
- Tree House Books
- Philadelphia Urban Creators and other civic groups
- 33rd Democratic Ward
- Basketball
- Various groups committed to carrying on a Philadelphia street basketball tradition from the late 1980s until the early 2000s (see Nathaniel 2014)
- Moore School
- Administration
- Staff
- Faculty
- Parents
- Students

Each interest cluster discussed their needs for the space. Holding these meetings within the school building, and frequently in the presence of Principal Stein or Vice Principal Green, emphasized that the plan must serve the students, parents, and faculty of the school above all else.

One other element to add to this picture is that 2015 was an election year in Philadelphia. Jim Kenney, the new mayor, had long been a progressive city councilman, and he came into office with promises both to improve the school system and revitalize neighborhoods. One of his first acts was to appoint a popular and visionary former high school principal named Otis Hackney as his chief education officer (Socolar 2013), a position that is not directly responsible for the school district but does serve to initiate special educational projects favored by the mayor. Dr. Hackney had gained attention for a new model he'd brought to the troubled school he ran in South Philadelphia, a model called "community schools" that has been tried with success in Cincinnati, New York, Chicago, and other places (Coalition for Community Schools 2016). This approach conceives of schools as hubs of social services for students from stressed urban communities. South Philadelphia High hosted regular visits from mental as well as physical health care professionals, social workers who could engage with family problems that might distract or stress students, and others who could bring targeted services to students and their families. In November 2015, a number of us working on the schoolyard project heard the news, confirmed by Principal Stein, that Moore was being considered as a candidate to become a community school. Our hope was that the redevelopment plan would add to the strength of Moore's candidacy, and that increased services, a newly enriched local landscape, and perhaps expanded science instruction based in a rain garden and greenhouse, could make the Moore School far more effective as a formal and informal learning environment.

MOBILITY AND NETWORKS OF LITERACY SPONSORSHIP

I'm acutely aware that local dreams can be dashed in a moment by shifts in government priorities, new fads in foundation giving, or just plain bad timing. As this chapter goes to press, forward motion has stopped and started on the Moore project for a number of exasperating reasons, even though the players I've mentioned are still hopeful that at least some version of the plan can be realized in the near future. The Water Department hasn't given up on recovering rainwater from that expanse of North Philadelphia pavement; however, for nearly a year the Water Department and the school district argued about who would pay the maintenance on any improvements to school facilities. Big Sandbox had trouble keeping its relationship with the Water Department viable; the Water Department itself changed leadership at the top. I had to suspend my involvement for many months when I was called suddenly to step in as interim chair of my troubled department. At the same time, the city didn't choose Moore for the first round of community schools; Moore remains on the short list for the next round. The dreams we had still glimmer ahead, but the struggle to improve any neighborhood depends not only on hard work and good intentions but also on luck and the kindness of strangers like city council people and foundation officers. Particularly in the politically fraught climate following the 2016 presidential election, when funding for the public good is constantly in question, so many projects compete for attention in one of America's poorest cities.

Although I dearly want to see major improvements in the physical, instructional, and support capabilities of Cecil B. Moore School, for the purposes of this chapter I must consider the larger implications of this relatively modest project, whether it's built or not. I regard the Moore Schoolyard Redevelopment as a literacy project, and as such it can teach literacy scholars and activists valuable lessons. The ending may eventually be happy or disconcerting, but the drama around the Moore schoolyard indicates possibilities for mobilizing literacy sponsorship networks in neighborhoods that seem locked in a matrix of violence, unemployment, and social neglect. Just as this collection's editors question the polarity between students who are either "stuck" or "going far" (5), imagining the Moore schoolyard redevelopment gives us a chance to see the potential for change and movement even where others might see stasis.

I have long admired Paulo Freire's challenge to the common picture of the "illiterate as the marginal man" (1985, 47). He rejects the notion that oppressed people stand "outside of" or "marginal to" society because this "necessarily implies a movement of the one said to be marginal from the center, where he was, to the periphery" (47). On the contrary, he asserts, the dispossessed do not choose to move to the margin, nor does the system "expel" them. A person in this condition is "a 'being inside of,' within the social structure, and in a dependent relationship to those whom we call falsely autonomous beings, inauthentic 'beings for themselves'" (48). I want to return to those "falsely autonomous beings" later in this chapter, but for now I focus on the contrast between beings *expelled* by the social structure and those *surrounded and captured* by the structure. If the "illiterates" are not like snow cleared from a city street or trees uprooted and tossed to the side of a plowed field, are they like fossilized insects encased in amber—immobilized and turned to stone—humans made dependent by a social world built on and around them? It is hard to grasp the possibility of agency in either analysis.

The current discussion of "mobility" in the context of Moore School helps me see the concept of "being inside of" in a new light. The children and parents in Moore's neighborhood are not paralyzed or fossilized—these metaphors would not do justice to humans with real hopes and dreams—but they are bound to dysfunctional systems such as underfunded schools, inadequate healthcare, and overcrowded prisons. These systems cost taxpayers considerable money, but they are not designed to move users into higher education, sustained and vibrant health, or higher paying employment; schools, hospitals, and prisons simply serve to maintain the target population at a level of existence that will not threaten the greater freedoms of more privileged citizens. In short, static social structures require considerable resources to maintain. Mobilization among oppressed groups, therefore, requires that seemingly "marginalized" people recognize that taken-for-granted structures such as school, health care, or law enforcement systems masquerade as fixed and altogether natural, when in fact they can be challenged and changed.

When one looks at the graduation rates, the low test scores, the high number of African American and Latinx people incarcerated from neighborhoods with the least effective schools, it's hard not to recognize the situation as a shameful social choice to contain a large population within the bowels of an unresponsive social order. I don't believe this is a consciously calculated plan devised by Machiavellian rulers; most state legislators are neither sharp enough nor energetic enough for that level of manipulation. Those in power channel funds to stabilize institutions they see as bulwarks against chaos and their own loss of control. They cannot or will not picture a truly inclusive world with the well-being of everyone as a priority. The racist and classist effects of this failure of imagination remain devastating: a tacitly accepted arrangement based on the unexamined assumption that certain populations will never be economically productive or politically strong enough to deserve more than minimal social services.

Imagine, for example, that all the comprehensive high schools in Philadelphia truly produced engaged graduates ready and eager to enter college. The competition for places in regional post-secondary schools would increase, and the state higher education system itself would require a great deal more funding. Philadelphians in wealthy sections of the city, not very many blocks from the city's most strained neighborhoods, avail themselves of services black and brown citizens in North Philadelphia can't afford or can't use. Those in the predominantly white suburbs (physically on the margins of the city) command pathways to universities and offices that the poor can live beside but enter only in small numbers. As one friend has remarked, it's a curious and shameful zero-sum economic game whose costs—in lost talent and expensive prisons—even some conservative politicians are recognizing as already unsustainably high.

One example brings this situation into stark focus. When Principal Stein took over Moore School, he noted a stunning indicator of educational mobility. Even though his K–8 school is four blocks from George Washington Carver High School of Engineering and Science, one of the city's special selection high schools, only one student in the previous ten years had graduated from Moore and enrolled at Carver, with its 100 percent college acceptance rate and $12.3 million in scholarships earned by the class of 2015 (Great Philly Schools). The math and science instruction at Moore, producing some of the lowest scores in the district, was not effective enough to prepare students for the rigors of Carver, whose students are 77 percent African American and 67 percent eligible for free or reduced lunches, but who are culled from schools all over the city. Students at Moore simply could not compete for admittance to high achieving schools at the next academic level. Instead they entered schools where dropout levels after ninth grade are high, and disruptive violence frequently prevents learning.

Freire's call for transformational consciousness lays a heavy burden on oppressed people and their educational collaborators to change dehumanizing structures that trap and silence those contained within. Even the best-intentioned educators wonder how to support people engaged with "a difficult apprenticeship in naming the world" (1985, 49). Nonprofits not directly beholden to schools or other mainstream structures can encounter children and adults in more focused and creative ways, placing empowerment above correctness and invention above convention. They are sites of informal sponsorship, spaces where learners grow their own food or make their own video or design their own website without judgment from a state-wide test or certifying body. An art center or urban farm can authorize participants by sponsoring their literacy around projects that grow directly from experience; as authors of their own realities, participants feel neither marginalized nor frozen inside a dominant culture. Freire's profound goal requires commitment and attention within trusted relationships between teachers or caregivers and their learners or clients. Especially today, when public schools and state higher education alike are under fierce fiscal attack and social scorn, such nurturing situations, aimed at self-motivated development rather than grading and ranking applicants, are neither common nor cheap, but they are crucial.

At the same time, we can't expect nonprofits like Tree House Books to save a system in crisis. Nonprofits are nearly always small, with limited funding and restricted reach compared to city school districts or metropolitan healthcare systems. One of the best and largest after-school enrichment programs I know, Philadelphia Futures, served 600 students from the city in 2015, following 9th graders through graduation and on into their college years, sometimes into employment or graduate school (Philadelphia Futures 2014). Yet the difference they make by the numbers seems slight: public, alternative, and charters schools supported by tax dollars enrolled a little more than 190,000 students in 2014 (McCorry 2014). Judging purely by the numbers, Futures barely makes a difference in the collective educational life of the city.

But numbers don't tell the whole story. The urgency to find innovative, effective, and focused responses to systemic educational dysfunction in Philadelphia and other urban areas drives our most successful nonprofits in community arts, restorative justice, immigrant support, or urban farming. Any solution must necessarily start on a small scale, and perhaps well-designed programs must stay at this scale. I have witnessed locally focused organizations acting effectively out of the distinctive character of their constituency. Tree House builds thematic units in their after-school program based on African American entrepreneurs or health care workers or civil rights lawyers. Asian Arts Initiative, based in Philadelphia's Chinatown, mounts powerful arts exhibits and presents lectures, spoken word, music, and dramatic works by artists of Asian ancestry born in America or abroad. Art Sanctuary, originating in a North Philadelphia church two blocks from Moore, sponsors discussion groups and online interviews with black authors, supports North Star arts and performance programming primarily for African American children and youth, and stages the Hip H'Opera every year in collaboration with Philadelphia Opera. Curricula designed for an entire city or state, textbooks written to sell nationwide, must necessarily become more generic and deracinated, less sharply focused on the pressing issues and joyful moments in the lives of particular learners. What nonprofits may lack in numbers they can make up for in specificity, inventiveness, and commitment to a community.

What my experience with Moore taught me is that, given the right circumstances, small agencies such as Big SandBox, Tree House Books,

Philadelphia Urban Creators, and local basketball associations can connect with public schools and even public utilities in a way that opens up possibilities for spirited dialogue and genuine change. A single parent like Denise, fierce in her convictions, can organize a drill team that galvanizes neighbors to fight for better conditions at their own school. Individually, any one nonprofit can make a difference for its constituency, and some who are helped at first transform into leaders who help others later. Collectively, nonprofits with similar or complementary interests can make a great impact on the fate of a neighborhood or the region, especially if they join forces with larger governmental and educational institutions.

My experience with Moore also taught me I need not run away from my association with Temple as long as I'm wary of the institution's unwieldy gravitational force. I was able to contribute to the effort because of my privilege as a professor and a long-time resident of Philadelphia. Unlike colleagues who came to Philadelphia for a faculty appointment and never really connected with the life of the city, my more rooted position allowed me to draw on associations that, in some cases, went back twenty or more years. Being rooted is not the same thing as being static; roots can feed dynamic relationships that can lead to productive new networks. In this instance, I could call on former students, a grown man I coached as a kid, and people I had worked with on other projects. My contributions were modest compared to Lois's energy for organizing neighborhood groups, Principal Stein's leadership in the school, or the Water Department's access to federal storm water management funds. Still, Temple did enable me to meet many people over the years; these connections sparked cooperative efforts that grew in response to the needs of Moore School.

Two underlying questions about literacy sponsorship persist for me in the face of the massive challenges in a city like Philadelphia:

1. How do people of good will and greatest need come together to create and sustain institutions that sponsor an empowering literacy, fulfilling Freire's vision of beings "naming the world"?

2. How do programs and agencies convert "education" into an avenue of mobility rather than bondage "inside" dysfunctional social structures?

Perhaps these two simply rearticulate the same question from different perspectives—one aligned with community organizing and the other institution-building—but I fear no one can answer either version adequately. I would like to conclude, however, with some thoughts about the power of networked literacy sponsors to address these questions and the role of higher education in such networks.

HOW LITERACY SPONSORS CAN FUNCTION IN NETWORKS

At one point early in the Moore project, many interested parties met around the table in Principal Stein's conference room. Beth and two other members of the Water Department sat at the table with Tamara, a representative from a local community development organization called North Lives, and two men from Neighborhood Improvements, Inc. Stein and Green from Moore School attended along with Denise, the parent who coaches the school drill team. Others included Alex from Philadelphia Urban Creators, three of us from Temple (a representative of the Vice President for Community Relations, a professor from Science Education, and me), as well as Lois from CU Denver and The Big SandBox. The facilitators for this meeting were three architects representing the Community Design Collaborative team who were drafting a preliminary plan. After initial introductions and an overview of the process, the architects walked us around the grounds and pointed out the possibilities and difficulties for the project.

The principal and vice principal, I think, found the meeting somewhat amusing. They spend so much of their time simply running a school under imminent threat of closure, internal strife, and supply deficit while this gathering of experts and outsiders was envisioning an elaborate facility transformation that might take three or more years to achieve, if anything happens at all. I found the event both wonderful and terrifying. I appreciated the various constituents coming together in one place and enjoyed the talk of playgrounds, environmental laboratories, rain gardens, and basketball courts, but I imagined how many other groups would need to be consulted in how many other meetings even before we could begin to approach any foundation for the money to break ground. I saw Stein and Green's skepticism and wondered if we were wasting their time when what they really needed was more teachers, smaller classes, and an ample budget.

A first-draft plan did in fact emerge from this and at least five other meetings. Some of the meetings were extremely contentious, especially around the plans for basketball courts that might or might not regain the glory days of basketball tournaments from twenty years before, with all the possible vending business, community pride, and gang trouble that might entail. My portion of the vision conjured an enhanced biology and chemistry program based on a living laboratory on the grounds, reinforcing the principal's hope to send Moore graduates to Carver High School of Science and Engineering down the street. I also wished Tree House could hold summer programs in the new schoolyard. Neighborhood Improvements saw the redeveloped yard

140   GOLDBLATT

as a place where elders from their building across the street could sit in the sun or watch their grandchildren play. Lois saw it as a part of The Big SandBox's larger plan to green at least fifteen schools around the district, with this one as a model of design integrated with school function. Urban Creators saw an urban garden to train neighborhood gardeners and introduce new fresh foods. Tamara from North Lives saw the possibility of jobs and organizing. The Water Department saw the Moore School pavement converted into an instrument for absorbing more than six acres of rainwater, federal dollars well spent and sewers relieved of overwhelming and polluted floods. Everyone had a piece of the vision, and not everyone's vision accommodated everyone else's. An idle fantasy and distracting pipedream, a complex social and technical engineering feat, a lawyers' battleground, a challenge to the uneasy harmony of a neglected neighborhood, and a chaotic literacy situation with many rhetors expressing themselves in multiple discourses. Would this go anywhere or lead nowhere?

Although I do not yet know the outcome of the effort, I would not choose to highlight the results here even if I could. This is not an account of a heroic project that succeeded or a community organizing campaign that failed valiantly. For the purposes of this discussion, Moore schoolyard is a node among intersecting networks of literacy sponsorship. I have indicated only six connecting networks in the accompanying diagram, figure 8.2, although I could easily name two or three others. If Moore becomes a community school, that number would immediately double, along the lines of health and social services that come into the building. Clearly no one will be able to reform the school district or other major urban institutions as thoroughly as the city needs right now. Nor will any one nonprofit, even with increased funding and enlightened administration, be adequate to respond to the urgent needs of students encased in dysfunctional systems. And yet, I am guardedly optimistic. I see the outlines of change in the connections small and large organizations, schools, and agencies can make without revolutionary upheaval. Networked sponsors can facilitate mobility through enhanced learning opportunities and an increased flow of resources to otherwise neglected neighborhoods.

THE ROLE OF HIGHER EDUCATION IN
LITERACY SPONSORSHIP NETWORKS

I return to Freire's bitter words about those who feel themselves above the dependencies of "illiterate" people. He calls them "falsely

Imagine a Schoolyard 141

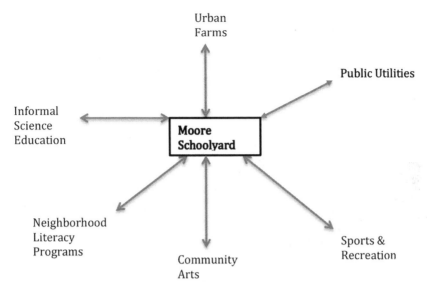

Figure 8.2.

autonomous beings, inauthentic 'beings for themselves'" (1985, 48). I have neither the space nor the inclination to temper his remarks; I often share his frustration when I encounter highly educated people who carry on as though disenfranchised people were not living so near the centers of upper-class power and learning. Suffice it to say that Freire's harsh tone calls academic researchers and privileged readers to account, forcing us to ask ourselves what responsibilities we bear for dysfunctional systems. Are we autonomous agents who can choose to turn away from unpleasant realities? Or are we implicated and complicit players in a game that has definite winners and losers? Can we help to make meaningful changes in dysfunctional systems without coming to terms with our own dependencies? I'm not calling for self-recrimination or group criticism for the sake of political purity, but some clarification on the place of university-based actors seems appropriate as we think about how networks operate, indeed *move and evolve*, across a range of institutional platforms.

Middle-class participants involved in community literacy projects such as the Moore Schoolyard or other promising ventures can fall into a conceptual trap. Our relatively more powerful positions as professors, builders, planners, architects, administrators, and community leaders can easily blind us to the reality that we all depend on sponsors to enable our literacy and earn us a hearing before certain audiences. Even more to the point, our positions as the *ones who know and can act* at a given moment cannot be severed from those who do NOT have access to pertinent information or *cannot control* a given situation. Decisions made by "leaders" must be carried out by and in relationship with others, and changes made without the consent of those who live with the changes often lead to failure or instability. At the level of individual experience, we also know that the *one who knows* may become one who does not know in the blink of an eye. Think of the surgeon struck down one Sunday by a heart attack or suburban parents worrying over an addicted teenaged child. Think of the drone pilot in war who blasts a hospital instead of an enemy.

What we do in redeveloping a playground reflects who we are within a system that produces and then tolerates failing and unsafe city schools. According to the 2014 independent report by Ransom et al., *A Promise Worth Keeping*, recent gains in graduation rates in Philadelphia indicate that greater commitment and attention to such problems can bring significant results, from a low four-year graduation rate of 43 percent for a 9th-grade-entering cohort in 2000–1 to a high mark of 64 percent for the 2008–09 cohort (2014, 9). This progress, facilitated in part by the hard work of Mayor Michael Nutter's administration that ended in 2015, gives educators hope. However, the persistent lack of funding for the district and the worrisome test scores remind us that any progress is slow and precarious. At the end of 2015, Paul Socolar of the independent journal *Public School Notebook* reported that

> school-by-school results show that only 10 public schools in the city, seven of them District schools [i.e., not charter schools], managed to have a majority of their students score proficient on last spring's PSSA [state standardized tests] math test. In six of those 10 schools, economically disadvantaged students are in the minority. . . . District schools had a median proficiency rate of 32 percent in science and 27 percent in English. (2015)

Our efforts at Moore School seem so miniscule and weak in the face of a challenge like this.

Yet paralyzing guilt or cynical despair are luxuries for those of us who can return to offices and homes as though, at the end of the day, the fate of children in the school district is not our problem. To me, those with exceptional mobility provided by literacy—those whose education and social support allow them to travel across continents and address influential audiences and consult with those who control resources—must do what we can to facilitate more flexible, capacious, and inclusive networks of literacy sponsorship. The university can work as a transit depot rather than a knowledge repository/dispensary, ensuring that people, no matter their education level or economic status, can move freely in a country that needs the contributions of all its inhabitants. The function of network building and maintenance may not be the traditional role of institutions of higher learning, but our first step must be to recognize that the static image of the university is a highly resourced but retrograde myth. To imagine both collective and connective functions for "higher education" is the moral imperative of a mobile perspective.

NOTES

1. In order to preserve some anonymity within a public space, I will use pseudonyms for the school, some of the immediate players, and their organizations. However, in the case of two nonprofits I have written about over the years, Temple University and Tree House Books, I see no utility in using false names for them. I also use real names for the governmental, arts, urban farming, and other organizations that represent the overlapping networks touched by this project.
2. Figures and characters for this essay date from final revisions made in 2017 unless otherwise noted.
3. In 2015, statewide testing was revised in response to Pennsylvania's version of the Common Core, which caused a drop in scores throughout the district and indeed the state. I am using 2014 test scores here in order to avoid this artifact. In some grades, 2015 proficient scores in math at Moore did not register above zero percent.
4. Space or focus doesn't permit me to consider how Pennsylvania supports education in rural areas, but I doubt less-affluent counties in traditionally agricultural areas benefit from the flow of state money either.
5. I serve on the board of PUC. Alex has agreed that I may use his first name and the name of the organization for this essay.
6. Brink and Gaffigan have agreed that I can use their real names and the name of their organization.

REFERENCES

Coalition for Community Schools. 2016. "What Is a Community School?" http://www
.communityschools.org/aboutschools/what_is_a_community_school.aspx. Accessed
January 20, 2016.
"Crime in Philadelphia." 2016. *Philadelphia Inquirer.* http://data.inquirer.com/crime
/neighborhood/north-philadelphia_west/. Accessed January 20, 2016.
Freire, Paulo. 1985. "The Adult Literacy Process as Cultural Action for Freedom." *The
Politics of Education: Culture, Power, and Liberation,* 43–66. Westport, CT: Bergin & Garvey.
Great Philly Schools. "George Washington Carver High School of Engineering and Science." http://greatphillyschools.org/schools/george-washington-carver-high-school
-of-engineering-and-science. Accessed January 20, 2016.
Jablow, Paul. 2015. "When it Comes to Education Funding, What's the Deal with Philly
Schools?" *Keystone Crossroads,* June 17, 2015. http://crossroads.newsworks.org/index
.php/local/keystone-crossroads/81319-when-it-comes-to-education-funding-whats-the
-deal-with-philly-schools. Accessed January 20, 2016.
Luetzow, Darcy, Lauren Macaluso, and Eli Goldblatt. 2014. "Garden in a Vacant Lot: Growing Thinkers at Tree House Books." In *Service-Learning in Literacy Education,* edited
by Peter Smagorinsky and Valerie Kinloch, 27–44. Charlotte, NC: Information Age
Publishing.

McCorry, Kevin. 2014. "Analyzing Enrollment Trends in Philly schools." *Public School Notebook*, December 1, 2014. http://www.thenotebook.org/articles/2014/12/01/analyzing-enrollment-trends-in-philly-schools.

Nathaniel, Isaiah. 2014. *16th & Philly*. http://16thandphilly.vhx.tv/.

Philadelphia Futures. 2014. "About Us." http://www.philadelphiafutures.org/about-us-overview. Accessed January 20, 2016.

Ransom, Julia, Heather Griffis, Jennifer Eder, Vaughan Byrnes, Benjamin French, Robert Balfanz, Douglas Mac Iver, and David Rubin. 2014. *A Promise Worth Keeping: Advancing the High School Graduation Rate. Project U-Turn*. William Penn Foundation. http://www.projectuturn.net/docs/PromiseWorthKeeping.pdf. Accessed January 20, 2016.

"School Spending." 2016. http://www.openpagov.org/school-spending/sdefault.asp. Accessed January 20, 2016.

Socolar, Paul. 2013. "South Philadelphia Principal Hackney." *The Notebook*, November 13, 2013. http://thenotebook.org/articles/2015/11/13/south-philadelphia-principal-hackney-to-be-chief-education-officer-kenney-says. Accessed January 20, 2016.

Socolar, Paul. 2015. "PSSA scores for District, charter schools: Philly students struggled in math." *The Notebook*, September 29, 2015. http://www.thenotebook.org/articles/2015/09/29/pssa-scores-for-district-charter-schools-philly-students-struggled-in-math. Accessed January 20, 2016.

PART TWO

Responding and Mobilizing

9

THE WORK OF MOBILITY

Anis Bawarshi

As this volume's introduction describes, a focus on mobility character-izes a range of *trans* approaches that currently occupy our attention in the field (transfer, translingualism, transmodality, transliteracies, trans-culturalism, translation). Naming mobility as a shared concern of these *trans* approaches calls on us to think critically and expansively about what, as the volume editors note, "constitutes mobility as a phenom-enon" so that we do not take mobility for granted, either as a deviation from a stabilized norm or as synonymous with movement and agency. One important characteristic of mobility as a phenomenon—a charac-teristic that appears across the chapters in part one of this volume—is the *work* that mobility involves, not just as a labor over and across and between meanings, genres, literacies, languages, modalities, identities, and differences,[1] but also as a labor that marks and creates artificial boundaries between stability and movement—indeed, a labor that marks different kinds of mobilities. In terms of writing studies, trans-lingualism and transfer research point to how mobility requires the work of cooperation and empathy (both moving and being moved by), a willingness to engage in trans-actions (inter and intra actions) as well as to critically engage the very boundaries implicated in these transac-tions. Rather than treating meanings as *residing in* particular formations (genres, discourse communities, language standardizations, modalities), the mobility phenomenon presented in this volume treats meanings as *negotiated across* boundaries, and these negotiations require work, includ-ing the work that marks the boundaries and terms of these negotiations. In short, a mobility paradigm shifts the emphasis of composition from the inhabiting/performance of a standard to the trans-acting work of communication across difference.

Mobility *work* in composition invites us to pay attention to the work that makes mobility possible, including the affordances, politics, mate-rialities, embodiments, tools, media, technologies, and affective factors

---

DOI: 10.7330/9781646420209.c009

148 BAWARSHI

that authorize, manage, and sponsor mobility. Mobility work is historical and needs to be historicized. At the same time, we cannot take boundaries for granted in mobility work. Mobility involves not only boundary crossing but also boundary-marking and boundary-moving practices, which always include issues of power. As Ann Shivers-McNair argues in her chapter, the marking of mobility (and the boundaries implicated in it) is a rhetorical and ethical concern. Eli Goldblatt's chapter draws our attention to the politics of boundary-marking and boundary-moving practices that are part of mobility work, especially when mobilizing new networks of literacy sponsors. Carmen Kynard's chapter likewise draws our attention to the critical cartographies of struggle as the student, Andrene, engages in respatializing and reterritorializing practices, which are part of mobility work.

What interests me most about mobility work is how it draws our attention to meso-practices of all kinds, the in-betweens, the seams: both what happens in the in-betweens and also how we can study what happens there. This has important implications for research in knowledge transfer, translingualism, and transmodality, all of which are concerned not just with spatial and temporal movements but also with the practices they involve and make possible. In the case of knowledge transfer, for example, Christiane Donahue, in her chapter, reinforces the extent to which transfer involves a lot more than just the carrying over of skills and knowledge across contexts, an instrumentalist view unfortunately implied in the term "transfer." Knowledge transfer, as Donahue explains, also involves mobility work in all the complexity described above, including the meaning-making and boundary-marking practices across which knowledge is presumed to move.

A mobility perspective on knowledge transfer invites us to see boundary-marking practices as both precursors to and consequences of knowledge transfer. In her book *Agents of Integration*, Rebecca Nowacek offers a salient example in the case of a Quaker student at a Catholic university who is assigned to write an argument paper about Thomas Aquinas for her religious studies class (2011). In order to mobilize her knowledge so she can write the paper, the student first has to grapple with a sense of identity threat she experiences in being a Quaker student at a Catholic university, including the sense she reports of feeling like the Aquinas paper is asking her to make an argument in defense of Aquinas and Catholicism. She negotiates this perceived threat to her religious identity by writing a dialogue between Aquinas and a deferential student instead of an argument about Aquinas. In this case, the student is able to mobilize knowledge she has learned in the course (and from a philosophy class she had taken, which introduced her to dialogue as a rhetorical strategy) not only after she has redrawn the boundaries of the assignment but also in ways that are entangled in and made possible by these very boundary-drawing practices. What might seem to an instructor (and researchers) as a student's inability or unwillingness to transfer knowledge becomes more complicated when we understand mobility work as entangled in boundary-marking and boundary-brokering practices. Rebecca Lorimer Leonard's chapter in this volume similarly provides insight into the differentiated movement of literate repertoires and their management in various spatial, material, and temporal contexts, including the impact of genre on literacy movement, as when the research subject, Nimet, reports that she finds letter writing allows her to "prevail with English writing" (Lorimer Leonard, chapter 4). As Lorimer Leonard explains, Nimet "is also talking about the literacy learning affordances of a letter in particular, a genre that, as Nimet says, 'makes a journey' or is made to move" (73).

Because of my intellectual tendency (or curse) to see genre everywhere, I was especially interested in how genres seemed to play an important role in the mobility work described in several of the chapters in part 1 of this volume. One of the ways that genres help us perform social actions is by directing rhetorical energy, moving it in typified directions to secure certain uptakes. But our genre performances can also redirect rhetorical energy in ways that secure alternative uptakes and open up new meanings and relations (as we see in the case of the Quaker student in Nowacek's research). For example, I am struck in reading John Scenters-Zapico's chapter by the role that updating his CV played in his mobility genealogy. After three years of futile attempts to lobby for increased funding for the university writing center, and amid growing resignation at the lack of response from administrators, Scenters-Zapico notes: "While I would continue my request for equity for the UWC . . . , I took on another strategy: one afternoon I updated my résumé" (62). In the "space of flows" of an academic year, faculty typically update their CVs as part of the annual merit review ritual, with the uptake being to secure a merit raise (the fact that at some institutions faculty continue to update their CVs even when there is no money available for merit speaks to how genre performances can become their own uptakes). In this case, Scenters-Zapico used the occasion of updating his CV to create the possibility for a different uptake: not only to document his achievements but also to begin the process of applying for other academic positions. In fact, it is interesting to note that it was after he updated his CV that Scenters-Zapico

150   BAWARSHI

began to consider the possibility of conducting a search. In this way, the genre mobilized a redirection, a swerve or pivot move that opened up new pathways and the possibility for new relations. In her chapter, Christiane Donahue cites Frédéric François's term *reprises-modifications*, which Donahue defines as the "simultaneous retaking-up-modifying" (20). Scenters-Zapico's updating of his CV can be understood as one such reprise-modification that mobilizes a different set of uptakes and relations within the space of flows.

Thinking about mobility in relation to genre work alerts us to the ways that genre uptakes are complex sites of transaction that challenge a view of mobility as synonymous with human agency and movement. For instance, in Anne Freadman's definition of uptake as "the bidirectional relation that *holds* between" genres (2002, 40; emphasis added), the pivotal term *holds* suggests a relational force or interplay that operates between genres. What makes uptakes especially interesting is that they compel us to pay attention to the historical-material conditions and dynamics of agency and power that function between, hold together, and shape genre performances. Such a historical-materialist view of uptake invites us to examine rhetorical movement in more complex ways—including how forms of cognition become "sedimented at a corporeal level where they are repeated as habits . . . lodged in bodily memory" (Coole and Frost 2010, 34)—and to recognize the interlocking systems and forces at play in mobility work.

As "the local event of crossing a boundary" (Freadman 2002, 43), uptake draws our attention not only to the relations between genres but also to how individuals move and translate across genres—to the pathways drawn, managed, and trans-acted across genres that enable and limit rhetorical and social movement. It is especially when they occur across intergeneric boundaries, Freadman notes, that uptake translations are "least automatic and most open to mistake or even to abuse" (44) since they are most subject to relations of power. As a result, we need to pay attention to how uptakes are brokered. Certain routinized uptakes, especially within bounded and regulated institutional contexts, follow well-worn, expected directions and are thus habitually received. But as Nowacek has demonstrated in terms of genre and knowledge transfer, other uptakes need to be explicitly "sold" and validated, and here too power and material conditions come into play in terms of which uptakes are sanctioned; who is granted authority to sell, see, and mobilize uptakes; the institutional affordances that enable or prevent the seeing, selling, and moving; and so on. Yet, as several of the chapters in this volume demonstrate, genres can also redirect rhetorical energy in ways that can secure new uptakes and also change the genres themselves in the process.

Scott Wible's chapter offers an example of how genre work and other mediational tools can be used to mobilize alternative uptakes. As students moved from the field (where they had conducted interviews and observations in order to identify and understand problems) back to the classroom, Wible describes two activities that helped them translate the field data they generated into unique insights and problem-solving practices: user empathy maps and point-of-view statements. Wible describes how students generated the user empathy map, for example, by using Post-it notes to translate key points from interview transcripts into a map that highlights what the interviewee feels, thinks, does, and needs. The Post-it notes allow for what Paul Prior (2009) and Clay Spinuzzi (2008) have described as "annotational genres," which are more idiosyncratic and improvisational and mediate and mobilize the use of other genres. The Post-it notes in this case can be understood as facilitating intra-actions between the transcripts and the user empathy map. As Wible describes, this set of genres allows students to move knowledge from their field data into the classroom and in so doing to mobilize alternative perspectives and uptakes on complex topics/issues in ways less possible through traditional classroom research. At the same time, Wible describes how the use of what he calls "prototyping genres" such as annotated sketches, storyboards, low-fi paper prototyping, and role-playing creates a more mobile relationship to knowledge-making as well as the possibilities for alternative uptakes.

If mobility involves transformation (of individuals, objects, boundaries, language, uptakes, knowledge), then the study of mobility in composition must become more attentive (and as Shivers-McNair argues, *accountable*) to the work involved in these transformations. Research on knowledge transfer has revealed that transformations, adaptations, and mobilizations are quite difficult to study with any direct measure. I would add that they are also quite difficult to study in indirect measures such as via various retrospective (and reflective) methods, which have tended to privilege human agency and metacognition as well as to isolate phenomena. Jody Shipka's chapter in this volume draws our attention to the ways that mobility work involves distributed agency, a complexly layered arrangement of human and nonhuman as well as of production, circulation, consumption, stabilizing, and systems of valuing. As Shipka concludes, "In addition, then, to attending to the ways humans and nonhumans move, and in turn, facilitate movement, our scholarship needs to begin attending to instances when they appear not to, when they wait, hesitate, stabilize, harden" (124). Stasis also involves mobility work.

Mobility and mobility work challenges us to consider methodologies and methods for studying and assessing transactions, meso-practices, transformations as well as stabilizations. In the *Prison Notebooks*, Antonio Gramsci writes, "The starting-point of critical elaboration is the consciousness of what one really is, and is 'knowing thyself' as a product of the historical processes to date, which has deposited in you an infinity of traces, without leaving an inventory" (1971, 323). How to account for these traces when an inventory is not available is a major challenge mobility work poses to composition research. Reflection journals, portfolio cover letters, retrospective interviews, writers' memos, heads-up statements try to inventory these traces, but these tend not to capture the heterogeneous, entangled arrangements and various kinds and degrees of movement and stillness that Shipka describes. Ann Shivers-McNair, in her chapter, offers Karen Barad's notion of diffraction as an alternative to reflective approaches to studying mobility work (2007). While reflective approaches tend to isolate phenomena, including separating the apparatus for reflecting from the phenomenon being reflected on, a diffractive approach explores how mobilities make waves as they move across, are moved and transformed by, and transform objects, boundaries, humans, meaning, and forms of mattering, including the transformations produced by stasis. The process journals Shipka describes can offer a partly diffractive method of studying mobility, as can the use of space-time diaries, video diaries, 3D interviews (which Shivers-McNair uses to document intra-actions between interviewer, interviewee, context, objects, and machines), uptake genres (intra-action genres that can allow students to inventory uptakes in process), and other means by which researchers can document mobility work in composition.

Mobility *work* in composition draws our attention not just to the work of moving between and across contexts, genres, modalities, languages, etc., but also to the work (material, political, racial, gendered, and economic) involved in marking, maintaining, and moving the very boundaries across which humans, objects, and knowledges are perceived to move. What gets made legible, how it is valued, what kinds of access it makes possible and forecloses, the management of direction and redirections—all this is part of mobility *work*. To understand that genres (re)direct rhetorical energy means also simultaneously to understand that genres are boundary-marking practices that frame what comes to matter as these marking-mattering practices (Barad, Shivers-McNair) are experienced by individuals in space, time, and material conditions.

In helping us understand mobility work as more than just negotiation and movement, the chapters in part one of this volume put pressure on us as teachers and researchers to explore the enmeshed, multidimensional work that mobility involves.

NOTE

There is, of course, an important and growing conversation about transgender orientations that I do not have space to address in this brief response.

REFERENCES

Barad, Karen. 2007. *Meeting the Universe Halfway: Quantum Physics and the Entanglement of Matter and Meaning.* Durham: Duke University Press.

Coole, Diana, and Samantha Frost, eds. 2010. *New Materialism: Ontology, Agency, and Politics.* Durham: Duke University Press.

Freadman, Anne. 2002. "Uptake." In *The Rhetoric and Ideology of Genre: Strategies for Stability and Change,* edited by Richard M. Coe, Lorelai Lingard, and Tatiana Teslenko, 39–53. Cresskill, NJ: Hampton University Press.

Gramsci, Antonio. 1971. *Selections from the Prison Notebooks.* Edited and translated by Quintin Hoare and Geoffrey Nowell Smith. London: Lawrence and Wishart.

Nowacek, Rebecca. 2011. *Agents of Integration: Understanding Transfer as a Rhetorical Act.* Carbondale: Southern Illinois University Press.

Prior, Paul A. 2009. "From Speech Genres to Mediate Multimodal Genre Systems: Bakhtin, Voloshinov, and the Question of Writing." In *Genre in a Changing World,* edited by Charles Bazerman, Adair Bonini, and Débora de Carvalho Figueiredo, 17–34. Fort Collins, CO: The WAC Clearinghouse and Parlor Press.

Spinuzzi, Clay. 2008. *Network: Theorizing Knowledge Work in Telecommunications.* Cambridge: Cambridge University Press.

10

MOBILITY AT AND BEYOND THE UTTERANCE

Andrea R. Olinger

"Everything *is* mobile," writes Christiane Donahue, "but at varying speeds" (24, emphasis in original). In "Mobile Knowledge for a Mobile Era: Studying Linguistic and Rhetorical Flexibility in Composition," Donahue assembles an array of scholarship from linguistics, literacy, writing, education, psychology, and translation studies to demonstrate this proposition. Arguing that mobility not only characterizes language use, including translingual practice, but also aligns with work on the transfer and adaptation of writing knowledge, she focuses particularly on language and writing at the utterance level. In "Managing Writing on the Move," however, Rebecca Lorimer Leonard treats language and writing both at and beyond the utterance. While describing how a multilingual writer, Nimet, composes in English, she traces the management of Nimet's literate practices and their social consequences. Through this ethnographic case study, Lorimer Leonard usefully elaborates Donahue's conceptions of *code* and *competence* as windows into the effects of mobility. Reading Lorimer Leonard's work alongside Donahue's theorizations, we may better understand linguistic and literate repertoires as co-constructed by individuals and institutions and, therefore, as inherently mobile. Awareness of these phenomena, I assert, is an important competence for speakers and writers to cultivate as they negotiate norms that are often conflicting and high-stakes. Finally, I argue that combining multiple research methods—such as textual analysis (Donahue's emphasis) with ethnography (Lorimer Leonard's method)—allows us to more fully comprehend the consequences of mobility for writers, texts, and contexts.

THE MOBILITY OF LANGUAGE AND WRITING

For Donahue, all language use is underlain by mobility, evidenced by, for instance, the ongoing evolution of language varieties and the

---

DOI: 10.7330/9781646420209.c010

composition of our own utterances. She draws on Frédéric François's concept of "reprise-modification" to analyze utterances, explaining that "the 'reprise'-simultaneous 'modification' echoes Bakhtin's description of utterances as always simultaneously a reuse of parts from a language system (and thus never 'original') and a transformation (always *new*)" (21, emphasis in original). In addition, the reprise-modification "co-constructs meaning in part by partnering with or resisting the meanings in the language, all it carries with it, its dialogic 'shot through' past" (20). Donahue recommends that researchers identify the work of reprise-modification through two research frames: *code* and *competence* (chapter 1). *Code* is a "way of studying the bits" of dialects, styles, and registers that we mix together and that "construct their meaning partly in use" (27), and *competence* is the flexible use of repertoire when interacting with different audiences and contexts, an "openness to uncertainty" in communication, and an ability to negotiate meaning (29).

The tools of code and competence could be applied in Lorimer Leonard's case study of Nimet's transnational literacy experiences and practices. Lorimer Leonard describes that when Nimet wants to send a laptop from the US to a friend in Azerbaijan, she arranges for a Finnish friend who lives in Turkey to deliver it. Notably, Nimet—whose repertoire includes Russian, Azeri, Turkish, and English—encloses in the laptop a letter that she wrote in English, with both friends as the intended audience. Nimet explains that she could have written the letter in Turkish, but her Finnish friend communicates better in English than in Turkish, and "it is easier for me to write it in English than Turkish" (72). Nimet also feels that the genre of the letter makes her English more fluent: "the informality of friendly correspondence . . . helps her to not 'care about the sentence' while the structure of the genre gives her a way to 'organize your ideas'" (72) and offers her linguistic templates like conventional greetings and closings. Not only does Nimet strategize which language and genre to use—a demonstration of Donahue's concept of "competence"—but readers can also infer that to compose the utterances in her letter, Nimet moves across multiple languages and her knowledge of the friendly letter genre in those languages to convey her meanings in English—an example of Donahue's concept of "code." As Donahue articulates, a mobility perspective can unite research on language and on writing transfer. Transfer researchers, for instance, might be interested in learning more about her reuse and transformation of the letter genre.

The mobility that permeates Nimet's language use and writing strategies, however, is not limited to the composition of her utterances.

156   OLINGER

Indeed, Nimet's experiences remind us to consider how any kind of movement ripples, that is, has an impact that extends beyond the utterance to the writer herself and to other agents, objects, and contexts. In describing her slow writing process for her US nursing courses, Nimet

> reveals that being stuck among languages is not just a matter of staring at a screen, but also a matter of converting one's identity. This takes time. It is no wonder, then, that what looks like stalled writing production on paper is the product of a shifting, often teacher-imposed 'cultural clash' that expects quick, efficient, and error-free writing (74).

Interaction with a new country and its cultures and schooling affects both Nimet's linguistic production and her identity, and she in turn shapes the programs and people she interacts with. For researchers of writing transfer, this experience aligns with King Beach's understanding of transfer as "consequential transition," which involves "changes in identity as well as knowledge and skill" (Tuomi-Gröhn and Engeström 2003, 28). "It is not only knowledge that moves—the entire human being moves," they gloss, "and in doing so reconstructs his or her relation to the context" (28). As Nimet finds herself in nursing school in the US and developing her literate repertoire by writing in new kinds of English for new purposes, we cannot help but expect changes beyond the utterance.

THE CO-CONSTRUCTED NATURE OF REPERTOIRES
AND THE LIMITS ON LINGUISTIC FLEXIBILITY

Although Nimet expands her repertoire over her time in the US, it is important to consider the ways in which she is prevented from freely exercising and developing it. Defining flexibility as the freedom to move, the quality of being able to move, Donahue posits that "linguistic, rhetorical, and discursive flexibility" are "motors of knowledge 'transfer' and translingual 'competence'" (17). Lorimer Leonard shows us, however, that the bits of languages, dialects, registers, genres, and styles that compose our inherently "truncated repertoires" (Blommaert 2010) are not equivalent, neutral, decontextualized tools in a toolkit; the effects of these bits are not solely under the writer's control. We may conclude, then, that the oft-used term *linguistic flexibility* risks erasing the fact that repertoires operate in contexts that are not always friendly.

The divergent responses to Nimet's linguistic repertoire in different contexts exemplify this tension. Although Nimet's multilingualism "is endorsed as both personal and professional asset before migration to the U.S.," it is "condemned as racial or cultural deficit afterward" (78). In Azerbaijan, Lorimer Leonard recounts, Nimet and her colleagues founded a professional organization for English teachers, got funding to create better teaching and learning materials that were independent from the Soviet model, and hosted conferences to train teachers, among other advocacy work. As a nursing student in the US, however, Nimet was compelled under "implied threat of expulsion" (76) to take a separate English class that did not improve her academic English and that stretched her time to degree from two to three years. Still, as "savvy multilingual writers," Nimet and her colleague Paj understand that the obstacles they encounter stem not from their "competence" in English but from the "'environment' of the program—the values and beliefs about 'English problems' held by faculty, staff, and students and fostered in the program itself" (76). The linguistic and cultural discrimination that Nimet, Paj, and their multilingual colleagues experience in nursing school and expect to experience in US workplaces points to the power of language ideologies to shape perceptions of people's literate repertoires and influence institutional procedures. As this case illustrates, the meanings of the linguistic and semiotic bits in our repertoires are constructed by different participants, and even institutions, who may have conflicting values and ideologies.

A COMPETENCE IN IDENTIFYING LANGUAGE IDEOLOGIES

With this in mind, I would argue that Nimet and Paj demonstrate a kind of competence at handling the management of their repertoires that would benefit all writers. Just as researchers have moved away from viewing competence as the "measurable, testable 'ability' of the individual autonomous subject," with ability and knowledge understood as static possessions (28), Nimet and Paj both show an awareness that their English literacy "skills" are not neutral, unchanging entities wholly under their control, but, rather, are read and "regulated" by individuals and institutions they may not be able to direct and whose interpretations may even clash with one another's. This competence aligns with that part of Ryuko Kubota's pedagogies for "border-crossing communication" in which students cultivate a "critical awareness of power and privilege" (2012, 64), of the "politics and ideology" behind diverse perspectives (65).

Wielding this competence, both Paj and Nimet understand that their difficulties stem not from an "English problem" but from "the environment" and from the fact that they must learn a great deal of medical terminology—which, Paj noted, is also a struggle for native speakers (76). Whereas Nimet could have dropped out or internalized

158   OLINGER

the program's implied view of her, she perseveres to graduation. Now, she is wiser to linguistic and cultural discrimination that she may continue to face in the workplace; complementing her own experience, she has learned from friends that when something goes wrong, non-native speakers are often blamed, so she is preparing to be on guard—"just keep an eye, or keep a good ear or listen with them, careful of misunderstanding" (78). By identifying the language ideologies embedded within practices and institutions and held by people, writers and rhetors like Nimet and Paj may be better able to persevere in the face of difficulty while preserving their writerly identities and confidence. Moreover, that entities such as "English" or even "academic writing" shift in meanings and conventions based on the interlocutors and the context is an awareness useful for all writers to gain.

CONCLUSION: METHODS FOR STUDYING THE MOBILITY OF LANGUAGE AND WRITING

Donahue's chapter theorizes the mobility of oral and written utterances, and Lorimer Leonard's case study implies utterance-level mobility while addressing the larger-scale workings of literate practices, such as their processes and perceptions. Both pieces attest to key aspects in the study of language and writing mobility: the natural presence of co-constructed, often conflicting interpretations and, thus, the limits on the free exercise of linguistic flexibility and the importance of writers' ability to identify the ideologies and politics at work in the people and systems with whom they interact.

This synthesis exemplifies, too, the utility of multiple research methods for exploring the mobile nature of language and writing. Donahue recommends textual analysis and, in particular, applying reprise-modification "as a tool for pulling apart the ways utterances are doing what they do" (26). She observes that this level of textual analysis has been overlooked by both translingual and transfer research, "the former having focused primarily to date on ethnographic work and 'key example' illustrations, the latter having shied away from utterance-level analyses, perhaps out of concern for the perceived a-contextuality of textual studies" (26). Indeed, textual analysis would help us trace Nimet's writing development more concretely. Other methods, including videorecording of the composing process and retrospective text-based interviews, would provide ways to connect her self-reported knowledge to her practice and could even disclose information about readers' uptake (cf. Prior 1998 on parallel discourse-based interviews).

As Lorimer Leonard's work demonstrates, however, ethnographic case studies are also essential, informing us about a text's production, circulation, and reception and linking textual details such as word choice to sociopolitical forces. Such combinations of methods allow researchers to more deeply explore the consequences of mobility for writers, texts, and contexts, as well as the histories and identities indexed by particular semiotic forms. For Lorimer Leonard and Donahue, and for future scholars, this approach to the study of language and writing lays rich ground for research on writing and literate activity—from utterances to practices and beyond.

REFERENCES

Blommaert, Jan. 2010. *The Sociolinguistics of Globalization.* Cambridge: Cambridge University Press.

Kubota, Ryuko. 2012. "The Politics of EIL: Toward Border-Crossing Communication in and beyond English." In *Principles and Practices of Teaching English as an International Language,* edited by Aya Matsuda, 55–69. Bristol, UK: Multilingual Matters.

Prior, Paul A. 1998. *Writing/Disciplinarity: A Sociohistoric Account of Literate Activity in the Academy.* Mahwah, NJ: Erlbaum.

Tuomi-Gröhn, Terttu, and Yrjö Engeström. 2003. "Conceptualizing Transfer: From Standard Notions to Developmental Perspectives." In *Between School and Work: New Perspectives on Transfer and Boundary-Crossing,* edited by Terttu Tuomi-Gröhn and Yrjö Engeström, 19–38. Bingley, UK: Emerald.

11

(IM)MOBILITIES AND NETWORKS OF LITERACY SPONSORSHIP

Laura Sceniak Matravers

In her chapter in this collection, Shipka argues that it is "difficult to ignore how . . . seemingly [still] images and artifacts [continue] . . . to move and transform" (113). She thus reminds us of the important role that seemingly static and nonhuman entities play in literacy experiences, urging us to recognize the agency of nonhuman entities. Her argument rests on the agency of *tangible* nonhuman objects (e.g., photo albums, diaries, and scrapbooks) in composing processes such as those of the individuals who participated in her "Inhabiting Dorothy" project—but what of the role of the *intangible?*

This chapter explores how intangible, nonhuman entities—space and context—comprise networks of sponsors (as described by Goldblatt, chapter 8) through which the literacy experiences of two students, Nimet and Andrene (as described by Lorimer Leonard, chapter 4, and Kynard, chapter 5), are both mobilized and immobilized, and the reciprocal relationship (Brandt 1998) these individuals share with the contexts within which they move. Just as the artifacts in Shipka's study are neither static nor passive, I argue, the backdrops of Nimet's and Andrene's literacy learning experiences—and those of other students like them—are similarly dynamic and agentive. Through this examination, I take up Shipka's call "for an increasingly dynamic focus," which "conceptualizes . . . composing processes as . . . complexly-layered arrangements of humans and nonhumans," and so "treats agency, action, and collaboration not as the special province of the human, . . . but rather, as distributed amongst various kinds of entities—human and nonhuman" (124).

NETWORKS OF NONHUMAN LITERACY SPONSORS

Shipka's chapter calls to mind the work of Blommaert (2007) and Canagarajah and De Costa (2016), who, like Shipka, recognize the

DOI: 10.7330/9781646420209.c011

(Im)Mobilities and Networks of Literacy Sponsorship 161

agentive potential of the nonhuman aspects at play within literacy events. Blommaert describes the intangible backdrop of space in sociolinguistic processes as "not a passive background but an *agentive* force" (2007, 2, emphasis in original). Similarly, Canagarajah and De Costa argue that "we have to consider how *context* might be agentive," because—though "context is often treated as a *container* of language interactions . . . , a passive backdrop to meaning negotiation and construction"—"object-oriented ontologies have made linguists sensitive to the fact that the material world is *agentive*" (2016, 4, emphasis added). Canagarajah and De Costa thus conclude that "context cannot be treated as separate from language and passive in its influence" (4). Context, then, is an active agent at play within literacy events.

As such, context—as described by Canagarajah and De Costa—like space (Blommaert), can be considered a literacy sponsor. Brandt defines literacy sponsors, her oft-cited paradigm of literacy learning, as "agents . . . who enable, support, teach, model, as well as recruit, regulate, suppress, or withhold literacy" (1998, 166). "It is useful," continues Brandt, "to think about who or what underwrites occasions of literacy learning and use" when examining the sponsors of a literacy experience (166). In short, literacy sponsors are agents who positively or negatively shape an individual's literacy learning experience by helping that experience come to fruition or by interfering with or hindering it in some way. Though literacy sponsors are most commonly human entities (Brandt 1998, 167), I propose that understanding the context of a literacy learning experience as a *nonhuman* literacy sponsor further illuminates the potential mobility—or immobility—of the student at the heart of that literacy event.

In the twenty years since Brandt's seminal article was published, the concept of literacy sponsors has been widely discussed, adapted, and modified. For example, in his contribution to this collection, Goldblatt extends Brandt's concept to an understanding of literacy sponsors as networked—not as discrete individual agents—and understands literacy experiences to be influenced by these networks of sponsors, ultimately conceiving of literacy sponsors as aggregate. In this chapter, I adopt Goldblatt's idea of networked literacy sponsors in order to consider how the intangible, nonhuman agents at work within literacy learning experiences might themselves comprise networks of literacy sponsors. It is here that the work of Blommaert and of Canagarajah and De Costa comes into play, with their arguments that those nonhuman entities, space and context—though intangible—are influential agents in language experiences, agents that shape literacy events—or, in Brandt's

162   MATRAVERS

terms, underwrite or sponsor them. This layered concept of networked, nonhuman literacy sponsors provides a useful framework for understanding the ways in which students' literacies are sponsored, and consequently mobilized or immobilized.

NIMET AND ANDRENE'S (IM)MOBILITIES

Goldblatt's understanding of literacy sponsors as networked, together with Blommaert's and De Costa and Canagarajah's conception of the spatial and contextual backdrops to literacy experiences as agentive, is useful for understanding the literacy sponsorship that exists in the case studies of Nimet and Andrene, as described by Lorimer Leonard and Kynard. More specifically, these concepts provide a framework by which to understand how those networks affect each woman's literacy learning experiences, and, consequently, their movements within and between different contexts. Lorimer Leonard's and Kynard's chapters detail the experiences of two women who exist, at times, outside of traditional American norms and conceptions of "academic" literacy, and the ways these two women go about demonstrating their literacies. Each chapter exemplifies the complexity of the dynamic relationships between literacy and mobility. These relationships, the networks of literacy sponsorship at play in the examples of Nimet and Andrene, and the different contexts through which these two women move, ultimately provide a fuller understanding of their literacy experiences.

The concept of a network of literacy sponsors and the profound impact of context as an agentive character in that network is seen clearly in Lorimer Leonard's chapter, in which she describes how Nimet's literacies are not always officially recognized as such, noting the "social and institutional agents" that manage Nimet's literate mobility as she moves through different cultural and educational spaces (67). Crucial to this understanding and to Lorimer Leonard's analysis of Nimet, a multilingual nursing student from Azerbaijan who migrated to the United States, is the plurality of institutional literacy sponsorship networks through which Nimet moves. In some contexts, such as in Azerbaijan, where she founded the Azerbaijani English Teachers Association and taught English to high school students and teachers, Nimet is considered an expert—and is arguably a sponsor of literacy herself—whereas in others, such as in her nursing classes in the US, her English literacy is deemed deficient. Indeed, as Lorimer Leonard describes, "while Nimet does wield agency as she manages how her literacies move, this is an agency that runs up against the power of institutions to move her writing around after immigration" (77). Nimet, then, can be counted as one among those whom Blommaert describes as "articulate, multilingual individuals [who become] inarticulate and 'language-less' by moving from a space in which their linguistic resources were valued and recognized into one in which they didn't count as valuable and understandable" (2007, 2).

What Blommaert describes as the "phenomenon" of "gaining or losing 'competence' by moves in space" is an apt description of what happens as Nimet herself moves between different networks of literacy sponsorship (Blommaert 2007, 2). Though these different contexts (the United States and Azerbaijan) have in common similarly rigid regulatory networks of sponsors, Nimet's control and ability to move through those systems is drastically different in each. In one, Azerbaijan, where "pedagogy was managed by the political system that regulated schools," Nimet is able to subvert and work within that system, whereas in nursing school in the US, the imposed bureaucracy of the university hinders Nimet's control over her own literacy practices and, as a result, impedes her timely progression through the nursing program (Lorimer Leonard, chapter 4). In Azerbaijan, the "official" literacy sponsorship network does not impede Nimet; in fact, because of its very rigidity, Nimet is compelled to work as a sponsor of literacy herself. Within the context of her American nursing program, however, the tables are turned, and the network of literacy sponsorship in which Nimet finds herself—a network established by the university—is immobilizing in its rigidity. Depending on the context of the literacy situation in which she finds herself, and the subsequent network of literacy sponsorship within which she is working, Nimet's control over her literacy practices—or the control she is presumably allowed or denied—fluctuates. In this way, these distinct cultural and institutional spaces act upon both Nimet's literacy experiences and her mobility.

Kynard similarly demonstrates the potential agentive force of context in a powerful way, through her description of the overwhelming success of Andrene's website "Pretty for a Black Girl." Kynard explains that on Andrene's website, Andrene

> is not using the polite, demure, subservient-apprentice etiquette that students are always expected to perform—a performance we sometimes mistakenly label "academic discourse." Instead, she mobilizes the discursive styles of African American Language via her strategic use of direct address. This is a conscious departure from the demands of school-based white linguistic etiquette which is especially hurled at students of color who are still often hopelessly rendered as people who have not mastered

the master code yet which can therefore justify all manner of dumbed-down, basic-skills teaching. (86)

Andrene's website, then, has the potential to be deemed unrecognizable as academic "literacy," per se, or even as a "legitimate" exhibition of literate skills that match institutional definitions or understandings of success or proficiency. This departure from "the demands of school-based white linguistic etiquette," as Kynard describes it here, is a conscious one—a decision that, arguably, contributes to Andrene's success, because it sets her ePortfolio apart from those that adhere to academic norms that are considered by other institutional forces to be more appropriate for a class assignment. Furthermore, because of the affordances of the digital context in which she presents her composition—one that reaches audiences beyond the institution of higher education in which she is a student and Kynard, her teacher—Andrene mobilizes her literacy via this website, a space that allows her to flex the full range of her rhetorical savvy. In the end, Andrene's website aids her mobility through at least two networks, as her ideas are spread via her online presence, and as the success of her website feeds her academic success, contributing to her movement through the institutional context of her university. Important to note, too, is that the publication of Andrene's website has had a profound impact on Kynard's classroom, playing an important role in the composing processes of other students as they, too, create their own websites (Kynard, chapter 5).

On the one hand, Nimet—despite her obvious control over a multilingual repertoire and literacy practices that mark her as "expert" in other contexts—is seen by her instructor and nursing program advisors as insufficiently literate in English, given their own singular understanding of American academic literacy as monolith. On the other hand, Andrene successfully subverts the rigidity of American academic norms of literacy and composes an influential web text, one that strikingly departs from those norms. In both cases, the spaces in which Nimet and Andrene are acting out their literacies in turn act upon their ability or inability to move through those very spaces. And, just as Nimet is afforded more control over her own literacy practices in another context, so too is Andrene's web text considered successful in an online context and by audiences that are not the "official" institutional sponsors of this particular literacy network—such as the other students Kynard teaches, who look to Andrene's website as an exemplary model of the kind of work they, too, want to produce, as well as her vast public audience online. Finally, as Nimet and Andrene move through the different contexts of various literacy sponsorship networks, there are seemingly many contradictions: namely, the perhaps paradoxical interplay between mobility and immobility, and the relationship between each woman's (im)mobilities and her (perceived) literacy skills in a given context.

CONCLUDING THOUGHTS

As their cases are described by Lorimer Leonard and Kynard, both Nimet and Andrene move through different situations or networks of literacy sponsorship in which they are considered "literate" to varying degrees, and that conception of literacy is tied to their ability or inability to mobilize. Furthermore, despite the clear differences between these two women (e.g., Nimet as a nursing student who migrated from Azerbaijan, Andrene as a young black woman living in New York City), the complicated relationships between their literacies and their movement through networks of literacy sponsorship are similar. For instance, in the case of Nimet, the context of her American nursing program, wherein she is deemed less-than-literate, immobilizes her and her literacy, stalling her academic progress. In contrast, in Azerbaijan, she mobilizes herself and her literacy practices. Similarly, Andrene and her literacy—via her website, a space that lies outside of the university's institutional structures—are also mobilized: just as Nimet subverts the power dynamics in the literacy sponsorship network in Azerbaijan, so, too, does Andrene in her own institutional context. Furthermore, Nimet and Andrene engage in reciprocal relationships with these literacy sponsors (Brandt 1998, 167), as both of their subversions profoundly impact those contexts, with Nimet's founding of the Azerbaijani English Teachers Association, and Andrene's transformation of Kynard's classroom and the composing processes of her successors therein.

The range of literacies possessed by Nimet and Andrene is ultimately shaped by the spaces and contexts in which they circulate, which they in turn also shape. In the particular networks of literacy sponsorship within their postsecondary institutions, their literacies are not always recognized (Nimet)—or have the potential to not be recognized (Andrene)—as such. Furthermore, the recognition of their literacy practices as legitimate is ultimately crucial to their successful movement through these institutions as they progress through their degree programs. Consequently, Nimet's and Andrene's experiences exemplify agentive contexts, as the contexts of the different networks they move through are active players in their literacy learning experiences. Nimet and Andrene interact with those contexts, their literacies both shaping and being shaped by them and their (im)mobilities, based on how their literacy is understood in and by those contexts. Such a perspective offers further understanding of the variety of forces at play in any sort of literacy learning experience, and the complicated relationships between those forces. Furthermore, such an examination allows us to see the need for change in certain of these institutionalized networks and for interrogating what is accepted as a legitimate "literacy" in the realm of American postsecondary education and the relationship between such legitimizing forces and students' mobility through institutional structures. As Goldblatt reminds us, "those with exceptional mobility provided by literacy—those whose education and social support allow them to travel across continents and address influential audiences and consult with those who control resources—must do what we can to facilitate more flexible, capacious, and inclusive networks of literacy sponsorship" (142).

REFERENCES

Blommaert, Jan. 2007. "Sociolinguistic Scales." *Intercultural Pragmatics* 4 (1): 1–19.

Brandt, Deborah. 1998. "Sponsors of Literacy." *College Composition and Communication* 49 (2): 165–185.

Canagarajah, Suresh, and Peter I. De Costa. 2016. "Introduction: Scales Analysis, and Its Uses and Prospects in Educational Linguistics." *Linguistics and Education* 34: 1–10.

12

RESISTING THE UNIVERSITY AS AN INSTITUTIONAL NON-PLACE

Timothy Johnson

It has been nineteen years since Porter et al. first explored the methodology of "institutional critique" (2000) as a way of understanding the spatial dynamics of work in Rhetoric and Composition. They argued that somewhere between the field's "macro-level national critique and the micro-level practices on individual campuses is space for an action plan informed by critique yet responsive to local conditions"—a space that has been occupied by institutions of varying size and nature (2000, 630). In turn, they argued that enacting "institutional change requires attention to the material and spatial conditions of disciplinary practices inside a particular institution" by making these practices visible. The primary method for generating this intermediary critical space is "storytelling" (631).

Institutional stories, as this collection makes clear, mark off otherwise invisible cartographies of power, personal development, and social movement. They help us to understand what we value, what we are, and—often—what we must work against. John Scenters-Zapico's chapter, for example, elucidates how "some institutions seem to work very hard to keep us in stasis (per what we can accomplish institutionally), and, on the other hand, by keeping us fixed they can also create frictional working conditions" (54). Rebecca Lorimer Leonard's chapter chronicles how "institutions control the pace and direction of Nimet's literate movement" in order to "maintain a literate power structure that grants their authority to keep writers in and out of their classrooms and, sometimes, the country" (76).

The stories and methods these scholars provide revive the spirit of institutional critique while also clarifying and adjusting this work in light of a world gone mobile. They highlight that institutional critique informs any study of mobility because institutions utilize the "world of fluidity"—as the introduction to this collection puts it—to produce and

DOI: 10.7330/9781646420209.c012

168   JOHNSON

maintain imbalances of power and equity. In the service of this claim, this essay works to combine these theoretical frameworks in order to better address a common enemy that speaks to the darker side of the world revealed by the mobility paradigm—"non-place."

Writing in 1995, Marc Augé turned to airports, highways, and waiting rooms as central examples of non-places. Augé explained that, rather than facilitating arrivals, these sites have been rhetorically designed to isolate individuals by trapping them within their flows of transit so that "place and non-place are rather like opposed polarities: the first is never completely erased, the second never totally completed; they are like palimpsests on which the scrambled game of identity and relations is ceaselessly written" (2008, 64).

Non-places function as a strategically-constructed set of institutional arrangements designed to evacuate both a sense of personal positionality (placeness) and any sense of institutions as fixed, reliable sites of communal action. For many institutions, the benefit of producing non-places is that they develop "neither singular identity nor relations; only solitude, and similitude" (103). Separate, but similar, occupants of non-place are more easily managed and more easily interchanged. If left unchecked, Augé argues, the "frequentation of non-places today provide an experience . . . of solitary individuality combined with non-human mediation" that can lead to the erosion of a number of important elements of local institutions (117–118). As a collective set of narratives, these chapters highlight that Augé's work was, in many ways, prophetic. Extending well beyond intentionally transitory sites, a mobility-driven "supermodernity" has come to fruition such that universities and hospitals must also combat the encroaching narratives of non-place lest they too become sites of solitary individuality and nonhuman mediation.

John Scenters-Zapico's work, for example, highlights the ways in which the production of a non-place can do more than produce a set of transitory spaces—non-place can sever existing ties to place by redefining institutional essence. I think we can all recognize the yeoman's work that Scenters-Zapico put into generating placefulness at UTEP—evidenced by a thriving writing center and a successful PhD program. Through his work, writing, rhetoric, and literacy became an occasion for the joining together of people and ideas. His work generated attachments, created inertia both internal (drawing individuals to the program and the center) and external (helping these individuals get jobs and circulate ideas). Yet, when the time for recognition of that place came around, UTEP changed the narrative. As Scenters-Zapico chronicles his own mobility story, it becomes clearer that this lack of

Resisting the University as an Institutional Non-Place   169

reciprocity was caused by changing spatial narratives. Scenters-Zapico's work is remarkable in this regard—the small-m-mobility model engages in the important work of providing tools for articulating micro-level concerns with professional and personal mobility.

Pairing this with institutional critique suggests placing this small m–mobility map in the context of the macro-national trends and that this combination might be key in the process of generating Scenters-Zapico's second construct: the big-M-Mobility model. Following this lead, I read Scenters-Zapico's work in the context of the Texas Congressional Bill HB 51, which sought to shift the way state schools would be funded in the state of Texas and recast them as non-places in the process. The bill created the Texas Research Incentive Program (TRIP) in which the state would match donations made to public universities for raising research profiles (Texas Legislature 2009). The bill first expressed disappointment that "only" three of the state's universities were considered "tier one" institutions and, in response, positioned all state schools as competitors for a set pool of resources allocated to three specific areas: raising research profiles (interestingly, this is articulated primarily as grant-oriented dollar amounts), generating PhDs, and the ability to raise at least $45 million expenditures in restricted research funds each year (Hamilton 2010, n.p.). We have seen, in the last several years, similar scenarios at the University of Wisconsin and the University of Illinois systems where policy statements have pushed to do more than allocate budgets—they have sought to redefine the very places of college campuses (Gardner 2016).

We must understand these moves as spatial arguments—as outside actors working to generate models in which educational outcomes, pedagogy, and/or quality of life for students and teachers—those elements that might count in understanding the nature or purpose of a place—rarely appear. The initiative recasts state schools as quintessential non-places of economic investment wherein taxpayer financing disappears and is expected to reappear with dividends that are measurable in economic registers, and these lead to an external competition over rankings. At a macro-level, these hollow out the places that exist between point A (investment) and point B (dividends). In this way, HB 51 opened up new rhetorical possibilities for the individuals in Scenters-Zapico's immediate institutional context—"I just don't think we have any money" (63) actually encodes a larger point—"thanks, but your work has been mapped outside of our institutional confines." The taxpayers have demanded a balanced budget at all costs; the state's governor and senate interpret this as reshaping the nature of the state's higher-education system along neoliberal lines (a competition for resources whose judgment points rely primarily on economic measures in the first place).

This move only works, however, when accompanied with a considerable degree of institutional solitude. As Scenters-Zapico notes, putting off facing the notion that a valuable member of UTEP as an institution was unhappy took the shape of a series of "delayed avoidance" phrases. Hands tied, the more immediate arms of this institutional circuit—dean and chair—simply sought to delay, and in so doing, keep the system in place without extending any additional resources to do so—"all" that they burned was social and communal capital. No one could really be blamed and, equally important, no one could really be addressed. By paying lip service to the problems of an underfunded writing center and ongoing issues with salary compression, the administrators were enacting precisely the kind of placeless work that Augé suggests institutions encourage. By gesturing always upward or not responding at all, the responsibility for eroding institutional continuity dissolved into the ether of the institution itself. For all of our belief in the power of discourse and persuasion, the only recourse for an individual trapped in the non-places of the neoliberal university was to leave and thus disrupt the system that positioned both him and the writing center as invisible.

How can we make clear that building mobility into the negotiating structures of the academic profession hurts scholars, students, and families by turning universities into non-places? What might we imagine by way of alternatives that take into account the various other capital expenses caused by the systemic use of mobility—both in terms of discourse and in terms of community? One option is to adopt the language of the marketplace. What if Scenters-Zapico had instead phrased his work as "contributing $300,000 of generated wealth to the university system" (using the basic logic that private tutoring in writing would cost the university $25/hour × 12,000 visits)? Might his requests have been heard more clearly? Could writing centers and/or writing programs ask that students record the ways in which their financial successes, or their employability, were dependent on critical thinking, communication skills, and understanding of genre? This seems fraught with problems—not the least of which is accepting the label of economic non-place—but it also creates a moment of fixity for negotiation. Asking these questions renders the work of writing visible on the economic maps drawn by various initiatives that seek to render it invisible. It suggests that if value is going to be mapped so resolutely in dollar amounts, writing can play that game.

The more palatable option is to work toward an administrative structure in which top-down initiatives like HB 51 cast wider nets for understanding institutional imperatives that recognize the "inertia starters," human or otherwise, that don't appear in the advanced metrics that focus on ends rather than means. This would mean consistently and loudly positioning universities as places that require attention and upkeep, not just imperatives and data—in this frame, Scenters-Zapico's ability to generate placeness in the form of a program and writing center would have been valued more clearly in the production of successful research initiatives and educational outcomes.

SIMILITUDE

Language, however, is not only rendered invisible by non-place. Language can also be used to produce non-place. Where Scenters-Zapico captures a state generating new forms of mapping and measurement for higher education institutions that rendered writing invisible, Lorimer Leonard's work accounts for individual decision-making positioning language as foundational to the institutional subjectivity of the nurse, in turn producing the non-place of a bureaucratic healthcare system. An instructor issuing an "ultimatum" to Nimet to improve her English language skills in order to continue on in nursing school highlights the ways in which institutional actors can discursively evacuate their own agency in the name of institutional logics and, in the process, institute those logics (75).

From a communal perspective, it would seem that this instructor disagrees with the institution's acceptance of ESL students and seeks to exclude them from the community of individuals capable of being productive nurses in the American healthcare system. In this frame, the *ad hoc* language requirement they develop seems to come from everywhere all at once and, therefore, nowhere in particular. For the instructor in question, the demand for more polished performances of American-inflected English is simply a part of the program, per the directors' thoughts as expressed in meetings. Though the mention is brief, much can be made of Lorimer Leonard's accounts for these occurrences being pitched in the dual terms of "student success" and "patient safety" (76). For this teacher, it seems, two communities are being imagined: first, a pool of patients, hostile to any sort of diversity while engaging with their medical treatments. In assuming a point like accent or speed would matter more to a community of patients than competence and ability, the instructor is also recasting the nurse as a service position rather than one of expertise and authority (a point highlighted by the claims that doctors are not subjected to the same anxieties over linguistic homogeneity).

Using a particular vision of language, the nursing classroom is recast not as a place filled with individuals working actively toward creating a more successful healthcare system, but a non-place transporting ideally literate cogs into an institutional chain of being in an equally non-placed hospital—the technocratic dream of a system made up of "non-human mediation." Ostensibly, in the non-place of the contemporary hospital, nurses are figures capable of ushering patients more clearly through the administrative structures of health care rather than figures generating places of care. All of this takes shape around a problematic understanding of language as a grounded, replicable object that reflects a single skill—replication.

Recognizing the nursing school as a lived place would have required assessing the state of the students and the needs of the community and then the place that language can play in such a location; as a non-place, however, the instructor is absolved of this kind of calculus. As a result, Nimet's extensive experiences with carefully considering how to phrase information, awareness of how to deal with multiple linguistic registers, and her awareness of how to move around within bureaucratic structures via language are rendered invisible.

The material outcomes of this mapping of the nursing curriculum equate to time and money for Nimet, but also in intellectual and communal terms as nurses get recast as figures whose primary role is to relay information clearly rather than produce information and contribute expert practices to institutions. All of this, then, gets mapped onto an understanding of language as itself a hollowed-out subject based primarily in the production of similitude—a human-less transfer of information. As scholars of language, developing and circulating mobility-based understandings of language and its transfer help to head off this argument and perhaps spare future nursing students all of the balderdash.

CONCLUSION

In sum, if "place is . . . a continually unfolding event of shifting character in response to tides of movement and pressure" (6) as the introduction to this collection points out, these events are often structured by institutional orderings staged for political power and inequity. Rather than creating place, the institutional orderings in each of these chapters render particular acts and identities transient or invisible in the smooth spaces of institutional life—each with detrimental effects. Whether it is working toward a mobility/Mobility model or identifying the spatial assumptions of literacy managers, remapping the institutional ethos of work in rhetoric and composition to account for the strategic production of non-places is integral to redressing these bureaucratic strategies that use solitude and similitude to render important elements of intellectual and literate activity invisible. These essays demand we ask what the consequences are when we don't measure, or don't provide clear notions of measurement, that articulate mobility in all of its complexity. We are place-makers, not just because place is what animates the environments we engage with, but because with increasing frequency there are forces working to erase and redefine the places constituted, at least in part, by the work of English/Language/Rhetoric/Writing Studies. Doing so will bring us a long way toward fulfilling the original vision of institutional critique—creating for the field a more focused point of analysis so that "institutions can be sensitized to users, to people, systemically from within and that this sensitizing can potentially change the way an entire industry perceives its relationship to the public" (Porter et al. 2000, 611).

REFERENCES

Augé, Marc. 2008. *Non-Places: An Introduction to Supermodernity*. Translated by John Howe. New York: Verso.

Gardner, Lee. 2016. "Turmoil Raises Specter of Faculty Exodus from Public Colleges." *The Chronicle of Higher Education*, June 19, 2016. https://www.chronicle.com/article /turmoil-raises-specter-of-faculty-exodus-from-public-colleges/.

Hamilton, Reeve. 2010. "Emerging Research Universities Vie for Tier One Status." *The Texas Tribune*, August 19, 2010. https://www.texastribune.org/2010/08/19/emerging -research-universities-tier-one-status/.

Porter, James E., Patricia A. Sullivan, Stuart Blythe, Jeffrey T. Grabill, and Libby Miles. 2000. "Institutional Critique: A Rhetorical Methodology for Change." *College Composition and Communication* 51 (4): 610–642.

Texas Legislature. 2009. Texas Legislative Session 81 (R), June 17, 2009. http://www.capi tol.state.tx.us/BillLookup/History.aspx?LegSess=81R&Bill=HB51.

13

(T)RACING RACE
Mapping Power in Racial Property Across Institutionalized Writing Standards and Urban Literacy Sponsorship Networks

Jamila M. Kareem and Khirsten L. Scott

By addressing race and bypassing race in their chapters, Carmen Kynard and Eli Goldblatt, respectively, exemplify how racial identity relates to property issues in both academic and nonacademic literacy mobility. Critical race theorists in legal studies and education describe the property values of race as features of racial identity that are exchangeable for tangible items (good textbooks, fresh produce) or for social ideals (home ownership, good health). People and institutions, often unintentionally, orient racial property along whiteness because cultural practices have shown that racial identity comes with the largest cultural capital. Critical race theorist Gloria Ladson-Billings proposes that racial property is more akin to the concepts of whiteness and blackness rather than actual phenotypical and cultural identification themselves. Where whiteness takes on properties of aspects such as "'school achievement,' 'intelligence,' 'middle classness,' and 'beauty,'" blackness belongs to cultural features like "'gangs,' 'the underclass,' and 'basketball players'" (1998, 9). In particular, the racial property of whiteness holds the most authority over literacy mobility in education-oriented enterprises because whiteness is thought to represent the lifelong success and influence that inspires institutional education. Giving attention to the way race, and especially whiteness, acts as a property in the circulation of literacy education encourages a perspective that necessarily places race at the center of literacy (im)mobility.

If educators and researchers view literacy practices as something people own, rather than something they simply do, we can envision how the ownership of whiteness-controlled literacies is exchangeable for a wider range of social and cultural material. The kinds of mobility available through whiteness-controlled literacies are power-based. These literacies are thought to aid mobility into a *better*, more *socially respectable*

DOI: 10.7330/9781646420209.c013

way of knowing. For example, the urban literacy network described in Goldblatt's chapter aims to help the less fortunate by setting them up with whiteness-controlled literacy offerings. By contrast, mobility accessible by blackness-controlled literacies are community-based. These literacies are believed to keep community customs and mobilize these customs and community expression into traditionally non-black spaces. Digital-based genres, like the ePortfolio that Kynard's students work with, move between the scales of whiteness-controlled and blackness-controlled literacy mobilities.

Here, we draw on the theory of sociolinguistic scales as Jan Blommaert applies it. For Blommaert, scales act as semiotic representations of the social practices made by language use. These representations hold various authority in different "TimeSpace" positions. For example, the blackness-controlled literacy practice of oral testifying holds high authority along blackness literacy scales, or Blommaert's lower scale. On the other hand, the whiteness-controlled literacy practice of the objective writing style holds stronger authority on whiteness literacy scales, seen as the higher scale because of its use by the culture in power.

Similar to the association of particular cultural tropes with concepts of blackness and whiteness that Ladson-Billings identifies, our culture places particular literacies along hierarchized scales of race. Academic literacies, scientific literacies, professional literacies, and other literacy practices associated with intelligence and prosperity are widely thought to be owned by whiteness. By contrast, blackness correlates to vernacular literacies, oral literacies, "mother tongue" literacies, and other common-folk literacy practices. Some literacy practices, like those based in digital genres, can operate on multiple racial scales depending on the practitioner. This flexibility inspires even stronger efforts by those invested in whiteness-centered literacies to coopt digital-based literacy practices into conceptions of whiteness. In doing so, these literacy practices are seen as useless or unattainable for particular segments of population—working-class black women, for example. As Kynard's naysayers declare, the visual rhetoric contained within digital literacy practices is thought to be a distraction and is considered irrelevant (90). The flexibility of these practices keeps them out of whiteness-controlled arenas. Relating mobility afforded through literacy to the cultural property of whiteness sheds light on the racialization of literacy mobility possibilities.

When marginalized literacies enter into spaces representing dominant cultural literacies, the dominant culture controls when and where those marginalized literacy practices are put into action. The dominant culture's "valorization of whiteness as a treasured property" (Harris

1995, 277) means that whiteness-controlled literacy practices will always hold more authority in white-imagined spaces in which blackness is othered. The resulting immobility of non-white literacies reinforces the forward directional literacy mobility of dominant whiteness. Where the predominantly Black students and parents in Goldblatt's urban literacy sponsorship network are immobilized by limited healthcare options, poor school funding, and almost mandatory incarceration, the "privileged" predominantly white university students and faculty benefit from these systems "simply serv[ing] to maintain the target population at a level of existence" (135). While Goldblatt lists schools as one of the systems meant for maintenance rather than forward mobility for the underprivileged community members, the AfroDigital creations discussed by Kynard push back against the expectation to adopt whiteness in whiteness-controlled academic spaces.

Institutional writing standards serve to structure whiteness-controlled writing practices as most desirable. They will most successfully assimilate others, like black women, into dominant society. As a result, whiteness is portrayed as the most coveted racialized way of being. Honoring whiteness as property through institutional writing criteria serves to colonize non-white literacy practices within the institution. Challenging this colonization, Kynard's subject Andrene, creator of "Pretty for a Black Girl," uses black English traditions in the digital environment to mobilize outside of her presumed intellectual and literacy placement within the white-invested institution. By using a feminist cartography, Kynard ascertains that institutional writing standards can work to limit the composing mobility of those at the intersection of race and gender oppression. If, as Goldblatt argues, "[t]hose in power channel funds to stabilize institutions they see as bulwarks against chaos and their own loss of control" and "[t]hey cannot or will not picture a truly inclusive world with the well being [sic] of everyone as a priority" (135), the majority of university representatives will see little legitimacy in financially and socially funding working-class black women's writing practices due to lack of authority in nonacademic literacy sponsorship. Kynard's resistant colleagues perceive Andrene as using the whiteness-controlled literacy practices of the academy for mobility through blackness-controlled literacies (chapter 5). They refuse to accept this "scale-jumping" because it diminishes the value of whiteness as the only way to forward directional literacy mobility. However, incorporating "Pretty for a Black Girl" as an example for all future classes of this course can potentially give university sponsorship, or at least English Department sponsorship, to the authority of these black women's literacies in this traditionally white space. The empowerment from this sponsorship allows Andrene and others to be the "authors of their own realities" (Goldblatt, 136).

Based on the institutional—and dominant cultural—standard of literacies for mobility, blackness-controlled literacy mobility is restricted by low sponsorship in institutional spaces. Blommaert's theory of sociolinguistic scales suggests that differing literacy spaces cause "[a]rticulate, multilingual individuals [to] become inarticulate and 'language-less' by moving from a space in which their [literacy] resources were valued and recognized into one in which they didn't count as valuable and understandable" (2007, 2). In applying a feminist cartographic approach, Kynard offers Andrene's ePortfolio as a case study that functions as both a site of analysis and a critique of the field's larger neoliberal representations of racialized pedagogy, often disguised as college- and career-readiness. She explores the "weight and risk" of the pressure of such structures on her teaching (Kynard 83), moving beyond these norms into spaces where technocultural competence is engaged and, further, resists the limited political imaginations of our schools and sanctioned research protocols (90–91). Kynard's "cartography of struggle," as analyzed through Andrene's "Pretty for a Black Girl," introduces dynamic possibilities for the racialized implications attached to mobility—possibilities that might have otherwise remained overlooked.

In the Moore School schoolyard development project that Goldblatt describes, implications of race play a critical role in the decisions made about the allotment of the grounds of the majority-black elementary school. For example, considering the types of literacy events promoted in working poor, majority-white neighborhoods, the influence of racial identity becomes more apparent in this black neighborhood. Revisiting the cultural features of blackness from Ladson-Billings, the question about whether "basketball courts that might or might not regain the glory days of basketball tournaments twenty years before" might foster gang and other criminal activity (Goldblatt 139) would not arise in working-class white neighborhood communities. Goldblatt concludes his exploration of literacy and mobility at the Moore School by positioning the university as "a transit depot rather than a knowledge repository/dispensary" with hopes of "ensuring that people, no matter their educational level or economic status, can move freely in a country that needs the contributions of all its inhabitants" (142–43). By positioning the university in this manner, Goldblatt passively remarks on the racialization of literacy practices in community work. While it may be obvious to some that *all* inhabitants would be inclusive of all racial groups, it is impossible to avoid the polarization of blackness and whiteness in this positioning. The university's attempt to avoid being understood as a "repository/dispensary" signals Goldblatt's attempt to be careful when discussing race. Whether his caution is influenced by identity or his own desire for neutrality, there is an inherent danger in avoiding race when discussing community work that diminishes the possibility of fully recognizing and engaging literacy practices and their potential to shift and shape communities. As we consider the relation of literacy education and sponsorship to issues of racial property, it is incumbent upon pedagogues, researchers, and community partners alike to carefully consider and engage racialized experiences. These considerations and the consequent unveiling of racism will reveal that issues of property are not only an issue of who can know what, but where and when they can.

If "people make physical space and time into controlled, regimented objects and instruments . . . through semiotic practices" (Blommaert 2007, 5), theories of racial property help denote where and when race-based literacy practices are permitted outside of their spacial[1] and temporal norms. These spacial and temporal possibilities become increasingly relevant in classroom and community interactions as Kynard and Goldblatt describe in their chapter. For Kynard, the racial property of literacy is sponsored through AfroDigital and technocultural means, and thus creates mobility of nontraditional literacy practices in TimeSpace outside of established norms. TimeSpace thus becomes ideological (Blommaert 5): the feminist cartographic lens on race highlights how institutional standards for writing dictate when (temporal) and where (spacial) black women's literacies are available, sponsored, mobilized, and silenced. Conversely, the property of whiteness, maintained by many of the social institutions in the literacy sponsorship network described by Goldblatt, influences where (e.g., at the Honickman Learning Center or in the school science classroom) particular literacy practices occur when (e.g., before, during, or after school hours). In either case, institutional representations of whiteness as the ultimate property influences when and whether blackness migrates with literacy practices in traditionally white spaces. As we look ahead, it is important to engage how we respond to ultimate property within our communities, classrooms, and institutions.

Concerned with social institutions as literacy sponsors, Goldblatt notes that dysfunctional spaces such as prisons and broke(n) schools cannot offer moments of empowerment to sponsor the literacy practices of disadvantaged citizens. We suggest that even sound educational spaces, invested in the hidden curriculum of whiteness property, fail to offer these moments as well. Instead, these spaces attempt to empower the destitute and less fortunate through assimilating them into dominant literacy traditions. In placing the burden on those with mobility provided by their literacy (140–43), Goldblatt places an equal, and potentially more impactful, burden on the individuals within those networks to understand and engage with the social implications attached to such sponsorships. These considerations invite questions related to the spacial and temporal constraints that influence not only literacy moments, but also the (im)mobility often attached with these moments—where and when are literacy moments possible? Who sponsors them? Who benefits from them? And so on. As Goldblatt describes the stark contrast between Temple University and the surrounding neighborhood, it becomes discouragingly clear that the burden present is one that is racialized, but also marked by material forces measured primarily through spacial considerations. The community is positioned in close proximity to the university within Goldblatt's view, but it is also positioned against the notion of the university as a site for enhancing temporal conditions. As literacy sponsorship networks determine how and when literacy migrates across racial and other socially constructed identity borders (Goldblatt, chapter 8), multiracial, first-generation, working class/poor students are denied equal access to white-owned institutional literacies at the moments when they need it most.

By advocating for respatialization as a means of promoting a culturally relevant writing curriculum, Kynard's position as professor is one that actively engages technocultural competence to encourage the TimeSpace moves across blackness and whiteness literacy scales. For black students, this "scale-jumping" (Blommaert 2007; Uitermark 2002) ultimately resists the construction of academic spaces as white where black bodies are merely visitors. This temporal and spacial manipulation fosters racial ownership that shapes the experiences presented in "Pretty for a Black Girl."

The first-year writing curriculum Kynard offers empowers black women to respond to the ways the institution tries to define them by mapping their racial and gender struggle and redirecting the "very directionality of learning and its processes" (88). By migrating across the digital divide and into the "histories of technology," which often exclude racially marginalized groups (90), the working-class black female students migrate across the intellectual boundaries historically denoted by whiteness and blackness. They do this through establishing the academic ePortfolio as a TimeSpace whereby they can express and define their blackness. It makes the classroom a space where all experiences, including those of working class and working poor black women, are relevant and logical within multiple scales (Kynard, chapter 5). On the other hand, more direct attention to race could afford Goldblatt a deeper exploration of literacy sponsorship networks in predominantly black and Latinx urban communities. Revealing the racial property of literacy sponsorship exposes one way sponsors determine who can use what literacies and under what circumstances. This approach opens up questions of whether these sponsors are simply transferring school-sanctioned literacies or whether there is potential to strip away boundaries (read: whiteness) in order to allow others the space and moments to move their own literacies.

The shift in attention to analyzing racial property in literacy for mobility encourages a different perspective of (im)mobility, one that places race at the center. Critical race theorists who interrogate race as property (Harris 1995; Ladson-Billings and Tate 1995; Leonardo 2004; Mills 1999) situate whiteness in a coveted position that determines educational outcomes. Ladson-Billings and Tate argue, about whiteness in school property, "when students [and community members] are rewarded only for conformity to perceived white norms or sanctioned for cultural practices (e.g., dress, speech patterns, unauthorized conceptions of knowledge), white property is being rendered alienable" (1995, 59). Cultural artifacts, such as literacies, invoking blackness are portrayed as inalienable, unable to be transferred or negotiated. Looking at whiteness as property with literacy mobility reveals why some literacy practices sponsored by social institutions grant mobility and others restrict it.

NOTE

1.   Kynard's spelling: p. 87.

REFERENCES

Blommaert, Jan. 2007. "Sociolinguistic Scales." *Intercultural Pragmatics* 4 (1): 1–19.
Harris, Cheryl. 1995. "Whiteness as Property." In *Critical Race Theory: The Key Writings That Formed the Movement*, edited by Kimberlé Crenshaw, Neil Gotanda, Garry Peller, and Kendall Thomas, 276–291. New York: The New Press.
Ladson-Billings, Gloria. 1998. "Just What Is Critical Race Theory and What's It Doing in a *Nice* Field like Education?" *Qualitative Studies in Education* 11 (1): 7–30.

Ladson-Billings, Gloria, and William F. Tate, IV. 1995. "Toward a Critical Race Theory of Education." *Teachers College Record* 97 (1): 47–68.

Leonardo, Zeus. 2004. "The Color of Supremacy: Beyond the Discourse of 'White Privilege.'" *Educational Philosophy and Theory* 36 (2): 137–152.

Mills, Charles W. 1999. *The Racial Contract.* Ithaca: Cornell University Press.

Uitermark, Justus. 2002. "Be-Scaling, 'Scale Fragmentation,' and the Regulation of Antagonistic Relationships." *Progress in Human Geography* 26 (6): 743–765.

14

MOBILIZING CONNECTIONS ACROSS DISCIPLINARY FRAMES

Megan Faver Hartline

Christiane Donahue's use of mobility as a heuristic for understanding disciplinary research frames in interaction offers a new way to think about how we understand current research practices across rhetoric and composition. Mobility allows Donahue to find connections between two seemingly disparate disciplinary areas of study, translingualism and transfer, and show how scholars of both can learn from each other to make new knowledge within their central areas of study and the discipline as a whole. In this response, I follow Donahue's example of connecting disciplinary frames via mobility to explore intersections between community writing, as presented by Eli Goldblatt, and design thinking, as presented by Scott Wible. Both of these areas of inquiry are receiving strong disciplinary attention at the moment.[1] But by thinking about them *together* through Donahue's model of disciplinary mobility—which involves recognizing, taking up, and modifying points of connection between subfields, thus inevitably transforming how we do research—we can gain a better understanding of specifically how community writing and design thinking are already connected and how to *mobilize* those points of connection to strengthen research practices in these two specific areas. More broadly, we can see how a mobility lens encourages all of us in rhetoric and composition to consider what we can learn from one another across subfields to deepen our scholarship.

At first glance, Goldblatt's discussion of networks of literacy sponsors and Wible's pedagogical strategies for his professional writing students seem to be in wildly different spheres of discussion, but thinking about them both through the lens of mobility (as modeled by Donahue) foregrounds aspects that the works share, showing how disciplinary knowledge from each area is already being used by the other. Community writing offers us a chance to think about how and where community members fit into the process of creating new knowledge in

---

DOI: 10.7330/9781646420209.c014

design thinking. Similarly, design thinking gives us a way to consider the process Goldblatt's networks use to pursue change through collaboratively creating an outdoor space for Moore School. But looking at where community writing or design thinking knowledge is present in other scholarship only shows us surface-level overlaps of writing studies research, not mobility. As Donahue explains it, mobility requires movement imbued with meaning (chapter 1), employing the idea of "reprise-modification" or "simultaneous retaking-up-modifying" as one way to show how movement is made into meaningful process. She sees "reprise, much like in music, as the reuse of material, and modification as the transformation that occurs in the reprising moment" (20). Using these ideas illustrated by Donahue, I explore how disciplinary knowledge that is already in the background of a scholar's work can be mobilized to transform research practices in new and exciting ways—how it can help us make more disciplinary connections across the field, rather than just in our own areas.

Because of the brief nature of this response chapter, I focus on two ideas that represent major tenets of community writing and design thinking and are present in both Goldblatt's and Wible's chapters: partnering with community members as reciprocal knowledge-makers and using an iterative process to generate solutions. Examining how each idea is used in both chapters, I argue that mobilizing these approaches across subfields could transform disciplinary knowledge in community writing and design thinking to produce research that better attends to concerns in our field about who is privileged in knowledge-making and how one designs collaborative projects that contribute to the public good.

COMMUNITY WRITING AND KNOWLEDGEABLE COLLABORATORS

One of the key tenets of community writing is the importance of approaching community members as knowledgeable collaborators, as a major part of the construction of the project rather than just the beneficiaries. This approach to community projects is central to Goldblatt's discussion of the redevelopment of the Moore School schoolyard. One way this can be seen is through the variety of people and types of knowledge described by Goldblatt as a part of the redesign process. Some members of the network had obvious professional knowledge to share about the schoolyard reconstruction plan—the principal and vice principal of Moore, members of the Water Department who provide necessary technical data, the team from the Big Sandbox who previously led similar environmental design projects. Each of those community members had the kind of logistical and technical knowledge that is necessary for this project, but Goldblatt also attends to other nodes in the sponsorship network—people who brought important knowledge to this project even if not directly related to the technical construction of the redevelopment plan. These alternative sources of knowledge include the young man who gave Goldblatt the necessary information about who owned the abandoned lot; Denise, who runs an after-school drill team and organizes the parent organization for Moore School; and representatives from other community organizations, including a group advocating for street basketball. Goldblatt discusses the contributions of *all* these groups, pointing out the importance of mobilizing knowledge from all sources—technical, social, neighborhood, and more—in order to transform the landscape of Moore School.

Design thinking's approach to community involvement is similar in that community members are central to defining local issues that need to be addressed, with designers going into the community to learn about how people are experiencing an issue. By going into the community during the empathy phase to learn more about a local problem, design thinkers aim to "deeply understand" people's attitudes and experiences with a problem before working to create solutions that improve those experiences (96). Wible shows that through design thinking processes and "get[ting] out of the building" (95), students learn to think deeply about the lived realities of community problems and how to address them in ways that they wouldn't be able to with other approaches. Where design thinking and community writing differ is that design thinkers seem to view community members as consultants in the designer's iterative process of problem solving *for* the community, rather than *with* them. Where community writing privileges long-term relationship-building and creating knowledge alongside community members, the design thinking process brings community members in only at specific moments—interviewing, observing, and getting feedback from them off and on throughout the development of solutions—making fully collaborative knowledge-creation less likely.

Although both Goldblatt and Wible are describing mobile experiences in which scholars and students move outside of the classroom to learn more about how to address a particular problem, one might consider how design thinkers might better mobilize understandings of community-university relationships from community writing scholars. In these chapters, while Goldblatt talks about significant contributions from multiple types of community leaders, showing how all types of knowledge were necessary when trying to put together the schoolyard project, Wible's approach focuses more on writing genres used for student learning and less on the relationship-building and knowledge-sharing process. Design thinking, in Wible's explanation, does value multiple perspectives on a problem; however, community writing scholars might push back against the reality of design thinking's work in "solving local, community-defined problems" (107) when community members are not fully integrated into the knowledge-making process, taking part only in problem-defining and solution-testing. Community members are, to an extent, being used as resources that can be assembled together for a particular goal, which, per Donahue, does not ultimately allow for *transformation*, or mobilization, of ideas, knowledge, and the lives of all concerned. For this community writing tenet to be truly mobilized in design thinking, Wible's students, and other design thinkers, would need to take up (as in "reprise") questions of who should have a seat at the table when defining *and* addressing community issues, allowing community members to engage in the full design thinking process alongside students and scholars by taking up and modifying questions at all stages of knowledge-making. Explicit conversations about relationship-building and collaborative knowledge-creation could lead not only to more significant transformations of design thinking, to a valuable reprise-modification, but also to transformations of the designers themselves, helping them better fulfill the "empathy mode" by learning to value knowledge from multiple sources and create more useful solutions in collaboration with community members. This transformation could move a writing studies version of design thinking even further toward the type of socially transformative research Wible hopes to achieve (110). Ultimately, design thinkers in writing studies could learn more about what is involved with "getting outside of the building" and how to navigate community relationships, not only drawing expertise from multiple sources, but also transforming that knowledge (and themselves) through bringing those sources together.

DESIGN THINKING AND ITERATIVE SOLUTION DEVELOPMENT

For community writing scholars, design thinking's process of iterative solution development might be valuable as they move forward with their own community-based, problem-solving projects. Wible walks readers through the five phases of design thinking, showing how designers work toward solutions purposefully and recursively, moving backward as well as forward through the phases to find appropriate ways to address local issues. This iterative process helps designers "deepen their understanding of the community context and the users they are designing solutions for" (97) and is particularly useful for moving students from "discovering an answer" to "inventing a solution" (Marback 2009 qtd. in Wible, chapter 6). For example, Wible shows how the ideate phase encourages students to generate a variety of possible solutions based on different dimensions (seen in the How Might We questions) of their original problem. Brainstorming so many possible solutions forces students to consider many ways of addressing an issue instead of going with the first possible answer. Throughout the process, design thinking requires a type of flexible mobility, a willingness to move and craft their possible solutions to better fit the people they are working with, which could be useful for community writing scholars as well.

Like design thinkers, Goldblatt seems to be committed to the possibility of multiple solutions and adaptable problem solving in his discussion of the Moore Schoolyard, a project that, as Goldblatt's description makes clear, requires a good amount of flexibility. He starts his piece with an empty lot near Moore School and Tree House Books, but he goes through multiple instantiations of what sort of community space might ultimately be built there. Goldblatt starts with a desire for Treehouse Books students to have a place to "investigate plants and animals as a way of motivating and grounding them in both academic and imaginative reading and writing" (130), and as the project transforms, he specifically points to ways that a "living laboratory" could help strengthen science education to enable Moore students to go to the nearby high achieving engineering and science high school. As Goldblatt listens to other stakeholders and accrues further knowledge and understanding of possible uses for the space available, he allows his initial goal to be transformed, a process which is also valued in design thinking. But beyond Goldblatt's personal flexibility, the full process of how various stakeholders come to a final decision about what should and should not be included in the new Moore schoolyard is unclear. Where design thinkers try to move iteratively through specific phases to address issues, community writing scholars do not often seem to explain their processes for forging partnerships and planning projects, obscuring what it is that these scholars actually do to create change and making their work difficult to replicate or even use as inspiration for other scholars' projects.

Wible and Goldblatt both describe the process of mobilizing a project out of a problem, but Wible's process, through design thinking, is more clear-cut and well-ordered, while Goldblatt's description of his process is, at best, less fully articulated, if not mysterious. For community writing scholars, their reprise-modification of design thinking could entail taking a more explicitly detailed approach to problem-posing and solution-finding with their community partners. I expect some community writing scholars would push back against using a more regimented process, but when relying on Donahue's description of reprise-modification as "reuse in transformation, transformation in reuse" (21), we can see a way to think about "knowledge reuse and adaptation across time and contexts" (25), which would allow community writing scholars to use and *transform* the design thinking frame and maintain their focus on relationship-building. Indeed, according to Donahue, they cannot not do so; we transform, inevitably, in taking up such frames, whether or not we recognize the transformations we effect. Using design thinking would not have to mean taking on an entrepreneurial mindset to community writing projects, but instead using a frame that already fits in some ways and mobilizing (and thus transforming) it to help others, both in the community and in the academy, more easily understand the specifics of community writing scholars' work. In fact, Wible is advocating for exactly this kind of approach to using design thinking within writing studies.

Additionally, seeing community writing through the lens of design thinking could encourage scholars to continually rethink how they are designing new projects and growing previously existing projects. The iterative approach to design thinking asks designers, or in this case community writing scholars, to always be thinking about process, regularly generating new solutions. Community writing scholars could transform this process to include ways to iteratively think about building relationships and producing knowledge with community members, always looking for new ways to address seemingly intransigent issues. In this way, a design thinking approach focused on iterative solution development gives scholars a model for navigating the difficulties of dynamic, collaborative work toward real-world solutions, and offers them a chance to transform a more business-oriented model of knowledge-making to become more collaborative.

CONCLUSION

Seen in the connections between community writing and design thinking illuminated above, disciplinary knowledge, which is already being applied across subfields, could be mobilized in order to strengthen both community writing's and design thinking's approaches to crafting research projects that work with and for local communities. Mobility allows us to, per Donahue, "explore shared motives, shared terms and consequences, and shared resistances" (18), and we can see here how community writing and design thinking *do* share similarities like those Donahue discusses. But ultimately, connecting disciplinary knowledge via mobility must involve *mobilizing* those similarities through conscious modification to transform our current research practices to be more pertinent to today's "mobile and superdiverse world" (Donahue 18), which leads to a transformation of the lives of those engaged in this process as well—researchers, designers, community partners, and students—as they learn to think differently about who has knowledge, what that knowledge looks like, and how it can be used for the good of their communities.

NOTE

1. Though community writing has been studied for over two decades, the recent Conference on Community Writing and work to change the special interest group (for the Conference on College Composition and Communication) in "Community Literacy, Service-Learning, and Public Rhetoric" to a standing group under the heading of "Community Writing" are markers of the growing energy and traction this subfield has right now. Similarly, design thinking is gaining power as a model for thinking about writing, as argued for by scholars like James Purdy (2014) and Richard Marback (2009). Over 100 panels and workshops at the 2016 Conference on College Composition and Communication referenced "design thinking," showing the increased use of this idea in the field.

REFERENCES

Marback, Richard. 2009. "Embracing Wicked Problems: The Turn to Design in Composition Studies." *College Composition and Communication* 61 (2): W397–W419.
Purdy, James P. 2014. "What Can Design Thinking Offer Writing Studies?" *College Composition and Communication* 65 (4): 612–641.

15

SOCIAL MOVEMENT FRICTION AND MEANINGFUL SPACES

Patrick Danner

Mobility work in composition studies—as this collection demonstrates—is intricately tied to physical and perceived realities of place. Our bodies, our composing processes, rhetorical capacities, and identities move from one place to the next, often finding our selves, discourses, actions, and identities constrained by the perceived appropriate practices of a given site. As a rhetorical idea, mobility work requires a close view of these places and the afforded means of invention therein. But I want to suggest that spaces are changed, too, as we or some objects move through them. In other words, I suggest a complicated relationship between space and mobility: Not only are spaces responsible for shaping the mobilities of bodies, but the mobilities of bodies, and the rhetorical capacities of those bodies, shape spaces as well.

Though Kynard and Scenters-Zapico engage the kinds of spaces that are informed by the mobility of objects, people, and ideas, the mobility paradigms at play in their work are largely about the institutional, psychological, affective, and political forces that inform movement, rather than those that can be informed *by* movement. This is a fruitful and necessary lens in our contemporary neoliberal moment, one that we can trace to Foucault's (1995, 2008) notion of static spaces disciplining bodies, if not back even further: movement—or stasis—of people is forced and directed by governmental practice, social norms, economic crashes, and so on (depending on, as Shivers-McNair reminds us in this volume, where observers draw the boundaries). But taking the other view, too, such movement changes our relationship to borders, economies, and spaces generally. I take Kynard's study to get at this very point. Kynard notes that the introduction of Andrene's digital portfolio "Pretty for a Black Girl" into her classroom space has fundamentally changed interactions within her class and, perhaps, among the student body at large: "The repeated expressions of Andrene's language by young women of

---

DOI: 10.7330/9781646420209.c015

color in my classes, no longer arguing their case, but highlighting a successful case in Andrene, allows a new uptake of political positions" (89). There's no doubt as to the implications of the movement of this object to and through the institutional setting. Kynard quite clearly spells out how political subjectivity within the walls of the institution is reframed by Andrene's—and her text's—movement among classmates and colleagues at her school: "young women of color in [her] classes" expand their repertoire of inventional techniques, pulling from "a successful case in Andrene" to take up new "political positions."

In other words, while the rhetorical means made available by Kynard's institution are expanded by Andrene's mobility, bundled up in the circulation and movement of this digital artifact and illustrated through changes among the student body, the opposite is true as well; the social institutions that house this mobile object-maker pair (even briefly) inform and circumscribe its uptake. Indeed, institutionally oriented perspectives such as this are often privileged in rhetorical studies: what forces or powers are present that limit or circumscribe perceived available action? Scenters-Zapico, writing of his own experience with his institution, notes "friction" that occurs whenever a mobile person or object begins, enters, or returns to a formative and changing space, what the author terms "Contingent and Emergent Events" based on their own protean character (55–57). Largely, Scenters-Zapico frames these as frictions sparked by institutional forces that prompt movement toward or away from another space. Such "frictions" take form as the motivating factors of mobility or stasis, "positive" or "negative" frictions (58).

Yet, if we are to take Scenters-Zapico's "friction" metaphor and Kynard's description of Andrene's politically influential mobility seriously, both views of mobility and its effects must be true: As space constrains or impedes or otherwise informs mobility, so too do mobilities inform the spaces they enter and pass through. "Friction," that is, can be understood to transfer rhetorical and symbolic energy simultaneously to both bodies as they meet, even if we don't readily perceive this energy (or the subsequent alteration effected by it) on one or the other surface.

A MOBILITY MODEL FOR SOCIAL MOVEMENT RHETORICS

Such bidirectionality of influence—space informing mobility and mobility informing space—is increasingly apparent in studies of social movement rhetoric (see Chávez 2011, Heaney and Rojas 2006; Pezzullo 2003; Warner 2005). Heaney and Rojas's study of anti-war protests in Fayetteville, North Carolina, is perhaps the most explicit in tracing the confluence, movement, accrual, and, of course, "friction" of meaning in social movement activity. As they remark in their study, Fayetteville is a site already rich in possible symbolic meaning: Fayetteville has a long tradition of military presence, hosted anti-war marches during Vietnam, boasts a Quaker heritage (evident in past anti–death penalty protests), and represents "a symbolic commitment to organizing in the South" (Heaney and Rojas 2006, 248–249). These are just some of the meanings available to protesters in Fayetteville, evident once an idea (here, an "anti-war" sentiment) sweeps through and informs how place is approached, discussed, and put to symbolic work. In other words, just as Kynard's classroom is a space for minority students to strike a new political sensibility in relation to Andrene's work, the introduction (and long history) of anti-war activity moving to and through Fayetteville provides "new" tools for protest rhetoric to take root.

Like Heaney and Rojas, Karma Chávez, too, notes the importance of meaning as constructed in movement between or among specific, meaningful sites: "First, activists interpret external rhetorical messages that are created about them, the constituencies they represent, or both. . . . Second, activists use enclaves as the sites to invent rhetorical strategies to publicly challenge oppressive rhetoric or to create new imaginaries for the groups and issues they represent . . ." (2011, 362). For Chávez, as for Kynard and Scenters-Zapico, meaning is derived within the spaces where action occurs. Though Chávez addresses the effect of movement from the enclave onto the public space, the creation of an enclave is itself an alteration of a space effected by mobility into and through that space. The enclave is transformed by media rhetoric, becoming a site for "new imaginaries" that alter the rhetorical self (for Chávez, the coalition of immigrant and LGBT activists) and imbue the space with movement meaning by coming to understand it as a space for inventing "rhetorical strategies."

Such creation via mobility became startlingly evident in my own participant observation research, conducted alongside organizers preparing for and acting in the 2015 National Adjunct Walkout Day (NAWD). As part of a larger network of movement action, the NAWD organizers in Louisville, Kentucky, coordinated two simultaneous teach-ins. During the organizing and planning stages, I tracked the group and took meeting minutes for the planning committee. Early meetings were held in local dive bars, and later moved to well-apportioned conference rooms after the conversation moved into administrative offices, signaling (for the organizers) administrative approval; those members of the group who affiliated with the local Industrial Workers of the World (IWW) carried conversations to their own meetings in coffee shops, libraries, and rented warehouse spaces; members with larger institutional roles carried conversations to department offices. In each instance places were granted symbolic meaning by committee members ("How often do adjuncts get to sit in *this* room on campus?") and the work done granted new meaning to old spaces ("*This* booth is where we strategize"). In both small and large ways, sites could become—could be *transformed into*—meeting places to discuss organizing for NAWD because of the movement of ideas through individual members. IWW meeting minutes during that time attest that a large portion of the meetings were devoted to updates about NAWD; the local bar became a space where members could go to air grievances about the planning process and organization. As one member's notebook became stuck to the bar top, peeling a layer off and discoloring the surface, that same end of the bar was given meaning as the corner where key tactical decisions were made.

This isn't to say that transformation of a space is as innocuous as the discoloring of a bar surface. Rather, there is evidence of real, rhetorical transformation effected by organizing members' mobilities and the past and future actions that will symbolically alter the way a place is approached or thought up. Dispersed among activist groups, administration, and precarious faculty at multiple institutions, and often serving two or more of these roles, the rhetoric of "adjunct rights" was seen and heard across spaces: bulletin boards in institutions and administrative offices, workplace mailboxes, and in conversation broadly. Moreover, the spaces that organizers and their rhetoric went through informed the delivery of this rhetoric and, to an extent, the available inventional tools. "Student first" discourse circulated in institutionally sanctioned organizing meetings held on campuses, "precariousness" discourse in informal meetings at bars and libraries. In other words, even at this local level, the accrual and alteration of symbolic meaning was evident in placed language and reflected in and by places in which such language is found.

As Chávez would have it, multiple "enclaves" were present in the planning of a movement action, particularly as organizers constituted a coalition of individuals with different stakes in the organization. Largely, however, Chávez's description of movement enclaves is a static one. Physical spaces become backdrops for rhetorical invention rather than vibrantly symbolic spaces that both inform and are informed by the rhetoric at work within them. In my view, conversely, a full understanding of mobility as symbolically altering the space in which it occurs is necessary to comprehend the very "frictions," to evoke Scenters-Zapico again, that constitute the conflict evident in social movement activity. If we are to argue, as Chávez does, that a coalition of migrant and queer populations is formed by the media space within which they operate, then we should acknowledge, too, that the physical space within which that operation occurs is transformed as well.

RECURSIVE MEANING IN MOBILITY STUDIES

Kynard's explicitness about the relationship between politics and mobility is somewhat counterbalanced by Scenters-Zapico. Whereas Kynard describes how Andrene's work moves through the monolithic cultural standards of writing instruction, illustrating how Andrene articulates new rhetorical possibilities inside the spaces that writing instruction touches, Scenters-Zapico emphasizes movement as resulting from a relationship between space and person. The politicized character of his mobility is largely that it was prompted by institutionally-specific labor concerns. Yet, he also suggests that foregrounding mobilities allows us to see spaces as morphing, emerging within specific institutional and political contexts. In other words, it is through mobility that spaces take on their full symbolic import, even though it appears that the inherent character of a space is what prompted mobility to begin with. Space is symbolically transformed by this initial friction, just as mobility begins.

Symbolic transformation of space reveals an accretion of meaning with the potential to broaden an individual's or collective's rhetorical toolbox; meaning prompts movement, and further meaning is created by it. In adjunct organizing, a conference room accrues meaning because of the discussion that moves into its walls—a different discussion and perhaps that meaning doesn't stick. A city parking lot can accrue symbolic meaning as one lead organizer notes the regular removal of part-time employee parking privileges when administrators visit campus—if not administrators, but a visiting scholar, and the meaning there perhaps doesn't stick. And as plans for an impromptu demonstration to be held in this specific lot were discussed, organizers were able to conceive of this space as interwoven with larger institutional issues: they now evoked not only questions of pay but also symbolic status, work conditions, and opportunity for part-time faculty. And problems of transportation of course became rhetorically connected to questions of ability to engage students and were evoked often during the teach-in I observed.

Thus, the play between objects and spaces can, and perhaps should, be read as one of mutual and emergent meaning-making. Movement through or into a space can alter both the symbolic meaning of that space and one's own rhetorical means. In other words, the "positive" or "negative" "attachments and attributes" Scenters-Zapico (57) notes may be as much a result of what meaning is made of a space as what meaning a space allows one to make. This interplay, moreover, parallels recent movement in critical and rhetorical theory, which imagines the collapse of borders and interconnectivity of bodies and individuals under contemporary neoliberalism (Hardt and Negri 2000; Greene 2006; Foucault 2008; Greene and Kuswa 2012). Working in the wake of Deleuze, such spaces that were once seen as beyond the scope of observation are transformed and given new meaning as we approach or address them (Deleuze 1988, 87). Or as Cary Wolfe suggests, scholars of the "outside," and what that outside means to those who interact with it, must reckon with "problems of circularity, self-reference, and the unpredictable effects of recursivity" (1998, xvii). Whether such an interplay between space and rhetorical output is circular, self-referential, or recursive is up for debate; of course, the examples of Fayetteville and NAWD above suggest to me that self-reference, rhetoric that is conscious of its speaker as placed, is ripe in social activism. Yet, such models of mutual emergence hint at the intricacies of how meaning emerges in placed rhetorical action, and how recursive or self-referential rhetorical output with regard to place can shift, become mobile, and evolve as it becomes mobile.

REFERENCES

Chávez, Karma R. 2011. "Counter-Public Enclaves and Understanding the Function of Rhetoric in Social Movement Coalition-Building." *Communication Quarterly* 59: 1–18. Reprinted in Morris and Browne 361–374.

Deleuze, Gilles. 1988. *Foucault.* Translated by Seán Hand. Minneapolis: University of Minnesota Press.

Foucault, Michel. 1995. *Discipline and Punish: The Birth of the Prison.* Translated by Alan Sheridan. New York: Vintage.

Foucault, Michel. 2008. *The Birth of Biopolitics: Lectures at the Collège de France 1978–1979,* edited by Michel Senellart. Translated by Graham Burchell. New York: Picador.

Greene, Ronald Walter. 2006. "Orator Communist." *Philosophy and Rhetoric* 39 (1): 85–95.

Greene, Ronald Walter, and Kevin Douglas Kuswa. 2012. "'From Arab Spring to Athens, From Occupy Wall Street to Moscow': Regional Accents and the Rhetorical Cartography of Power." *Rhetoric Society Quarterly.* 42 (3): 271–288.

Hardt, Michael, and Antonio Negri. 2000. *Empire.* Cambridge, MA: Harvard University Press.

Heaney, Michael T., and Fabio Rojas. 2006. "The Place of Framing: Multiple Audiences and Antiwar Protests near Fort Bragg." *Qualitative Sociology* 29: 485–505. Rpt. Morris and Browne 243–260.

Morris, Charles E., III, and Stephen Howard Brown, eds. 2013. *Readings on the Rhetoric of Social Protest.* 3rd ed. State College: Strata.

Pezzullo, Phaedra C. 2003. "Resisting 'National Breast Cancer Awareness Month': The Rhetoric of Counterpublics and Their Cultural Performances." *Quarterly Journal of Speech* 89: 345–365.

Warner, Michael. 2005. *Publics and Counterpublics.* New York: Zone Books.

Wolfe, Cary. 1998. *Critical Environments: Postmodern Theory and the Pragmatics of the "Outside."* Minneapolis: University of Minnesota Press.

16

MOBILITY THROUGH EVERYDAY THINGS

Ashanka Kumari

In this short response, I offer a reading of Shivers-McNair's case study through the lens of Scenters-Zapico's "Small m to Big M–Mobilities" model to outline alternative considerations of the implications of mobility in our research practices. Ann Shivers-McNair argues that we should not "treat 'mobility' as a given" (36). Instead, in "Marking Mobility: Accounting for Bodies and Rhetoric in the Making," she notes that mobility is "*marked*" similarly to how we conceive of language, and we must be attuned to the "definitions, knowledges, practices, bodies, spaces, and rhetorics we study and teach" (37). Shivers-McNair, through her description of a year-long ethnographic case study of a makerspace, offers us a theoretically based methodology for capturing the markings of mobilities and encourages us to consider the ethical implications of that methodology for how we research mobility. Everyone comes to mobility from different positionalities and places, which in turn impact how we both conduct and interact with research. As Shivers-McNair's study acknowledges, our diverse positions impact how we move in, between, and among spaces; our bodies both impact and are impacted by space(s). But her chapter complicates this view by noting the fluidity of those positions and spaces. Similarly, in "Small m to Big M–Mobilities: a Model," John Scenters-Zapico reminds us of temporality through recounting his experience moving from one university to another. He writes that our positions at universities are typically considered temporary while giving the illusion of permanence by the university. I would argue that this consideration also applies to our interactions with interpretations of research participants at our study sites. When Shivers-McNair concludes her study with the makerspace, the physical space and the people she interacted with will continue to move and transform while she and her study continue to move across other spaces, such as academic journals and conferences as well as the people who connect with it.

DOI: 10.7330/9781646420209.c016

Scenters-Zapico's model operates in three parts: 1. Small m–mobility stages, 2. contingent and emergent events, and 3. inertia starters. These mobility stages refer to Scenters-Zapico's choice to revise his résumé and apply for a new academic position after experiencing some friction at his previous institution. While Shivers-McNair's chapter does not focus on her mobility across institutions, her year-long ethnographic case study of a makerspace still involves a change of physical space, one that, by the inherent nature of research, requires her to make plans to go to the makerspace and interact with people there. In her study specifically, she uses what she terms "3D interviewing" as her primary form of documentation (41). This methodology elevates how attuned she is to the mobility of things in the space, such as the physical movement of machines or furniture surrounding bodies in the space. Scot Barnett and Casey Boyle, in their introduction to *Rhetoric Through Everyday Things*, direct us to a comparable *"rhetorical ontology* of things." This notion is not a movement away from thinking about language, which still "matters, of course," but toward thinking about the "thing power" of objects around us because "these things we find ourselves between possess a certain 'thing power' in the way they gather forces and actors and in so doing 'affect other bodies, enhancing or weakening their power" (Bennett 2010, 3, qtd. in Barnett and Boyle 2016, 5). Rereading Shivers-McNair's thirty-six-second interaction with Richard, we might consider the power of the object he is manipulating—a piece of plywood—and the laser-cutting machine as active, mobile participants in the interaction. Scenters-Zapico notes that mobility stages, in his small-m mobility model, are "dynamic" because "they can be planned, replanned, and unplanned" (35). Similarly, we might think about the dynamic and fluid nature of the bodies and things in the makerspace; Shivers-McNair and Richard plan when they meet while the warping of the plywood is unplanned and, in a way, replanned by Richard's interference with the machine. While we have the power to act on objects as Richard does with the plywood, so too do objects have power to act on us or on one another. Shivers-McNair's methodology offers a way to document the mobility of things and, when taken with Scenters-Zapico's model, affords fruitful considerations of "thing power."

The second part of Scenters-Zapico's model moves us to consider the dynamic nature of events as contingent and emergent. Mobility work does not assume a stable beginning to events but rather sees them as fluid and able to be transformed. Contingent and emergent events lie on the points of stability that make up complex interactions. As Scenters-Zapico notes, mobility work builds on points and positions.

Mobility through Everyday Things   197

With research, mobility work operates on our own identity positions, which are constantly negotiated and renegotiated. While Scenters-Zapico moves, he notes that he "morph[s] from researcher, observer, and ethnographer to passenger, memoirist, and subject" (60). Likewise, Shivers-McNair indicates her own position in relation to her interactions with people and things at the makerspace she studies as a cis-gender woman, researcher, and teacher, among other identities. When we are first introduced to Richard in her study, he is described with a set of identity traits: former graphic designer, founder of the makerspace, and a "white man with a beard and brown hair (save for a pink ponytail)" (45). These identities are contingent and emergent in that they reflect starting positions, but they are also fluid, mobile entities. Richard is self-taught and an expert on the technologies in the makerspace; Shivers-McNair grows over the time of her research from someone who is "uncertain" at first to someone who feels "less tentative and more intentional" by the time of her interaction with Richard eight months into her research fieldwork (43). While her study does not feature this aspect, we might also consider the impact of the spaces outside of the makerspace that affect Shivers-McNair's interactions with participants, such as spaces where she conducts research or writing before and after her interactions, moments of planning, and her transportation space to and from the site. We also get a small sense of her emotions that add depth to our interpretation of the interaction—she laughs "nervously," for instance (44, emphasis added). 3D interviewing allows an opportunity to witness the emotional and physical dimensions at work in her interactions, particularly those that might be involuntary, such as when Shivers-McNair's eyes widen after Richard interferes with the machine. In this thirty-six-second interaction, the dynamic evolution of contingent and emergent events is thus captured.

Additionally, as Scenters-Zapico writes, people have different "attachments" to different contingent and emergent events (56). Richard and Shivers-McNair, for instance, foster different attachments with the makerspace. I would argue that Richard primarily sees this space as one where he goes to play, design, and create, while Shivers-McNair's primary purpose for the space is as a research site. Of course, these are not the only or permanent purposes Richard and Shivers-McNair have for the spaces. Reading these spaces as contingent and emergent events allows us to consider how a researcher's involvement in the space naturally changes it. Shivers-McNair alludes to such changes when she describes her use of cameras and then the later inclusion of recording devices by the leaders of the makerspace:

> The purpose of the video camera was not ethnographic filmmaking, but a means of accounting for mobility, bodies, knowledges, and rhetorics in the making—including the making of the research study through my active participation in the space. By that December, my mobility in the makerspace had been re-marked: I felt much more comfortable with the people, the machines, and processes in the makerspace, and I felt comfortable asking their permission to video record parts of my participatory interactions, particularly since, by that point, there were web cameras installed throughout the space and on or in several machines so that the CEO and the regulars could monitor activity. (44)

The recording of interactions in the makerspace became a regular component of the space through the installation of web cameras, which then could also monitor Shivers-McNair as a participant of the space who might not be able to capture herself otherwise with the cameras on her own body, and whose presence is likely to have changed the interactions when not recorded. Shivers-McNair's 3D interviewing method offers a unique way to capture contingent and emergent events.

Finally, we can consider Scenters-Zapico's model as a way of thinking about what mobilizes research and writing. Adapting a term from physics and aircraft engines, the third part of Scenters-Zapico's model draws us to inertia. Scenters-Zapico offers us the *OED*'s definition for inertia as "that property of matter by virtue of which it continues in its existing state, whether of rest or of uniform motion in a straight line, unless that state is altered by an external force" and ties it to the idea of an inertia starter on a plane, which was a manual way to start an aircraft engine before electric starters ("Inertia" n.d.). Inertia starters can be external or internal: Scenters-Zapico experiences external friction from his former institution, while internal inertia starters refer more to unseen psychological feelings that happen before movement. Drawing another term from physics, Shivers-McNair offers Karen Barad's definition of diffraction as a way for us to think about the boundary-marking tendencies of mobility work. Diffraction allows Shivers-McNair to approach her methodology in a way that attends and holds accountable to both the bodies of participants, but also her own researcher position. Barad defines diffraction as "the way waves combine when they overlap and the apparent bending and spreading out of waves when they encounter an obstruction" (2007, 28, qtd in Shivers-McNair 38). Shivers-McNair's 3D interviewing methodology can help draw conclusions about both internal and external inertia starters and, like Shivers-McNair in a moment of editing her footage that drew her attention again to the laser-cutting interaction with Richard, "diffract—to draw on Barad's framework—the words and movements on camera with relationships,

Mobility through Everyday Things 199

understandings, and experiences that happened off camera both before and during" the interaction (Shivers McNair 45–46). For a researcher writing about her research, as Shivers-McNair does in her chapter, the internal inertia starters come from reflecting on and reviewing data that prompt writing, while calls for papers operate as an external inertia starter. As Scenters-Zapico clarifies, "internal inertia starters inform possible movements and trajectories—but do not fully determine them" (63). While calls for papers such as the one underlying this collection can prompt researchers to write on a topic, they do not define the parameters of the work. Returning again to Shivers-McNair's case study, we see another example of inertia starters in the laser-cutting interaction; Richard functions as an inertia starter when he manipulates the plywood after it begins to warp.

However, inertia starters are not always clear. While we have Scenters-Zapico's perspective on his choices to apply for a new position and leave his institution, we do not get perspectives from the members of the institution otherwise. Another example of this absent dimension occurs in Shivers-McNair's discussion when she notes that women she met in the early part of her study who developed the space left the space over time. She presents that this disappearance is not necessarily an exclusion of this typically gendered space, but potentially as an alternative. In other words, the women might have been disinterested or lost interest, or decided they wanted to spend their time in other spaces. This movement out of the space might also reflect movement into another, similar space, especially as the existence of makerspaces and maker culture continues to grow around the world. While a person or object seems immobile in one space, she or it might be mobilizing in another.

In this response, I have offered a rereading of Shivers-McNair's case study through Scenters-Zapico's small-m to Big-M-Mobility model towards considering the implications of this model for interpreting and conducting research. Using video- and audio-recording methods can allow for rich, multidimensional data as Shivers-McNair proves but can also be potentially overwhelming. How do we account for missing dimensions, for instance? How does it impact the space for a researcher-participant, like Shivers-McNair, to be wearing a camera strapped to her head? In her study, Richard's actions show his privilege in the makerspace because of his ethos developed as a cofounder and experienced operator of the machines. As Shivers-McNair notes, if she had tried to touch the machine as he did, she would have been "stopped immediately" (46). How might her interactions be shaped if she continued this study for years and developed her maker ethos? Reversed,

Shivers-McNair's method offers additional ethical considerations about surveillance. Scenters-Zapico could not capture his movement from institution to institution using the same method; however, getting the insights of others involved in the interactions he described would add further dimensions to his reflections. Scenters-Zapico's model paired with Shivers-McNair's 3D interviewing method offer insight for us to view multiple dimensions of mobilities and new ways to conduct and interpret research.

REFERENCES

Barad, Karen. 2007. *Meeting the Universe Halfway: Quantum Physics and the Entanglement of Matter and Meaning.* Durham: Duke University Press.

Barnett, Scot, and Casey Boyle. 2016. "Rhetorical Ontology, or, How to Do Things with Things." In *Rhetoric Through Everyday Things*, edited by Scot Barnett and Casey Boyle, 1–14. Tuscaloosa: University of Alabama Press.

Bennett, Jane. 2010. *Vibrant Matter: A Political Ecology of Things.* Durham, NC: Duke University Press.

"Inertia, n." n.d. OED Online. July 10, 2017. https//en.oxforddictionaries.com/definition/inertia.

17

STAGING INGENUITY
A Pedagogical Framework of Mobilizing Creative Genre Uptake

Elizabeth Chamberlain

Writing instructors frequently task students (and themselves) with a "wicked problem" (Marback, qtd. in Wible, chapter 6): They want students to mobilize their knowledge critically and creatively, but creativity is often stifled by limitations—from students' prior genre knowledge to the brevity of the academic term. Several chapters in this volume describe media and genres that, combined with particular prompts, foster innovative uptakes. What pedagogical practices combined with what presentations of genre and media, I ask, best foster knowledge mobility? To develop a pedagogical framework of creative genre mobilization, I turn to prompt genres from Scott Wible, Carmen Kynard, and Jody Shipka. Wible calls for writing studies-wide attention to the creative problem-solving of design thinking; in this chapter, I define a frame for integrating innovative thinking into the foundational pedagogical practice of writing-assignment design. I focus on three shared qualities that I argue mobilize the potential for innovative uptake: a mix of familiar and unfamiliar media, a series of well-defined productive limitations, and a location within an ongoing genre system. These shared qualities reflect the mobilities paradigm's rejection of the stability norm, embracing the inherent dynamism of rhetorical situations. These prompts, as in most natural rhetorical situations, require that students make choices about media and genre, destabilizing their expectation of writing prompts that prescribe calcified genres.

CONSTRUCTING THE BOX: INNOVATION AND GENRE UPTAKE

I begin with the assumption that writing prompts, as all genres, sanction and provoke a particular range of uptakes; yet neither the prompts nor their uptakes are stable representatives of a genre. I use "uptake" in Anne Freadman's sense, via Anis Bawarshi (2003, 2006), to describe

DOI: 10.7330/9781646420209.c017

how genres mediate and construct social actions in textual production. When students take up a prompt, Bawarshi says, they write within "a genred site of action" that requires them to "acquire and negotiate desires, subjectivities, commitments, and relations before they begin to write" (2003, 127). That is, writing prompts and their associated uptakes are genred (structured by genre expectations), but not static genres. Genres exist only in performances, which always reshape the genres they represent. As Bawarshi puts it, "genre difference . . . [is] the norm of all genre performance" (2016, 244); Christiane Donahue similarly reminds us that "all discourse is reprise-modification, reuse in transformation, transformation in reuse" (21). Genres are always mobile, never stable—but perhaps they are most mobilized at the moment of uptake.

Students, in taking up a writing prompt, must balance the newness of that prompt against their understandings of its requested genre, mediated by their prior genre knowledge. Bawarshi describes this student negotiation between "imitation and invention" as "exist[ing] on a genre-defined continuum," with uptake thereby positioned along "the ideological interstices that configure, normalize, and activate relations and meanings within and between systems of genres" (2008, 79–80). Making these interstices visible to students—what Bawarshi elsewhere calls "inviting students to practice the iteration of a convention" (2016, 247)—can encourage them to be inventive and intentional about their uptakes.

This goal of making genre relations visible is inherent in all three qualities I highlight in Wible, Kynard, and Shipka's[1] prompts. By mixing familiar and unfamiliar media (or using familiar media in unfamiliar ways), the prompts ask students to reimagine genre expectations in service of an insistently new rhetorical situation. By defining a series of productive limitations, the prompts guide students regarding some of the most challenging aspects of generic uptake, namely "what must be acknowledged and what can be assumed as known; when to reappropriate or recontextualize (in short, transform) what's imitated as one's own invention" (Bawarshi 2008, 81). By locating the prompt within an ongoing genre system of the class, instructors offer clues about how students might take up the opportunity of the prompt to "define [their] own opportunity in relation to the prompt" (Bawarshi 2008, 81). Thus, defining a stable relationship between genres in the class, charting out how each assignment builds into the next in the sequence, is just apparent stability; it encodes multifaceted opportunities for student mobilization of genre knowledge. The prompts in these chapters create such stable systems with provocations toward mobility.

MIX OF FAMILIAR AND UNFAMILIAR MEDIA

New media-oriented pedagogies sometimes approach assignment design with a process that might be described as "add new media and stir": remediation assignments abound (à la Bolter and Grusin 2000), asking students to turn a traditional print essay into, say, a three-minute video. Yet this style of remediation, which prescribes a new medium and genre instead of providing constraints of a new rhetorical situation, produces precisely the kind of "friction" that the introduction to this collection suggests may keep even the most creative students "in place" (see introduction, this volume); students may produce interesting projects but are unlikely to take up the remediation conceptually, revising their questions or approach. Thus, early definition of a topic may foster conceptual stagnation.

Stagnation may also lurk within familiar genres. One way to foster innovational uptakes, according to Heather Bastian, is to ask students to critique unfamiliar genres. Bastian suggests that students may struggle to critique a genre that they encounter frequently because it often requires investigating "their own self-interests and privileges" (2010b, 33). In her earlier dissertation study of prompt/response sets and classrooms, Bastian similarly calls for "a pedagogy of uptake awareness and disruption that is situated within the interpretations and productions of alternative, innovative texts and that values and promotes innovation alongside convention" (2010a, 19). This pedagogical move reflects the understandings of language and genres sponsored by the mobilities paradigm, both of which Donahue positions as fluid and always changing, since all language is "retaking-up-modifying" past language (20); every text is some mixture of new and old, and being explicit about that mixture helps students see how best to mobilize their knowledge.

How, then, to mix the familiar and unfamiliar? How to promote the production of "alternative, innovative texts"? Instead of asking students to mix genres in their uptake (a stymying suggestion), prompts should draw on both familiar and unfamiliar genre practices. Wible presents one such vision: though students in his professional writing course were asked to "ideate" with familiar brainstorming materials—butcher paper and Post-it notes—the multi-step process demanded that they use these materials at unfamiliar times, in unfamiliar ways. These are typical tools for concept maps, which students are often asked to create at the outset of a project, constructing broad hierarchical overviews. Instead, Wible had students wait several weeks into their research project before they encountered the butcher paper and Post-its, after they had already done the "empathy research" of interviewing stakeholders and developing character profiles. Further making strange the tools, Wible presented them in the context of the "How Might We" genre.

Another take on how blending familiar and unfamiliar genre practices can inspire student innovation is central to Kynard's pedagogy of AfroDigital design. By emphasizing the potentials for black vernacular narrativity and visual storytelling in her prompts and examples, Kynard inspires innovative uptakes of the ePortfolio genre. Helping students see the metacognitive potential of a creative ePortfolio design gives them what Bawarshi calls "the opportunity for intervening in and resisting normalized uptakes" (2008, 80).

Shipka's "Inhabiting Dorothy" project prompted participants toward innovative uptakes also by mixing familiar and unfamiliar genres. After uploading Dorothy's photos to Flickr, Shipka put out a broad call for participants willing to "inhabit" the photos somehow. In that call, she pointed to a familiar "inhabiting" genre: the "projects where people restage or reenact their own family photos" (115). But the Dorothy project genre was truly unfamiliar in the sense that the images to be inhabited were originally taken by complete strangers. In typical restagings or reenactments, artists are limited by attempted fidelity to the original materials—photos include the same people, in similar clothing and poses. Shipka's project asked participants to imagine "inhabiting" without that impulse to fidelity. In response, some of the forty participants did indeed attempt to create "a new photographic image that replicates or updates" a Dorothy picture; but "inhabitations"/uptakes also took six other forms, including original artwork and videos (116).

WELL-DEFINED PRODUCTIVE LIMITATIONS

The mobilities framework identifies the inherent fluidity in all genre uptake, exploring how rhetors operate at the intersection of familiar and unfamiliar genres. To make visible these interstices, writing instructors ought to articulate the rules of the desired uptake. Angela Rounsaville highlights the value of presenting "sort[ing] through . . . prior genre knowledge" as a "dynamic" and explicit challenge, to help writing students achieve "high-road transfer"; she cites Mary Jo Reiff and Anis

Bawarshi's definition of "'not' genres," which are "a way of naming that transitory space between familiar and unfamiliar writing tasks." These generic rules are different from the abstract, arbitrary rules that Kerry Dirk found so often define writing prompts, such as, "You must include at least three quotations in your paper," and "The essay must include an original and interesting title, using a colon." "Yet such requirements," Dirk points out, "are not constraints of a genre but constraints determined by the teacher" (Dirk 2012, 10); in fact, they are likely to make students slavish to the rules, even "citing the prompt explicitly in a way that shatters the illusion of self-sufficiency we desire students to create" (Bawarshi 2003, 134). Better prompts help students define the typified rhetorical actions expected of any given uptake.

Wible's "How Might We" brainstorming rules, for instance—deferring judgement, building on each other's ideas, visualizing, and "headlining"— all define what the writing should do rather than prescribing particular surface features. I do not mean to suggest surface features are unimportant; indeed, Wible describes how the content and form of the Post-its become defined by the "Headline" rule. Bastian similarly recommends the "game rules" genre as a means of "delay[ing] habitual uptakes of writing assignments" (2010a, 126). Yet these rules maintain the focus on action, not form.

Andrene's call-and-response "data analysis" section is another example of how strict limitations can nevertheless prompt creative responses when the rules of the genre are presented as focusing on social action rather than specific surface features. Kynard required that the research project follow a fairly strict IMRAD format, but within sections, Andrene had more play. Kynard demonstrates how Andrene uses literal boxes to think outside the typical data analysis box. This performance aligns with Bawarshi's definition of "genre agency," a "strategic genre performance . . . within asymmetrical relations of power" (2016, 246).

Though Shipka's prompt was more open than Wible's or Kynard's (calling on participants to "inhabit" Dorothy's images), the images themselves create specific limitations, what Friedrich Kittler calls the "distinguishing particulars" of imprinting media (1999, 83). Dorothy's piles of laundry, her proto-selfie, and her 1957 birthday cake are all insistently, distinguishingly particular. Shipka's interviews with participants suggest that many interpreted that particularity to develop genre cues and rules; Michaels' uptake, for example, seized upon the cake as a genre, which led her to muse on the familiarity of another typified social action, "trying to replicate some food photo that I saw online" (120).

LOCATION WITHIN AN ONGOING GENRE SYSTEM

The final shared quality I'll address in these three writing prompts is well-trod, and thus I will be briefer: Many who have written about classroom genre uptake have emphasized the importance of locating writing within a larger activity system. If we accept (as we do) that genres are "typified rhetorical actions based in recurrent situations" (Miller 1984, 159), then we must establish generic exigency and avoid presenting classroom assignments in a rhetorical vacuum. When we don't do so, Dirk suggests, we may be "teaching students how to use a piece of sporting equipment that belongs to no specific game" (2012, 6). Thus, Wible presents the butcher paper and Post-it activity within the context of a term-long design thinking project. Kynard presents the ePortfolio as a capstone, organizing and showcasing a semester of work. And Shipka presents the "inhabiting" prompt in the context of her own previous work with the Dorothy archive, including her "Past, Present, Presence" video. For contrast, consider the prompts Dirk collected that presented "the 'research paper'" as a self-evident, "isolated utterance" (2012, 2). We must not pretend that classroom genres can be acontextual; there is no genre without context, and all genre performances transform their contexts.

TOWARD A FRAMEWORK

Though I am reluctant to suggest that there is a formula for creativity, I do mean to argue that there is a formula for writing prompt genres that are better at mobilizing creative uptakes. Some rules stifle; others open up possibilities. The ongoing challenge of assigning writing, then, is finding rules that create a stable space for experimentation while minimizing the "friction" that keeps students from destabilizing uptakes. The best prompts, I argue, invite students to reimagine genres as a mobile framework of remixable rules and expectations, resources available for a writer's marshaling. Wible, Kynard, and Shipka's prompts point toward one potential mobile framework. These genres have a whiff of the familiar, put to new rhetorical ends; they constrain uptake playfully and productively but not arbitrarily; and they are positioned within long-standing genre systems that work toward clear social actions. Together, they paint a picture of a writing classroom that, ideally, will help students at once develop writing knowledge and literacies that can transfer to other rhetorical situations, and mobilize that knowledge toward creative ends—even perhaps, as in Andrene's case, toward critical consciousness.

NOTE

1. I recognize that Shipka's prompt is not classroom-based, not mandatory or graded, and did not prescribe a strict timeline for participants; in these ways, it is a somewhat different genre than the classroom prompt. Yet, for the purposes of this chapter, I will be treating it as part of the "prompt genre."

REFERENCES

Bastian, Heather. 2010a. "Disrupting Conventions: When and Why Writers Take Up Innovation." Dissertation, University of Kansas.

Bastian, Heather. 2010b. "The Genre Effect: Exploring the Unfamiliar." *Composition Studies* 38 (1): 29–51.

Bawarshi, Anis. 2003. *Genre and the Invention of the Writer: Reconsidering the Place of Invention in Composition.* Logan: Utah State University Press.

Bawarshi, Anis. 2006. "Taking Up Language Differences in Composition." *College English* 68 (6): 652–656.

Bawarshi, Anis. 2016. "Beyond the Genre Fixation: A Translingual Perspective on Genre." *College English* 78 (3): 242–248.

Bawarshi, Anis. 2008. "Genres as Forms of In(ter)vention." In *Originality, Imitation, and Plagiarism: Teaching Writing in the Digital Age,* edited by Martha Vicinus and Caroline Eisner, 79–89. Ann Arbor: University of Michigan Press.

Bolter, Jay David, and Richard Grusin. 2000. *Remediation: Understanding New Media.* Cambridge, MA: MIT Press.

Dirk, Kerry. 2012. "The 'Research Paper' Prompt: A Dialogic Opportunity for Transfer." *Composition Forum* 25.

Kittler, Friedrich A. 1999. *Gramophone, Film, Typewriter.* Stanford: Stanford University Press.

Miller, Carolyn R. 1984. "Genre as Social Action." *Quarterly Journal of Speech* 70: 151–167.

Rounsaville, Angela. 2012. "Selecting Genres for Transfer: The Role of Uptake in Students' Antecedent Genre Knowledge." *Composition Forum* 26.

18

GENRE UPTAKE AND MOBILITY
Making Meaning in Mobilized Contexts

Keri Epps

At the 2016 Watson Symposium, Anis Bawarshi encouraged participants to consider how genres direct and manage rhetorical energies. This (re)direction of genres is often understood as genre *uptake*, which Anne Freadman explains as "what happens when you accept an invitation to a conference, or agree to rewrite a paper for publication . . . , or disagree with, or explore, a proposition in theory" (2002, 39). Defining *uptake* as "the bidirectional relation that holds between [genres]," Freadman uses "bidirectional" to underline the ways genre uptake involves a give-and-take with antecedent and emerging genre(s) (Freadman 2002, 40).[1] Freadman's definition reinforces a notion that I further investigate here in the context of mobility, which is that genres are constantly *shaping* and being *shaped by* the contexts in which uptake occurs, and consequently, enabling the "management and direction of rhetorical energies (or mobilities)," as Bawarshi remarked in his conclusions at the symposium.

What I hope to make more explicit in this response is how the give-and-take between genres involves several agents—namely, the genre *users* and their nonlinear genre choices—and is made more visible by mobility models. More specifically, the mobility models offered in the collection reveal the power structures and ideologies embedded in genres that both enable and often constrain or challenge mobility (understood as *movement plus meaning*). Ann Shivers-McNair, for instance, questions how we mark mobility and who/what "counts" or "matters" (36). Other authors in this collection similarly interrogate the complexity of mobility and use mobility models and theories to highlight the dynamism, fluidity, flexibility, and even pacing of interactions among language-users, written and oral texts, and their sociocultural contexts. I use this understanding of mobility as dynamic and flexible to explore genres and their uptake in the essay's examples and thus illustrate how genres direct users' actions, meaning-making,

DOI: 10.7330/9781646420209.c018

and responses in ways that can be beneficial to them, but in several cases make the user's vulnerability in certain contexts more visible (e.g., John's professional move and Nimet's navigation of different institutions and bureaucratic processes). Thus, this response, also an example of genre uptake, considers a selection of the chapters' mobility models to offer a clearer view of the reciprocal relationship between genres, language, users, and contexts and how users can use genres as resources for navigating inhibiting power structures and making those structures more visible.

Exploring such issues, I lean on Freadman's theory of uptake and respond to Anis Bawarshi's argument in his *College English* article "Beyond the Genre Fixation," which asks genre researchers to recognize the limitations of studying genres as "sites" or as stable structures that can be explicated for specific characteristics or conventions. He writes: "In our preoccupation with genres as sites of access, we have tended to privilege genres as things that can be made explicit through explication, and we have fixated on trying to figure out which genres are best taught when and where" (2016, 244). Though Bawarshi's argument focuses on a pedagogical exigence, I follow his lead here to further suggest the mobility models introduced in this collection, although they do not focus explicitly on rhetorical genres, support the argument that the fixation on genre explication is not enough. The chapters, for example, show many ways that genres are taken up, propel genre users into action (in often limited ways, given power structures in play), and change the contexts in which that action is occurring. Further, the mobility models make inhibiting power structures more visible or able to be marked, as Ann Shivers-McNair calls for in her chapter. Such power structures inhibit the genre users represented in the essays, or push and pull them into a temporary "stasis" that then leads to future mobility. A closer look at genre use in the examples offered by Rebecca Lorimer Leonard, John Scenters-Zapico, and Christiane Donahue reveal genres as resources for discerning meaning in highly volatile situations and for navigating shifting power dynamics and ideologies in such contexts. Using mobility as represented in these essays and considering several agents of genre uptake, we can better understand how (1) genre and genre uptake involve complex, necessarily messy relationships between user, contexts, languages, medium of delivery, and other genres and (2) help users see *meaning*, the second part of mobility, that users are trying to *make visible* or *expose* through genre to negotiate power structures that are sometimes (or often) working against them in mobilized contexts.

AGENTS OF GENRE UPTAKE

The pieces in this collection offer insight into how we might see several dimensions of genre uptake at work, and importantly, how structures of power are embedded and reinstantiated in rhetorical genres. The essays also highlight the potential of genres to facilitate mobility even through false starts or moments of stasis (Scenters-Zapico). In other words, such moments arise when the writer feels stalled because of institutional or cultural barriers that at first seem to *prohibit* mobility, but actually *facilitate* it. Further, the models and examples explored here reveal some of the complex decision-making taking place as the writers/genre users find themselves navigating unstable, constantly shifting contexts and trying to find meaning in situations they have not previously encountered.

In "Managing Writing on the Move," Rebecca Lorimer Leonard analyzes Nimet's rich repertoire of literate practices and addresses the different types of mobility—including mobilities across various repertoires and the "regimes" of work and school—that Nimet manages (69). Discussing the fixed and fluid literacies that Nimet shapes and is shaped by, Lorimer Leonard offers an insightful example of Nimet's experience with letter writing, a personal genre that offers Nimet the opportunity to exercise a great deal of control that is not possible in the other institutionalized genres discussed elsewhere in the essay. In the interview, Nimet discusses the letter as a genre that "makes a journey," and she details the process of writing the letter's salutation and closing and the ways she grappled with language choices (73). Specifically, she notes her struggle to decide on correct verbs and synonyms to replace words she felt were "wrong." As Lorimer Leonard's analysis shows, the process Nimet describes reveals that she also sensed a tension between the modalities of orality and letter writing. Yet while she experiences some difficulty with certain genre choices, Nimet also explains the unique way she delivered this letter to her friend in Azerbaijan by folding the letter and putting it inside of a laptop she was delivering as a gift. Her decision to change the medium of delivery for her letter by combining old and new media thus shows Nimet creatively and thoughtfully making decisions that influence the reception of her letter, adding yet another dimension to Nimet's management of mobility and her management of genre uptake.

In analyzing this excerpt, Lorimer Leonard concludes that the letter allows Nimet to manage mobility on a number of levels, some of which include "sending a gift to a friend, staying in touch with another friend, thinking among her languages, and intentionally composing only in

English" (73). In other words, Nimet makes thoughtful, layered genre decisions to meet her intended rhetorical ends. Although this personal genre eliminates much of the need to negotiate deeply embedded power structures like those illustrated in the nursing school assignment examples, which Lorimer Leonard posits are controlled or managed institutionally, we nevertheless see ways that genre users can take control and direct their own mobility when they have the resources—material and linguistic—to do so (chapter 4). Yet even in situations where Nimet was able to "control" her literacy repertoire, some of her letter writing choices still caused her great anxiety as she went through the writing process—arguably, some of the same decisions that caused her anxiety in navigating her nursing assignments and the institutional processes required for obtaining her degree. Thus, in Lorimer Leonard's example, we can see Nimet shaping the genres through her careful movements across literacy repertoires, regimes, and cultural contexts, and in turn, see the genres and their uptake also reciprocally shaping Nimet's own experience, including her anxiety, with participating in different language systems and genres and experimenting with different forms of delivering her message(s).

Contrasting Nimet's experience with a personal genre with which she felt both comfort and anxiety, John Scenters-Zapico's model of mobility involves several formal and institutional genres that enabled and prevented his professional relocation from UTEP to CSULB. He introduces the piece explaining his dissatisfaction with not knowing the *hows* and *whys* of the many academics who make similar moves to his own. In other words, moves are treated as static events or as "news" rather than complex, dynamic processes (51). The author wants to make such processes, and the many logistics and affective responses involved, visible. To do so, he offers a mobility model that accommodates a range of mobilities—including those that underlie moments of dissatisfaction or stasis that later facilitate mobility. This model, which he calls the "small m–mobilities paradigm," offers several points that highlight how certain genres can shape and *force* genre users' actions in specific contexts in which power structures are deeply sedimented and quite difficult to navigate.

In discussing the small-m mobilities model, Scenters-Zapico recognizes that "[m]obility spaces, in order to be studied, need some form of visible or even defined unseen area of examination" (55). Although he is not specifically referencing genre here, his argument aligns well with my own proposition that mobility models can make certain interactions between agents of genre uptake, in these "flow" spaces, much more

212   EPPS

visible. And if the interactions are more visible, we can also recognize how the genres being used or transacted reinforce power structures and/or help genre users subvert them in ways that allow them to move forward, or move at all, like in this author's case. For instance, Scenters-Zapico explains his interactions with several genres that facilitated his relocation. Noting the genres working together here—including multiple email correspondences, job postings, job application documents, and a new job contract—we can more clearly see the many considerations and actions occurring in the "flow" spaces that both stalled and enabled John's mobility.

Though Scenters-Zapico offers multiple examples of genres relevant to this response, this brief summary shows a number of connected genres that are being taken up by John and other agents to ensure his professional relocation; yet, as the author's framework of internal and external inertia starters suggests, the relationship between the genres also depends on his willingness to wait or prolong his forward movement to respond to individual correspondences, to decide when and how to update his résumé for returning to the job market, and to negotiate deeply complex institutional settings. For instance, the author describes in detail the many emails and face-to-face interactions that took place after he received his new job contract at CSULB, but the delayed responses by the administrators, especially their delay in putting together a counteroffer, ultimately forced his and UTEP's hands and led him to accept the offer at CSULB. Even though UTEP was supposedly trying to keep him, John ultimately had to tell them it was too late (chapter 3). What I find most compelling about this example is that John's genre choices and responses to several delays demonstrate how the genre user(s) must carefully consider possibilities for genre uptake to ensure their mobility amidst institutionalized power and must be attentive to timing—or the kairotic moments in which they respond that allow them the most "gains" in their movement. His example is, thus, an appropriate one to show how the genre *user* and his or her needs should be accounted for and made visible in genre uptake to better understand how genres connect not only to each other, but also facilitate mobility among genres, contexts, users, media, and languages.

EXPOSING AND MAKING MEANING THROUGH GENRE

Premises that led me to select these essays included the authors' reflections on specific genres and their uptake and their common argumentative thread of mobility as dynamic and recursive meaning-making. More specifically, in situations like John's relocation or Nimet's experiences with letter writing and nursing school assignments, we see how the meanings derived from genre use actually made or shaped *them* and required extra effort and resources to shift the power dynamics in ways that could, in fact, help mobilize them. Christiane Donahue's theoretical explanation of how transfer, translingualism, and mobility intersect has several useful points for thinking about how genre and genre uptake allow for meaning to be made and for power hierarchies to be negotiated at this intersection. For instance, she draws on Bakhtin's theory of speech genres to theorize *code*, writing, "the 'code' in question can be no longer an overall descriptor of a stable language entity but a way of studying the bits (Bakhtin's 'language system') that *combine and recombine in an unending transformative mobile activity of production of* utterances, and that are themselves not stable bits, as they construct their meaning partly in use" (27, emphasis mine). The constant combining and recombining possibilities with each code reinforce the notion that even something that *seems* stable (at least momentarily) or capable of being disassembled and moved around in stable bits, like a *code* or a *genre*, can be more adequately understood as constantly mobile and endlessly generative of new utterances, genres, and meanings.

In addition to Bakhtin's theory, Donahue leans heavily on perhaps an even more useful theory for contemplating how genres help make meaning-making and power negotiation possible: Frédéric François' theory of *reprise-modification*. Donahue explains that in English *reprise* is primarily relegated to music, meaning "reuse of material"; its original eighteenth-century French meaning, however, is defined as "taken up again" and used in a much broader context (20). Donahue shows through her discussion that *reprise-modification* helps us theorize and see that "*All* language use is always re-use, making the new from the existing: all composing is recomposing" (20). One important result of Donahue's use of this theory is that it has the potential to reveal the cracks or fissures in language where new meaning-making can occur, and likewise, where power can be redirected by and to the genre user. In other words, as every "new" use of language, or a genre, occurs, so does more potential for change and (arguably) displacement of former uses and power dynamics associated with the language and/ or genre.

I want to expand on Donahue's (re)theorization a bit by adding genre uptake to the mix and recognizing how genre change occurs from always making *new* meaning through users' responses to changing contexts, especially in regard to time, place, and specific circumstances.

214 EPPS

Considering genre uptake in relation to *reprise-modification* is important to mobility studies because it includes and reveals the ways users must face power structures and ideological bearings that may stall mobility. As we saw with Nimet's reprise of the letter genre, for instance, even though we cannot be sure of its reception, the letter genre being written in a certain language and delivered through a very unique medium had great potential in changing the context in which it was delivered, read, and perhaps used. By calling on Donahue's use of *reprise-modification*, we can see that genre change, as it occurs because of the particulars of the singular moment in which it takes place, can lead to creating "new" genres through its repetition and uptake and can expose the cracks/ fissures that allow for new meaning to occur and for the potential shifting of power that makes mobility possible for users in somewhat vulnerable positions (because of race, class, gender, cultural background, etc.).

CONCLUSION: SOME IMPLICATIONS FOR GENRE UPTAKE AND MOBILITY STUDIES

The essays in this collection helped make clear that mobility models can make the many agents of genre uptake—namely, the genres, languages, users, media, and contexts—more visible and show how the complex relationships between them enable and require the negotiation of power hierarchies. As this selection of essays attests, studying mobility and genre uptake is messy, and seeing the two together, reciprocally informing the other, allows us to account for the many moving parts that are contributing to meaning-making. Using and expanding on Anne Freadman's theory of uptake to examine the examples the authors in this collection offer allows genre and mobility researchers to think about ways to get beyond the flat relationships existing just between genres or just between genre users, etc. Rather, using uptake enables a more comprehensive understanding of the dynamic, messy relationships occurring among genres, languages, users, media, and contexts involved in negotiating power dynamics in ways that both inhibit and instigate desired mobilities. Ultimately, this comprehensive framework can help us see who and what "count" and get marked as visible and valued in mobilized contexts.

NOTE

1 Other helpful explanations of genre uptake can be found in Bawarshi and Reiff (2010) and Tachino (2012).

REFERENCES

Bawarshi, Anis. 2016. "Beyond the Genre Fixation: A Translingual Perspective on Genre." *College English* 78 (3): 243–249.

Bawarshi, Anis, and Mary Jo Reiff. 2010. *Genre: An Introduction to History, Theory, and Pedagogy*. West Lafayette, IN and Fort Collins, CO: Parlor Press and WAC Clearinghouse.

Freadman, Anne. 2002. "Uptake." In *The Rhetoric and Ideology of Genre: Strategies for Stability and Change*, edited by Richard M. Coe, Lorelai Lingard, and Tatiana Teslenko, 39–53. Cresskill, NJ: Hampton University Press.

Tachino, Tosh. 2012. "Theorizing Uptake and Knowledge Mobilization: A Case for Intermediary Genre." *Written Communication* 29 (4): 455–476.

19

REGARDING OUR DISCIPLINARY FUTURE(S)
Toward a Mobilities Framework for Agency

Rick Wysocki

> [T]he representations of agency that we make available to ourselves are not the result of determining how to formulate and apply a rule (or a theory) but of our feelings about the possibilities of consequential action and how we recognize and justify what we do.
>
> —Trimbur (2000, 288)

In this passage, excerpted from his 2000 *JAC* article, John Trimbur offers a method for conceiving of agency that has, for me, become equal parts heuristic and mantra. I take Trimbur to mean that how we think about the locations, the holders, and the possibilities of agency both reflects and *in*flects our understandings of futures within and outside of rhetoric and composition. Focusing on the chapters of Scott Wible, Jody Shipka, and Christiane Donahue, in this response I attempt to tease out at least three possible trajectories emerging from our disciplinary imaginary that call attention to the intersections of agency, our work, and our disciplinary future(s) in productive and challenging ways. Furthermore, I claim that each author constructs certain paradigms of rhetorical activity through their representations of agency and that their representations frame what "counts" as the work of composing in new ways. As Ann Shivers-McNair suggests in this collection, "the boundary marks we draw shape who and what come to matter, and who and what are excluded from mattering—not only in physical spaces but also in onto-epistemological spaces" (38). To borrow the terms taken up by Shivers-McNair, it behooves us to consider how the boundaries we draw around agency inflect our *disciplinary* onto-epistemologies—that is, our *being* and *knowing* as a field.

With this in mind, I argue for embracing mobility and positioning ourselves in such a way that we are able to mobilize Shipka, Wible,

DOI: 10.7330/9781646420209.c019

and Donahue's paradigms, entering them into productive entanglements (Shivers-McNair, chapter 2). I am informed in this respect by Tim Cresswell's argument that "a focus on empirical mobilities necessitates both mobile theorization and mobile methodologies in order to avoid seeing mobility from the point of view which privileges notions of boundedness and the sedentary" (2011, 552). A mobilities framework for agency that takes up the spirit of Cresswell's call, as I will suggest at the close of this essay, can help us to recognize and design futures that assert human, semiotic agency alongside the real agencies of technologies and nonhuman actors generally.

DESIGN AGENCY

Wible, in his chapter, articulates a pedagogy based on the principles of design thinking, charting the similarities between writing and designing and stressing the need for mobile, human-centered approaches to each (chapter 6). Design thinking, which he describes as "a theory and method aimed at developing solutions through direct, regular engagement with people," offers a way of thinking through how writing and ethnographic research can be synthesized in order to imagine innovative or novel approaches to "wicked problems" (95).[1] Furthermore, Wible's pedagogy traverses media and modes, integrating and taking seriously the semiotic affordances of seemingly "traditional" forms of writing, oral performance, and short-form composing made mobile through Post-it notes that are valued precisely *because* of their constraints (100). Drawing connections between the ideational practices described by design thinking methodologies and practices of invention relied on by our field, Wible asks us to reconsider the relationship between writing, multimodality, and design.

That this relationship implicates conceptions of agency is both suggested by Wible and also articulated explicitly by design theorists. The New London Group, for example, called for a reconception of the composing process based on the metaphor of design, asserting that "we are both inheritors of patterns and conventions of meaning and at the same time active designers of meaning. And, as designers of meaning, we are designers of social futures—workplace futures, public futures, and community futures" (1996, 65). By thinking about composing through the lens of design (as both verb and noun, practice and aim), we can then recognize semiotic practice as an endless, agentive process of redesigning the materials available to us. This human-centered perspective, to be sure, resonates with discussions of learning by "making" in higher education. As one example, the organization Agency by Design developed through Harvard's Project Zero has sought to explore how designing and making practices can be taken up in education to develop better environments for learning (Agency by Design 2016).

Wible's contribution is therefore necessary, as it extends the work of scholars familiar to our field—the New London Group (1996) and Richard Marback (2009), among others—to argue for the relevance of rhetoric and composition within shifting educational apparatuses. However critical one might be of the influence of design thinking and "making" practices within universities and the economy generally—and there are compelling reasons for criticism—Wible shows that there is, or should be, a seat for us at the table. He thus broadcasts one possible future for rhetoric and composition, one in which we consider more seriously design agency—human-centered activity that is, by definition, mobile, transformative, and unfixed—as both an influence on and a description of what we do. Furthermore, Wible's transformation of design thinking to meet the purposes of rhetoric and composition reveals not only the author's own design agency but also the mobile nature of agency itself, a phenomenon that—as indicated in the introduction to this collection—should be considered not as a deviation but the norm (chapter 6). That Wible's own framework will also certainly be repurposed in scholarship and in teaching only further demonstrates this mobility.

DISTRIBUTED AGENCY

But, as Shipka contends, objects also have designs on us. In her chapter, Shipka resoundingly calls for widening our conception of agency to include nonhuman as well as human actors and for a radical expansion of what "counts" as both composing and as the work of our field. Furthermore, as Shipka's title suggests, the relationship between presence and collaboration is productively called into question: the author illustrates ways that composing traverses both spatial and temporal vectors, going so far as to suggest that the recompositions she discusses function as "collaborating with the dead" (114). If Wible's pedagogy is based on the principles of human-centered design, Shipka calls attention to the ways that humans and their agencies are *re*-centered not only through their negotiations with other people but also by the objects and artifacts with which they interact.

It is, from my perspective, increasingly difficult to argue with the idea that agency is distributed among human and nonhuman actors.

As Erik Brynjolfsson and Andrew McAfee have argued in their research on the promise (threat?) of a "second machine age" rivaling that of the Industrial Revolution, "Computers and other digital advances are doing for mental power—the ability to use our brains to understand and shape our environments—what the steam engine did for muscle power" (2014, 7–8). While, like design thinking, there is much to be wary of in this technological transformation, there is, at least, hope for composing. As Brynjolfsson and McAfee note, while technological advances are accelerating toward artificial intelligence, self-driving cars, and fully-automated labor power, one thing that researchers have yet to figure out is *ideation*. Furthermore, the authors explicitly frame composing as an example of this limitation: "Programs that can write clean prose are amazing achievements, but we've not yet seen one that can figure out what to write next" (191).

Though I seem to have digressed, I contend that Shipka's insights become not only useful but fundamentally necessary in the possible future depicted by Bynjolfsson and McAfee. First, Shipka's forceful attention to the interaction between various types of actors in not only digital but material compositions can attenuate the reservations some might have about the future of composing in increasingly technological scenes. While there are important differences between "material" and "digital" composing, Shipka reminds us that *all* compositions emerge from the intersecting agencies of humans, objects, and contexts (chapter 7).[2] Second, her focus on how composing spans modes and media intimates a second possible future for the work of rhetoric and composition. While neither Shipka nor I would advocate for the abandonment of either alphabetic text or the importance of human phenomena, seeing these as mobilized within complex, distributed environments of possible modes and agencies provides another set of potentialities for our field.

TRANSLINGUAL AGENCY

Turning to Donahue's chapter, it is tempting to double back and claim that she, like Wible, is interested in design agency as a model for the discipline. This is true to a degree, but whereas Wible is interested in the actual methodology of design thinking and its potential for our work, Donahue is more interested in design as a metaphor for a translingual orientation toward the mobility of linguistic practices. Drawing on Frédéric François's concept of "*reprises-modifications*," an orientation that calls attention to how language is practiced by way of transformative transportation, Donahue asserts that both translingualism and knowledge transfer are necessarily marked by mobility (chapter 1).

From this perspective, she articulates a form of translingual agency[3] that frames individuals as always agentive as they linguistically (re)design the world (chapter 1). In addition, Donahue puts pressure on the notion of object-agency discussed above by writing that "[t]he kind of *writing* knowledge needed today is mobile knowledge, movement from mooring to mobility, a movement across not just time but space, and above all a movement that only matters if the writer has imbued it with meaning" (22). In other words, the translingual agency described by Donahue is necessarily (and solely) human because it requires the agentive transformation of language through the situated linguistic practices of individuals.

I have already revealed my opinion that an attention to nonhuman actors and agencies is necessary for our increasingly technologically-driven world (though, as I also mentioned in relation to Shipka, composing has always required the employment of composing technologies). This does not discount Donahue's human-focused argument for the relationship between mobility and translingualism/knowledge transfer. We must always, as Donahue claims from a Serresian orientation, attend to the transformations that take place during transportation. In the language of Bruno Latour (a student of Michel Serres), language is a mediator; its output always exceeds its input.[4] By attending to the translingual, transformative capacities of language use, Donahue projects an interdisciplinary future in which we draw more heavily on the insights of linguistics. As the author claims, these insights are necessary for the field's attention to both translingualism and knowledge transfer as we respond to an increasingly globalized, mobile world (chapter 1).

A MOBILITIES FRAMEWORK FOR AGENCY

I have so far attempted to map the three articulations of agency produced, respectively, by Wible, Shipka, and Donahue in their chapters. Furthermore, I have sought to discern what sorts of futures they might mobilize for our field. It might seem enticing, at this point, to set these ideas against each other, to make them do battle in the critical arena in order to determine which conception of agency is "correct." As I conclude this response, however, I want to suggest that this would be misguided, because doing so would render these frameworks as fixed and stable, thus contradicting each of their careful contributions to our understanding of mobility. As discussed in the collection introduction, mobility should not be "approached as a problem to be solved in order to return to what we imagine should normally happen" (4).

Any articulation of agency—that is, any attempt to define or circumscribe, permanently or impermanently, the contours of how the world moves—might seem at first glance to require that we stabilize its subject. How else could the agencies of people, technologies, and objects be scrutinized other than to pin them down and subject them to the critical gaze? Paradoxically, however—and within this insight lies the true purchase of mobility studies—these articulations are the *product of mobility*, and as soon as they are assembled, they themselves also begin to move. My argument for recognizing the distribution of agency across various forms of actors, for example, may be read as a definitive statement fixed in text, but in reality it is an event emerging through the mobility between myself, Wible, Shipka, Donahue, the various other authors I discuss, my computer, the coffee I drink as I write, and so on. Most important, it is an anticipation of future mobilizations not fully under its control: the various *reprises-modifications* it will be subjected to when read.

Wible, Shipka, and Donahue's work is essential because they each depict various moves through which we can "get at" the ways that activity travels through and mobilizes the world. Each of the futures these scholars forecast is marked by negotiation—of disciplinary boundaries, of the distributed agencies of humans and nonhumans, and of the transformations produced by language-in-use. To meet these futures, we should privilege a conceptual fluidity capable of discerning the multifarious actors and agencies that make and remake the landscapes we study. Doing so requires, as my title suggests, that we remain mobile in the ways we interpret and exert agency, and that we attend to the ways that agencies mobilize and are mobilized in the world.

NOTES

1. Wible draws the concept of "wicked problems" from Richard Marback (2009), who describes them as "wicked because they are never fully solvable; they are contingent problems of deciding what to do that require resolution 'over and over again'" (W399).

2. That being said, we can (and, I would argue, must) remain critical of the effect of technological automation, and the neoliberal "flexibility" that often accompanies it, on labor practices.

3. By "translingual agency" I refer to the idea that language is constantly and necessarily reshaped through use and the related idea of linguistic difference as the norm. For articulations of translingual agency (besides the one offered by Donahue in this collection), see Lu and Horner (2013); Pennycook (2010); and Canagarajah (2013).

4. "Mediators transform, translate, distort, and modify the meaning or the elements they are supposed to carry" (Latour 2005, 39).

REFERENCES

Agency by Design. 2016. "About Us." *Agency by Design.* Project Zero. http://www.agency bydesign.org/.

Brynjolfsson, Erik, and Andrew McAfee. 2014. *The Second Machine Age: Work, Progress, and Prosperity in a Time of Brilliant Technologies.* New York: Norton.

Canagarajah, A. Suresh. 2013. *Translingual Practice: Global Englishes and Cosmopolitan Relations.* Abingdon, UK: Routledge.

Cresswell, Tim. 2011. "Mobilities I: Catching Up." *Progress in Human Geography* 35 (4): 550–558.

Latour, Bruno. 2005. *Reassembling the Social: An Introduction to Actor-Network-Theory.* Oxford: Oxford University Press.

Lu, Min-Zhan, and Bruce Horner. 2013. "Translingual Literacy, Language Difference, and Matters of Agency." *College English* 75 (6): 582–607.

Marback, Richard. 2009. "Embracing Wicked Problems: The Turn to Design in Composition Studies." *College Composition and Communication* 61 (2): W397-W419.

The New London Group. 1996. "A Pedagogy of Multiliteracies: Designing Social Futures." *Harvard Educational Review* 66 (1): 60–92.

Pennycook, Alastair. 2010. *Language as a Local Practice.* Abingdon, UK: Routledge.

Trimbur, John. 2000. "Agency and the Death of the Author: A Partial Defense of Modernism." *JAC: A Journal of Composition Theory* 20 (2): 283–298.

20

MAKING MOBILITY WORK FOR WRITING STUDIES

Rachel Gramer and Mary P. Sheridan

Writing studies researchers have a long tradition of examining the possibilities and pitfalls of importing methodological frameworks, ideally interrogating how and why we borrow from and adapt other fields' methodologies (see Sheridan 2012). The chapters in this collection enact this move as they interweave mobility studies frameworks with methodologies more familiar to us as a discipline. Some scholars try out terms and frameworks; others highlight deep alignments across frameworks; still others fully embrace and intermingle multiple frameworks to work toward new inquiries. As writing studies scholars invested in methodological reflection, we applaud such efforts that help us see what mobility studies might afford us as a framework. As feminist writing scholars more specifically, we are interested in how mobility studies might address persistent methodological questions about power's often unmarked presence, an issue central to meaning-making in sites of literacy and education. Given this commitment, we are dedicated to asking how intersections between mobility and writing studies might be methodologically generative for studying writing and the power that constrains and enables knowledge-making, research, and teaching in our discipline.

In this response, we examine how three chapters intermingle and interrogate mobility as a new framework. To do this, we offer a brief history and analysis of mobility studies as it has been constructed by chapter authors. Then, we analyze three chapters—by Scott Wible, Eli Goldblatt, and Carmen Kynard—with two purposes. First, we explicate how each chapter uses mobility alongside other methodologies and toward what end(s). Second, we suggest how writing studies scholars might engage mobility studies in future iterations to address long-standing questions of power. We conclude by remaining open to the potential for mobility studies as a methodology in writing studies that can support us in

DOI: 10.7330/9781646420209.c020

improving how we study *what* moves while also addressing *how* and *why* bodies, ideas, and identities move in relation to embodied power. Yet we also caution against adopting a methodological trend without vigorously *making it work for us* to pose questions that speak back to and challenge entrenched power in needed ways.

HOW DOES MOBILITY WORK?

Often marked as coalescing in the early 2000s, mobility studies developed as a social sciences critique of an implicit sedentarist bias in research paradigms that historically presumed things—cultures, people, ideas, rights, networks—were still and stable as a standardized, unmarked norm. Oft-cited mobility scholars Tim Cresswell and Peter Adey are credited with formulating mobility studies as an area of inquiry interested in movement and power that emerged out of research trajectories in cultural studies and anthropology from the 1980s and 1990s. Scholars in this collection reference foundational works by Cresswell and Adey, in which we see three pertinent concepts in mobility studies that point to the slipperiness of terms and the complex omnipresence of mobility and power. The first is that mobility is not the same as movement. Movement can be understood as a fact or event too easily decontextualized or flattened; that someone moves (and where), for example, is a fact or sequential event. By contrast, mobility studies aims to interrogate why and how someone's mobility is constrained or sustained. Not wanting to limit mobility to terms that carry specific privilege (or not) (e.g., travel, migrate), Cresswell situates mobility as a capacious umbrella term to describe any movement that is socially produced and contextualized (2001, 19–20). The second concept is that mobility is a complex norm that historical (and contemporary) binaries fail to illuminate. Mobility scholars maintain that, theoretically, mobility has been held in suspicion or celebrated (Cresswell 2001, 19), grounded in sedentarist bias or transgressive power (Adey 2006, 77). Yet Adey debunks the binary of sedentary and nomadic approaches, suggesting that mobility is an ontological absolute, that even seemingly immobile things move or change if we observe them long enough, and that the world is continually changing, "brought anew" over time (2006, 82). This view further challenges the treatment of mobility as activated only in visible movement, suggesting that, if we are to see the world—and our ways of knowing it—as mobile (Cresswell 2001, 17–19), we need to understand mobility as a complex omnipresent norm that is neither inherently constraining nor liberatory.

We see the third concept, emerging from and expanding upon the first two, as especially salient for feminist writing research because it concerns power. If mobility is about socially produced meaning and culturally recognized norms, then mobility studies must attend to questions of power. Creswell writes that mobility is "a meaningful and power-laden geographical phenomenon" that "is produced and given meaning within relations of power. There is then no mobility outside of power" (2001, 20). For Creswell, key mobility questions are not only who moves, but how, who benefits, and how does mobility become meaningful (25)? Adey suggests that "[t]here is not an innate or essentialist meaning to movement. Mobility instead gains meaning through its embeddedness within societies, culture, politics, histories" (2006, 83), arguing that "[i]f we are to take the 'mobility turn' seriously, academic scholarship should not fail to realize the relations and differences between movements" (91). Adey's seemingly simple statement hints at the deep methodological complexities involved in studying differences in *what* moves (people and ideas, which are both vital but should not be conflated) (see Creswell 2001, 14–15), *how* things move, and how these movements are *related*. For writing researchers who want to discover how a deep engagement with mobility studies might work for us, Adey's assertion points us directly to the challenges of studying mobility and meaning within and across dynamic social relationships characterized by uneven movement inextricably tied to (often, though not always, invisible) power.

PUTTING MOBILITY TO WORK IN WRITING STUDIES

Given these characterizations of mobility, we see several possibilities and pitfalls for adopting—and adapting—mobility studies as a methodology in writing research. The core concepts we (and others) have identified are replete with potential for studying socially produced meaning (see also Ann Shivers-McNair's chapter in this collection); but existing folk and academic associations with mobility can easily result in a slipperiness of terms and concepts. Further, mobility studies as a framework might help us to deepen our methodological understanding of how to trace power in and across expanded units of analysis in writing research; yet this possibility also raises questions about how mobility works in relation to other concepts (e.g., design, community, literacy) and frameworks (e.g., critical pedagogy, usability studies) we already deploy in writing research. These affordances of mobility studies highlight our need to define our terms and clarify what we want the methodology to do for us—both of which should be informed by a deep engagement with mobility studies as an imported interdisciplinary methodology (and not simply a borrowed folk term). Here, we analyze three chapters, looking in particular at how scholars operationalize mobility studies as a methodology in relation to other frameworks and how these chapters can inform how we put mobility to work in future iterations of writing research.

In "Mobilizing Knowledge Through and For Research Practice: Lessons from a Design Thinking-Oriented Writing Course," Scott Wible describes a course he taught in partnership with his university's Academy for Innovation and Entrepreneurship in which students articulate community-identified problems and design (and revise) solutions. Wible focuses on knowledge mobility (via education researchers Tara Fenwick and Lesley Farrell) and the role of texts in mobilizing knowledge across campus spaces and various stakeholders as students work iteratively through the stages of design thinking. Throughout his chapter, Wible puts mobility to work in service of design thinking as a methodology more central to his current project, with usability studies ever-present. His intention is commonplace and still needed in our field: to improve how students engage in invention for problem solving, especially professional writing students who can/should learn inquiry and invention via situated interactions, rather than only engaging in decontextualized library research or imagining solutions to self-identified problems for abstract audiences. Yet such interactions bring with them a set of relational complications involving power. Wible acknowledges these in his chapter's closing, suggesting that mobility studies might be a productive way for technical and professional writing scholars to interrogate design thinking and reconsider how we might use knowledge mobilization not as market research but as socially transformative research (110) in writing studies to ask questions about, for instance, "the social and cultural dimensions of health" (109).

In a move common to early explorations of a newer methodology, Wible's chapter posits possibilities for using mobility to address issues of power in usability studies, design thinking, and community research—yet does not fully enact mobility studies to interrogate power from the outset, leaving its potential unrealized within the scope of his current text. While he points to how mobility studies might influence design-thinking pedagogy, such an influence is not yet clearly enacted here, where he focuses primarily on how design thinking might influence knowledge mobilization. A more recursive engagement with mobility studies as an interwoven framework would directly attend to the power dynamics involved in entrepreneurial frameworks, neoliberal university programs, and academic research practices from the beginning and throughout the process. For instance, Wible notes that writing studies and design thinking share an epistemology: "a belief in the social nature of knowledge and the collaborative nature of knowledge construction" (108). Leading with the tenets of mobility studies, rather than subordinating them to design thinking, would be one way to directly attend to the systematic, often invisible power involved in the social and collaborative nature of invention and qualitative research. With mobility studies at the forefront, we might address (and redress) concerns about who benefits from the ethnographic work required for usability studies and service-learning frameworks to succeed, as well as persistent concerns about how individual users and communities are represented (or omitted) in our research. In any case, further embracing mobility as a framework could push us to further question how entrepreneurial frameworks—as well as the bounds of the academic semester and university relationships—shape our study of meaning- and power-laden mobilities in professional writing contexts.

In "Imagine a School Yard," Eli Goldblatt traces the movement of knowledge and action across and throughout networks of literacy sponsors in a North Philadelphia neighborhood as diverse groups mobilize networks of material and semiotic resources to propose a schoolyard redevelopment plan. This project, Goldblatt posits, "dramatizes mobility within relationships among a variety of literacy actors on an urban stage" (127). Careful not to tout mobility as inherently liberatory or celebrated—or certainly equally accessible—Goldblatt points us to how "[t]he definition, glory, and violence of literacy emerge from the way symbol systems encourage, enact, and restrict human movement" (127). Throughout his chapter, Goldblatt puts mobility to work for other frameworks commonly invoked in our field: literacy studies, community engagement, and critical pedagogy (via Paulo Freire). For Goldblatt, mobility is understood in relation to literacy and power, with especially weighty consequences for those who have been historically understood and positioned as "*expelled* by the social structure" or "*surrounded and captured* by the structure" (134, emphasis in original), which Freire rejects and which Goldblatt notes is not a particularly agentive construction. Goldblatt's chapter demonstrates how mobility studies can align with multiple frameworks toward familiar writing studies research goals: to trace how literacy is embedded in community action and can be recruited, activated, and supported (or not) by networks of local sponsors for the benefit of "neighborhoods that seem locked in a matrix of violence, unemployment, and social neglect" (134).

A scholar long committed to these more familiar frameworks, Goldblatt also makes a common methodological move: finding strong alignment between established and newer frameworks. And yet, the close alignment of Goldblatt's multiple frameworks raises questions of what mobility studies brings that is not addressed through existing methodologies we already rely on to study literacy and education with overt attention to power. Writing researchers have long used literacy as an object and means of analysis to study bodies, practices, and ideas mobilized toward social change. Further, community engagement scholars analyze knowledge-making and relationship-building as socially produced phenomena and ontological absolutes within specific localized conditions and instantiations of power. And we have long turned to Freire's body of work, as Goldblatt does, to call ourselves (and others) to take up the transformational consciousness work that education can—and should—perform for those historically oppressed and marginalized. These familiar frameworks interrogate macro power relations that localized practices destabilize and reproduce and, as such, already function as a means to study and account for the "power-laden geographical phenomenon" of movement (Cresswell 2001, 20). Thus, Goldblatt's text makes it difficult to see the utility of the new methodology because of its tight alignment with other frameworks already in use.

In "Pretty for a Black Girl," Carmen Kynard focuses on mobilizing the concerns of black women to speak back to the systematic denigration of black college students as evident in sedimented assumptions of their digital production (chapter 5). Kynard details how Andrene's Pretty for a Black Girl website both enacts Andrene's complex visual and linguistic identities and becomes an inspiration for black women in and beyond the academy who are changed by its circulation. Throughout her chapter, Kynard puts mobility to work in relation to black feminist digital design and Fred Moten's notion of mobile black sociality, which Kynard declares "moves us away from simplistic narratives of space, place, time, and mobilities in a racialized western academy" (84). Kynard underscores that spacialized and racialized mobility is both digitally mediated and always embodied within a set of "social imaginaries . . . where ideas, identities, and experiences in a racist world are always in *practice*, constrained and enabled simultaneously" (84), with discursive and material consequences for black women whose bodies have been bound and literally burned by the privileging of white beauty and white, middle-class norms of embodied and linguistic correctness. Interweaving Moten's thinking with Creswell's notion of microgeographies and Katherine McKittrick's critical cartographies, Kynard in effect flexes and reshapes mobility as a framework toward her aim of speaking back to normative paradigms that flatten and erase the everyday lives, activities, and mobilities of black women that precede, exceed, and infuse the constructed bounds of any academic map.

Kynard embraces the possibilities of mobility studies frameworks even as she interrogates how the unmarked whiteness of mobility (and writing) studies methodologies—and the power that enables and perpetuates this—skew meaning-making from the outset. Kynard's essay offers dynamic remappings of how it feels to be black and female in cultures that mask their active privileging of whiteness and maleness beneath values embedded in everyday institutional apparatuses (e.g., the neoliberal formulas that authorize ePortfolios). For instance, Kynard's notion of "vernacular technocultural expressivity" (87) points to a collision of critical challenges in studying black students' digital design: (1) the entrenched misconception of African American youth's digital technology creation; (2) the institutional mechanisms required to assess digital portfolios/texts; and (3) the ease of erasing the relationships between the bodies that produce those texts and the mobile devices they use to do so. To illuminate how deeply we have normed disciplinary practices (in this case, writing assessment), Kynard interweaves a host of relevant, *needed* work from other fields that can enable us to address power and redress our privileging of white scholarship currently at the core of mobility studies. If mobility studies affords us the opportunity to question how power functions to create unspoken, invisible norms, then we might use the central tenets of mobility studies to question how mobility as a methodology has emerged from, and remains largely entrenched in, privileged white male scholarship—despite the evidence in Kynard's essay of mobility thinking and scholarship from black authors and academics whose work is robustly interdisciplinary, methodologically sound, and certainly concerned with power. By fully embracing the tenets of mobility studies while also remapping whose ways of thinking and being are visible and valued, Kynard's essay shows how writing scholars might complicate our use of another field's methodology, interrogating anew how we conduct disciplinary practices while using the affordances of a new methodology to speak back to power.

CONCLUSION

Based on our analysis of how these collection chapters have taken up mobility studies to address pervasive cultural questions, we offer two final points about the affordances of mobility as a complex framework concerned with locating, tracing, and interrogating power. First, we as a field have much to learn from the interanimation of mobility studies with other methodological frameworks and disciplinary questions. For instance, mobility studies supports our inquiry into studying how power in and behind the scenes of writing constrains and enables our knowledge-making, teaching, and research; and mobility studies also illuminates our ongoing struggle for appropriate units of analysis to trace the movement of complex concepts and practices that we are committed to (e.g., invention, literacy, composing). Second, even within this richness, there linger methodological questions and challenges when importing key terms or frameworks from another discipline. Given the foundational assumptions of mobility studies, it seems especially vital to note that methodologies themselves are not simply "imported" but transformed; and any "borrowed" framework recursively transforms the movement of knowledge as well as the knowledge-making process and research practices across scholars, sites, and disciplines. Consequently, we encourage scholars to interrogate what aspects of *any* methodology we import, adapt, or eschew as we articulate how to make methodologies work for contemporary writing research.

REFERENCES

Adey, Peter. 2006. "If Mobility Is Everything Then It Is Nothing: Towards a Relational Politics of (Im)mobilities." *Mobilities* 1 (1): 75–94.

Cresswell, Tim. 2001. "The Production of Mobilities." *New Formations* 43: 11–25.

Sheridan, Mary P. 2012. "Making Ethnography Our Own: Why and How Writing Studies Must Redefine Core Research Practices." In *Writing Studies Research in Practice: Methods and Methodologies*, edited by Lee Nickoson and Mary P. Sheridan, 73–85. Carbondale: Southern Illinois University Press.

ABOUT THE AUTHORS

Anis Bawarshi is Professor of English at the University of Washington, where he specializes in the study and teaching of writing, rhetorical genre theory, writing program administration, and research on knowledge transfer. He is co-editor of the book series *Reference Guides to Rhetoric and Composition* and until recently was co-managing editor of the journal *Composition Forum*. His publications include *Genre and the Invention of the Writer: Reconsidering the Place of Invention in Composition*; *Genre: An Introduction to History, Theory, Research, and Pedagogy* (with Mary Jo Reiff); *Scenes of Writing: Strategies for Composing with Genres* (with Amy Devitt and Mary Jo Reiff); *Ecologies of Writing Programs: Profiles of Writing Programs in Context* (coedited with Mary Jo Reiff, Christian Weisser, and Michelle Ballif), and *Genre and the Performance of Publics* (coedited with Mary Jo Reiff).

Elizabeth Chamberlain is Assistant Professor of English and Director of First-Year Writing at Arkansas State University. She is an Associate Editor of *Kairos: A Journal of Rhetoric, Technology, and Pedagogy*. Her mixed-methods research examines the intersection of writing technologies and culture, and her work has appeared in *Kairos, Computers and Composition Online, The Journal of Interactive Technology and Pedagogy*, and *Wired*.

Patrick Danner is Assistant Professor of English at Misericordia University, where he specializes in professional and technical writing. His recent projects include ethnographically-informed work on collaboration, storytelling, and creativity in technical writing spaces. He is currently researching the circulation of technical information for social change.

Christiane Donahue is Associate Professor of Linguistics and Director of the Institute for Writing and Rhetoric at Dartmouth College. She is the author of *Writing at the University: Comparative Analysis, France-United States* and co-editor of *University Writing: Selves and Texts in Academic Societies*, among several other books and articles, and is the recipient of the 2009 Fulbright Research Scholar award for the project titled, "University Student Writing in Cross-National Perspective: Types, Difficulties, and Interventions." Donahue's areas of expertise include writing research methods, international writing studies, discourse analysis, and knowledge transfer. Her scholarship and expertise have led her to projects like "Re-envisioning Composition: Assessment, Knowledge Transfer, and Emerging Literacies," a three-year assessment and innovative curriculum project targeting the Dartmouth first-year writing program. She teaches first-year writing, courses on science writing, and linguistics topics courses such as The World's Englishes as well as courses on US composition research and theory in the US and abroad. She is a member of several European research groups and is grounded in the European research landscape. She organizes the annual Dartmouth Summer Seminar on Writing Research.

Keri Epps is Assistant Teaching Professor of Writing and Academic and Community Engaged Faculty Fellow at Wake Forest University. Her teaching, research, and administrative projects at Wake Forest investigate and enact feminist principles of community writing. She is also currently working on a feminist genre and media analysis of women's letter writing across three time periods marked by media transition. Her work has appeared in *Community Literacy Journal* and *Kairos* and the edited collections *Composing Feminist Interventions: Activism, Engagement, Praxis* and *Making Future Matters*.

232   ABOUT THE AUTHORS

Eli Goldblatt is Professor Emeritus of English at Temple University and former director of New City Writing, an institute focused on community-related literacy projects in North Philadelphia. His scholarly work includes *'Round My Way: Authority and Double-Consciousness in Three Urban High School Writers*, *Writing Home: A Literacy Autobiography*, and *Because We Live Here: Sponsoring Literacy Beyond the College Curriculum*, which won the 2008 National Council of Writing Program Administrators' Best Book Award. The Conference on Community Writing presented him with the Outstanding Scholar Award in 2015. With David Jolliffe of the University of Arkansas, he is currently finishing a book entitled *Literacy as Conversation: Learning Networks in Philadelphia and Arkansas*. Goldblatt's poetry collections include *Sessions 1–62*, *Speech Acts*, *Without a Trace*, and the recently published *For Instance*. His two books for children are *Leo Loves Round* and *Lissa and the Moon's Sheep*.

Rachel Gramer is Assistant Professor of English and Director of the University Writing Program at Illinois State University. Her work as a feminist researcher, teacher, and administrator attunes to the stories we tell (and those we don't) as teachers, as a field, and as social groups in positions of power. Gramer has overlapping research commitments to narrative, feminist methodologies and pedagogies, new writing teacher preparation, digital composition and pedagogies, and writing program administration. Her work has appeared in *JAC*, *Kairos*, *Computers and Composition Online*, *College English*, and the edited collection *Writing for Engagement: Responsive Practice for Social Action*.

Megan Faver Hartline is Assistant Professor of English at the University of Tennessee at Chattanooga. Her scholarship examines institutional structures for community engagement, focusing on how emerging engaged scholars learn to navigate these structures. She earned a PhD in rhetoric and composition at the University of Louisville, and her work has been published in *Community Literacy Journal*, *Reflections*, and *Computers and Composition Online*. Her co-edited collection *Writing for Engagement: Responsive Practice for Social Action* (with Mary P. Sheridan, Megan Bardolph, and Drew Holladay) was published by Lexington Books in 2018.

Bruce Horner is Endowed Chair in Rhetoric and Composition at the University of Louisville, where he teaches courses in composition, composition theory and pedagogy, and literacy studies. His recent books include *Crossing Divides: Exploring Translingual Writing Pedagogies and Programs*, co-edited with Laura Tetreault, *Economies of Writing*, co-edited with Brice Nordquist and Susan Ryan, and *Rewriting Composition: Terms of Exchange*.

Timothy Johnson is Associate Professor of English at the University of Louisville. His research interests include visual, spatial, and institutional rhetorics; professional and technical writing; and critical studies of political economy (particularly via studies of corporate rhetoric). His work has appeared in *Rhetoric Society Quarterly* and he has a forthcoming book on Ford Motor Company's film rhetoric in the first half of the twentieth century from Penn State University Press.

Jamila M. Kareem, PhD is Assistant Professor of Writing and Rhetoric at the University of Central Florida, where she teaches first-year writing and upper-division courses in writing and rhetoric. Her essays have appeared in the *Journal of College Literacy and Learning*, *JAC: A Journal of Rhetoric, Culture, and Politics*, and the collection *The Good Life and the Greater Good in a Global Context*, and she has an essay forthcoming in the journal *Teaching English in the Two-Year College*.

Ashanka Kumari is Assistant Professor of English at Texas A&M University-Commerce after earning her PhD at the University of Louisville. Her research focuses on rhetoric

About the Authors   233

and composition doctoral students and how this population negotiates their professional expectations of graduate study and academia with their lives, identities, and many other obligations. Her work has appeared in *Kairos: A Journal of Rhetoric, Technology, and Pedagogy*, *Composition Studies*, *WPA Journal*, and the *Journal of Popular Culture*.

Carmen Kynard is the Lillian Radford Chair in Rhetoric and Composition and Professor of English at Texas Christian University. She interrogates race, black feminisms, AfroDigital/African American cultures and languages, and the politics of schooling with an emphasis on composition and literacies studies. Carmen has been published in *Harvard Educational Review, Changing English, College Composition and Communication, College English, Computers and Composition, Reading Research Quarterly, Literacy and Composition Studies*, and more. Her first book, *Vernacular Insurrections: Race, Black Protest, and the New Century in Composition-Literacy Studies* won the 2015 James Britton Award and makes black freedom a twenty-first-century literacy movement. Her current projects focus on young black women in college, black feminist digital vernaculars, and AfroDigital humanities learning. Carmen traces her research and teaching at her website, "Education, Liberation, and Black Radical Traditions" (http://carmenkynard.org).

Rebecca Lorimer Leonard is Associate Professor of English at University of Massachusetts Amherst where she teaches undergraduate and graduate courses on literacy studies, language diversity, and research methods. Her work has been published in *College English, Composition Studies, Literacy in Composition Studies, Research in the Teaching of English, Written Communication*, and *WPA: Writing Program Administration*. Professor Lorimer Leonard's book, *Writing on the Move: Migrant Women and the Value of Literacy*, received a 2019 Outstanding Book Award from the Conference on College Composition and Communication as well as an Honorable Mention for the 2018 Winifred Bryan Horner Outstanding Book Award from the Coalition of Feminist Scholars in the History of Rhetoric and Composition.

Laura Sceniak Matravers is Assistant Professor of English at Chattanooga State Community College, where she teaches courses in composition. She earned her PhD in rhetoric and composition at the University of Louisville. Her recent scholarship interrogates the role of two-year college faculty within Composition Studies. Her work has appeared in *Kairos*.

Andrea R. Olinger is Associate Professor of English and Director of Composition at the University of Louisville. Her scholarship articulates a sociocultural approach to the study of writing styles and explores the role of the body in writers' talk and interaction. Her work has appeared in journals such as *Research in the Teaching of English, Rhetoric Review*, and *Linguistics and Education* and the edited collections *Retheorizing Literacy Practices: Complex Social and Cultural Contexts* and *Style and the Future of Composition Studies*.

John Scenters-Zapico (PhD Arizona) held WPA positions in Texas and is presently WAC Director, GWAR Coordinator, and English Professor at California State University, Long Beach (CSULB). Early in his research career he focused on epistemologies of meaning-making, specifically enthymemes and Vygotskian socially situated theory and pedagogy, because both consider initially missing, misunderstood, and hidden assumptions in both teaching and learning. Taking what he learned about enthymemes and Vygotskian thought, he began focusing on reading and writing literacies to better understand the learning experiences of understudied groups. This led to his ethnographic studies for the last two decades on traditional and digital literacies in multilingual settings. Most recently he completed a pilot writing across the curriculum study on experiences learning and teaching writing with three distinct yet intertwined CSULB audiences: students, alumni,

234   ABOUT THE AUTHORS

and instructors. He hopes the findings help make writing a CSULB priority. He spends his free time with his family, especially his four dogs.

Khirsten L. Scott is an Assistant Professor of English at the University of Pittsburgh where she teaches undergraduate and graduate seminars on black rhetoric and material culture, critical literacy, and writing pedagogy. She is currently working on an archival-based study centered on Tougaloo College's institutional narrative, which argues for revision to top-down historical narratives through the use of student voice as testimony. Her work has appeared in *Kairos* and *Kentucky Teacher Education Journal* and she has contributed to the edited collections *Bridging the Gap: Multimodality in Theory and Practice* and *The Routledge Reader of African American Rhetoric: The Longue Dureé of Black Voices*. Further, she serves as co-founder of Digital Black Lit (-eracies and -eratures) and Composition (DBLAC), a digital and in-person network that seeks to support and mentor black-identified graduate students across the fields of literacy studies, literature, and composition.

Mary P. Sheridan is Professor of English at the University of Louisville where she teaches and investigate questions relating to digital composing, community engagement, and feminist methodologies. Sheridan has written *Girls, Feminism, and Grassroots Literacies: Activism in the GirlZone* and *Design Literacies: Learning and Innovation in the Digital Age* (with Jennifer Rowsell) and co-edited multiple collections, including *Making Future Matters* (with Rick Wysocki), *Writing for Engagement: Responsive Practice for Social Action* (with Megan Bardolph, Megan Hartline, and Drew Holladay), and *Writing Studies Research in Practice: Methods and Methodologies* (with Lee Nickoson). Her articles have appeared in *CCC, Computers & Composition, Kairos, JAC, Written Communication, Feminist Teacher, Composition Studies,* and *Journal of Basic Writing*. Sheridan's work earned the Winifred Bryan Horner Outstanding Book Award from Coalition of Women Scholars in the History of R/C and the Book of the Year Award from *Reflections: A Journal of Writing, Service-Learning, and Community Literacy*.

Jody Shipka is an Associate Professor of English at University of Maryland, Baltimore County where she teaches courses in the Communication and Technology Track. She is the author of *Toward a Composition Made Whole* and the editor of *Play! A Collection of Toy Camera Photographs*. Her work has appeared in *College Composition and Communication, Computers and Composition, Enculturation, Kairos, Text and Talk,* and a number of edited collections, including *Writing Selves/Writing Societies, Exploring Semiotic Remediation as Discourse Practice, Multimodal Literacies and Emerging Genres in Student Compositions, First-Year Composition: From Theory to Practice, Assembling Composition,* and *Exquisite Corpse: Studio Art-Based Writing Practices in the Academy*.

Ann Shivers-McNair is Assistant Professor and Director of Professional and Technical Writing in the Department of English at the University of Arizona. She serves as an associate editor of *Technical Communication Quarterly*, and her work has appeared in journals such as *Learning, Culture, and Social Interaction; Computers and Composition; Across the Disciplines; Technical Communication; Kairos: Rhetoric, Technology, and Pedagogy;* and *College Composition and Communication*.

Scott Wible is Associate Professor of English and Director of the Professional Writing Program at the University of Maryland, College Park (UMD). Since 2014 he has collaborated with UMD's Academy for Innovation and Entrepreneurship in developing a range of design thinking-oriented rhetoric and writing courses at both the undergraduate and graduate levels; delivered design thinking workshops at the Council of Writing Program Administrators Conference and for UMD's campus-wide ePortfolio Initiative; and taught design thinking courses for private companies in the Philadelphia region. His current research project examines how social entrepreneurs and civic innovators use rhetoric and writing in their design work as well as how they conceptualize their social and civic work in relation to the private sector and public sphere.

Rick Wysocki is Assistant Teaching Professor of English at Ball State University and holds a PhD in rhetoric and composition. As an archival researcher, his work intersects conversations on queer archives and rhetoric, new materialisms, and media studies. Additionally, he has been involved in a number of digital publishing efforts, most notably as a co-editor of *Making Future Matters*, a born-digital edited collection published with Computers and Composition Digital Press, and as an Associate Editor at *Kairos: A Journal of Rhetoric, Technology and Pedagogy*. For more information, see www.rickwysocki.com.

INDEX

Academy for Innovation and Entrepreneurship, 108
Adey, Peter, 39, 40, 41, 63, 119, 123; mobilities make waves, 121; on tourist activity, 118
African American Language, 86
AfroDigital black feminism, 84, 92
AfroDigital black vernacular, 83–87
agency: design, 217–18; distributed, 218–19; mobilities framework for, 220–21; of tangible nonhuman objects, 160; translingual, 219–20
Agents of Integration, 148
Altman, Irwin, 56
anachorism, 59
anachronism, 59
Anderson, Erin, 115
Archibald, Alasdair, 29
Arola, Kristin, 38
audience-making, 87–88
Augé, Marc, 168
Azerbaijan English Teachers Association (AzETA), 70–71, 77, 162, 165

Bach, Jackie, 119
Bakhtin, Mikhail. M., 18–21, 25; language system as code, 27; theory of speech genres, 213
Barad, Karen, 38, 39, 40, 41, 42, 45, 152, 198
Barnett, Scot, 196
Baron, Jaimie, 123
Bastian, Heather, 203, 205, 208
Bawarshi, Anis, 10, 37, 60, 201–2, 204–5, 209
Beach, King, 23
big M–Mobilities, 51, 52, 58–59, 169, 195, 199
black digital migrations, in curriculum and design, 88–89
Black Girl, 82–84; migrations in color caste systems, 82–83
Blackledge, Adrian, 27
#BlackLivesMatter, 91–92
black navigational messaging as ethos, 85–86
blackness-controlled literacy mobility, 177

blackscapes, 92; multimedia, 85
black technocultural creativity, 87–88
Blank, Steve, 99
Blommaert, Jan, 37, 161, 162, 163, 175, 177
Bolter, Jay David, 122
boundary-marking processes, 37–38; accountability for, 38
Boyle, Casey, 196
Brandt, Deborah, 161
Brink, Lois, 131
Brown, Michael, 84
Brynjolfsson, Erik, 219

California State University, Long Beach (CSULB), 51, 58, 63, 211, 212
Canagarajah, A. Suresh, 25, 29, 160–61, 162
Cecil B. Moore School, 128–29; budget for school, 129; funding, 129; literacy sponsorship, 133–43; parent association, 128; schoolyard redevelopment plan, 130–33
CEE. *See* Contingent and Emergent Events
Chamberlain, Elizabeth, 11
Chávez, Karma, 191, 192
Chiseri-Strater, Elizabeth, 107
Christian, Barbara, 84
Chronicle of Higher Education, 108
code, 26–28, 154, 155, 213; language system as, 27; as stand-in for language, 26; switching, 26–27
"codemeshing," 26, 27
"codeswitching," 26, 27
Cogo, Alessia, 29
collaboration: with dead, 114–17; intermundane, 115
collaborative solution design, mobilizing knowledge for, 99–107; composing multimodals to reshape knowledge with stakeholders, 104–7; composing questions to enable empathetic travel, 99–100; composing texts for collaborative invention, 103–4; composing to synthesize research and define user problems, 100–103

238 INDEX

color caste systems, 82–83
colorism, microgeographies of, 84
communication: design, 25; expressive nature of, 19
communicative competence, 28, 30
Community Design Collaborative (CDC), 130–31
community schools, 133
community writing, 183–85
competence, 28–30, 154, 155; communicative, 28, 30; in identifying language ideologies, 157–58; multicompetence model, 28–29; orientation as, 29; writers' language, 29
Contingent and Emergent Events (CEE), 55–57, 190, 196, 197
Creese, Angela, 27
Cresswell, Tim, 6, 52, 58, 59, 60, 64, 82, 114, 217; movement and stillness, 124; representations of mobility, 122–23
Crowley, Sharon, 38
cultural-spatial contouring, 84–85
Cushman, Ellen, 24, 38

Danner, Patrick, 11
Deans, Thomas, 107
De Costa, Peter I., 160–61, 162
delay-as-avoidance tactics, 62
Deleuze, Gilles, 194
design agency, 217–18
design thinking, 95; collaborative solution design, 99–107; community involvement, 184; define mode, 97; empathy mode, 97; ideate mode, 97; and iterative solution development, 185–87; knowledge mobilization to reshape, 107–10; pedagogy, 96, 98; problem solving, 96–97; in professional writing course, 96–97; prototype mode, 97; stages, 96–97; test phase, 97; transform, 187; writing course, defining knowledge mobility for, 97–98
diffraction, 38–40, 198
Dirk, Kerry, 205, 206
discrimination, 79; gendered or raced, 85; linguistic and cultural, 78, 157, 158
disruption, 121–23
distributed agency, 218–19
D'Mello, Marisa, 59
Dolmage, Jay, 38, 43
Donahue, Christiane, 8–9, 10, 11, 154–55, 159, 182, 183, 187–88, 202, 209, 216, 217, 219–20, 221; knowledge transfer, 148; linguistic reprises, 20; reprise-modification, defined, 150;

(re)theorization, 213–14; transfer, translingualism, and mobility intersection, 213
Dunn, Patricia, 25

empathy, 99, 100
Engels, Friedrich, 70
English as Lingua Franca (ELF), 29
English-language intelligibility, 78–79
English-language skills, 74, 75–76, 78
English problem, 76, 157
Epps, Keri, 11, 60
ESL (English as a Second Language) course, 81

Farrell, Lesley, 98, 110
Fenwick, Tara, 98, 110
FieldWorking (Sunstein), 107
Foucault, Michel, 189
Fox, Sarah, 41
François, Frédéric, 18, 27, 150, 155; and reprise-modification, 20–21, 213
Freadman, Anne, 150, 201, 208, 214
Freire, Paulo, 134, 136, 140
"friction," 190

Gaffigan, Jake, 131
genre agency, 205
genres, 201–3; ePortfolio, 204; exposing and making meaning through, 212–14; location within ongoing system, 206; mixing familiar and unfamiliar, 203–4; in performances, 202. *See also* genre uptake
genre uptake, 208–14; agents of, 209, 210–12; implications for, 214; innovation and, 201–3
Gilmore, Ruth Wilson, 92
Goggin, Gerard, 90
Goldblatt, Eli, 6, 9, 10, 11, 107, 148, 161, 162, 166, 174–80, 182–84, 186
Goldstein, Lauren, 118
Gramer, Rachel, 11
Gramsci, Antonio, 152
Grusin, Richard, 122

Hackney, Otis, 133
Hahn, Hans Peter, 113
Hall, Joan Kelly, 29
Hamilton, Mary Lynn, 52
Haraway, Donna, 38, 39
Hartline, Megan Faver, 10
Heaney, Michael T., 190–91
Helfand, Jessica, 114
HMW questions. *See* How Might We questions

Horner, Bruce, 19, 20, 29, 37, 64
How Might We (HMW) questions, 103–4
Hutchins, Edwin, 106

ideation, 104, 219
immobility, 42
Industrial Revolution, 219
Industrial Workers of the World (IWW), 191–92
inequality, literate mobility and, 68–69
inertia, 168; definition of, 198
inertia starters, 57–59, 171, 198–99; in Texas, 61–64
Ingold, Tim, 115, 116
"Inhabiting Dorothy" project, 115, 121, 160, 204
innovation, 201–3
intentional disparity, 121–23
intermundane collaborations, 115
"isolated utterance," 206
iterative solution development, 185–87

Jackson, Michael, 83
Jamison, Leslie, 99, 100
Jenkins, Jennifer, 29
Joe, Fat, 83
Johnson, Nathan R., 60
Johnson, Timothy, 10
Jolliffe, David, 107
Jonnaert, Philippe, 28

Kareem, Jamila, 10
Kenney, Jim, 133
Kerschbaum, Stephanie, 38
Kittler, Friedrich, 205
knowledgeable collaborators, 183–85
knowledge mobilization, 3, 9–10, 98; for collaborative solution design, 99–107; for design thinking writing course, 97–98; iterative process of developing solution, 106; to reshape design thinking, 107–10
knowledge transfer, 22, 28, 98, 151; "adaptive reuse," 30; mercuriality and degree of stability, 24; and mobility work, 148; writing, 25
knowledge transformation, 23, 98
knowledge translation, 98
Kristeva, Julia, 18
Kubota, Ryuko, 157
Kumari, Ashanka, 11, 43, 46
Kynard, Carmen, 6, 9, 10, 11, 21, 37, 42, 148, 162–65, 175–79, 189–91, 193; pedagogy of AfroDigital design, 204; presents ePortfolio, 206; prompt genres from, 201, 202, 206

Ladson-Billings, Gloria, 174, 175, 177, 180
language, 171–72; *ad hoc* requirement, 171; code as stand-in for, 26; competence, 29; ideologies, 157–58; mobility of, 154–56, 158–59; pedagogy, 70, 71
language-in-use, 17, 18–20, 30; Bakhtin's model of, 18–19; "linguality," 18; from lingual to translingual, 21–22; linguistic flexibility, 21
Larsen, Jonas, 116
Latest Trends in ELF Research (Archibald), 29
Latham, Alan, 119
Latour, Bruno, 220
Leander, Kevin M., 88
Le Boterf, Guy, 23
legitimate literacy, 166
Lenin, 70
Leonard, Rebecca Lorimer, 9, 10, 11, 42, 149, 154, 155, 156, 158, 159, 162, 165, 167, 171, 209, 210–11
"lingual," 21–22
linguistic flexibility, 156–57
literacy: directing, 75–76; learning affordance, 73; legitimate, 166; marginalized, 175–76; materials, 71–73; multilingual, mobility of, 69; pacing, 73–74; technology, 72; whiteness-centered, 175; whiteness-controlled, 176
literacy sponsorship networks, 133–38, 182; function, 139–40; higher education in, role of, 140–43; nonhuman, 160–62; "official," 163
literacy sponsors/sponsorship, 127, 133–43; function in networks, 139–40; mobility and networks of, 133–38; questions about, 138; social institutions, 178–79
literate mobility, 69–76; directing literacy, 75–76; and inequality, 68–69; management of, 69–76; pacing literacy, 73–74; passing pedagogies, 69–71; schools, 73–73; sending materials, 71–73; struggle and success in, 76–80; writer's, 69–73
Lorde, Audre, 92
Low, Setha M., 56
Lu, Min-Zhan, 19

makerspaces, 41–45, 195–99; attachments with, 197; bodies and things in, 196; existence of, 199; interactions in, 197, 198; mobility-marking in, 43; physical space and practices in, 43; re-marked mobility in, 44

Marback, Richard, 104, 218
marginalized literacies, 175–76
marking mobility. *See* mobility-marking
Martinet, André, 18
Marx, Karl, 70
Massey, Doreen, 78
materials, 115–18; categories, 116; literacy, 71–73; vs. objects, 115
Matravers, Laura Sceniak, 10
McAfee, Andrew, 219
McKittrick, Katherine, 87
media, 203–4
Memorable Contingent and Emergent Events, 56
merged proficiency, 29
Michaels, Jen, 118, 120, 121
"micro-celebrity status," 88
migration: black digital, 88–89; and color caste systems, 82–83; and multilingualism, 78
Miller, Peter N., 108
Miller, Richard, 52
"mobile black sociality," 84
mobile phones/mobile black sociality, 90–91
mobilities approach, definition of, 58
mobilities paradigm, 3, 4–7, 127
mobility, 3–4, 52–54; in composition studies, 189; Contingent and Emergent Events, 55–57; directions and rates of, 42; and inequality, 68–69; Inertia Starters, 57–59; of language and writing, 154–56, 158–59; linguistic perspectives and, 18–22; literate, 68–69; making, 41–47; making waves, 121–23; marked, 36; and movement, 5, 52–53; Nimet and Andrene's (case study), 162–65; prohibit, 210; representations of, 122; small m–mobility, 54–55; through everyday things, 195–200; "transfer" and, 22, 23–24
mobility-marking, 36–40, 41–47; boundary-marking processes and, 38; maker-spaces, 41, 43; significance, 45–47; workplace culture and processes, 43
mobility work, 147–53, 196–97; composition, 147–48, 152–53; and meso-practices, 148; mobile processes for, 7–11; onto-epistemologies of, 37–41
Molina, Clara, 29
Moore School. *See* Cecil B. Moore School
Moten, Fred, 84
movement: mobility and, 5, 52–53
multilingual migrants, 78
multimedia blackscapes, 85

National Adjunct Walkout Day (NAWD), 191–92, 194
networks: literacy sponsorship, 133–43; of nonhuman literacy sponsors, 160–62
New Literacy Studies (NLS), 4–5
New London Group, 18, 25, 217, 218
nonhuman literacy sponsors, networks of, 160–62
non-place, 167–73; of bureaucratic health-care system, 171; economic label, 170; function, 168; individual trapped in, 170; recasts state schools, 169; similitude, 171–72; transitory spaces, 168
Nowacek, Rebecca, 148, 150
Nutter, Michael, 142

objects: materials vs., 115; nonhuman, 160; "thing power" of, 196
Olinger, Andrea, 10
onto-epistemologies: of mobility work, 37–41
"ontological absolutes," 4
orientation: as competence, 29; writing knowledge, 24

paraphrase, 20
pedagogy: for border-crossing communication, 157; design thinking, 96, 98; effective language, 70, 71; media-oriented, 203; passing, 69–71; political system and, 70; racialized, 177
Pennycook, Alastair, 21
Perrenoud, Philippe, 23
Philadelphia Green School Alliance, 131
"phone down," 90–91
physical space, 43
physical space and time, 178
Piekut, Benjamin, 115
point-of-view (POV) statements, 100, 101–3, 107, 108
Porter, James E., 167
Post-it notes, 100, 102, 103–4, 151, 203
POV statements. *See* point-of-view statements
Powell, Katrina, 39, 40
Prior, Paul, 151
Prison Notebooks (Gramsci), 152
productive limitations, well-defined, 204–5
prohibit mobility, 210
Project Zero, 218
A Promise Worth Keeping (Ransom), 142
prompts, 11, 201–3, 204; collaborators, 104; HMW questions, 103; "inhabiting," 206; writing, 201–2, 205, 206
Purdy, James P., 18, 25

race, 174–80
racialized pedagogy, 177
Ransom, Julia, 142
recursivity, 193–94
Reiff, Mary Jo, 204
repertoires, co-constructed nature of, 156–57
reprise-modification, 20–21, 27, 155, 213–14
reprises, 20–21
respatialization, 179
Rhetoric and Composition, 98, 122, 167
Rhetoric and Writing Studies program, 51
Rhetoric Through Everyday Things (Barnett), 196
Ríos, Gabriela, 40–41, 42, 43
Rojas, Fabio, 190–91
Rose, Mike, 53
Rosner, Daniela, 41
RWS program. *See* Rhetoric and Writing Studies program

Sahay, Sundeep, 59
Sánchez, Raúl, 40
Sandberg, Sheryl, 83
Sano-Franchini, Jennifer, 38
Sayers, Jentery, 41
Scenters-Zapico, John, 6, 9, 10, 11, 149–50, 167, 168–71, 189–93, 195–200, 209, 211–12
Scott, Khirsten L., 10
Sheridan, David, 41
Sheridan, Mary P., 11
Sherrill, John, 41
Shipka, Jody, 9, 11, 151, 152, 160–61, 201, 216, 218, 219, 221; "Inhabiting Dorothy" project, 204; presents "inhabiting" prompt, 206; prompt genres from, 201, 202, 205, 206
Shivers-McNair, Ann, 7, 9, 11, 148, 152, 195–200, 208, 216
similitude, 171–72
small m–mobilities, 52, 54–55, 59, 195–96, 199, 211; assumptions for, 60–61; of writing program administrator, 60–61
Smith, Laura, 52
social movement rhetorics, 190–93
Socolar, Paul, 142
space-making: and AfroDigital black vernacular, 83–87; black navigational messaging as ethos, 85–86; critical cartographies, 87; cultural-spatial contouring, 84–85; multimedia blackscapes, 85
Spinuzzi, Clay, 151

Stanyek, Jason, 115
stasis, 5, 54
Steele, Fritz, 56
Stevens, Sharon, 39
stillness, 123–25
Suchman, Lucy, 47
Sunstein, Bonnie Stone, 107
symbolic transformation, of space, 193

Takayoshi, Pamela, 39, 40
Takhi, Jaspreet, 27
Tate, William F., 180
Taylor, Charles, 84
Texas Research Incentive Program (TRIP), 169
"thing power," 196
Thomas Watson Conference on Rhetoric and Composition, 2016, 8
Thrift, Nigel, 119
"transfer," 17–18, 22–30, 31; and mobility, 22, 23–24, 30; translingualism and, 23–25
transformation, 185; of space, 192; symbolic, 193
transformational consciousness, 136
translation, 25
"translingual," 21–22
translingual agency, 219–20
translingualism, 21–22, 31; mobility and, 23–24, 30; and "transfer," 23–25
Tree House Books, 107, 130, 137
Trimbur, John, 216
TRIP. *See* Texas Research Incentive Program

Ulgado, Rachel, 41
University of Maryland's Academy for Innovation and Entrepreneurship, 95, 96
University of Texas, El Paso (UTEP), 51, 52, 55, 58–59, 61, 63, 168, 170, 211, 212
University Writing Center (UWC), 59, 61–62
user empathy maps, 100–103
UTEP. *See* University of Texas, El Paso
utterances, 18, 19; isolated, 206; production of, 27; as reprises-modifications, 20, 21
UWC. *See* University Writing Center

Varlack, Christopher Allen, 117

Watts, Laura, 61
Weiss, Hadas, 113
whiteness-centered literacy, 175

242   INDEX

whiteness-controlled literacy, 176
whiteness-controlled writing practices, 176
Wible, Scott, 11, 18, 25, 151, 182, 183, 216, 218, 219, 221; community writing, 184–85; "How Might We" brainstorming rules, 205; mobility work, 37; pedagogy, 217; prompt genres from, 201, 202, 206
Wilson, Darren, 84
Winfrey, Oprah, 86
Winsor, Dorothy, 106
Wolfe, Cary, 194
Worthington, Kristen, 52

writing: community, 183–85; as "knowledge-making activity," 98; mobility of, 154–56, 158–59; process, 73–74; role of, 3. *See also* writing knowledge; writing skills
Writing Across the Curriculum initiatives, 51, 61
Writing and Community Action (Deans), 107
writing knowledge: orientation, 24; reuse, 22; "transfer," 17
Writing Program Administrator (WPA), 51, 52, 55, 61
writing skills: English-based, 74; transfer of, 5
Wysocki, Rick, 11